T0210664

Lecture Notes in Computer Science 9467

Commenced Publication in 1973
Founding and Former Series Editors:
Gerhard Goos, Juris Hartmanis, and Jan van Leeuwen

More information about this series at http://www.springer.com/series/7412

Guorong Wu · Pierrick Coupé
Yiqiang Zhan · Brent Munsell
Daniel Rueckert (Eds.)

Patch-Based Techniques in Medical Imaging

First International Workshop, Patch-MI 2015
Held in Conjunction with MICCAI 2015
Munich, Germany, October 9, 2015
Revised Selected Papers

 Springer

Editors
Guorong Wu
University of North Carolina at Chapel Hill
Chapel Hill, NC
USA

Brent Munsell
College of Charleston
Charleston, SC
USA

Pierrick Coupé
Bordeaux University
Bordeaux
France

Daniel Rueckert
Imperial College London
London
UK

Yiqiang Zhan
Siemens Healthcare
Malvern, PA
USA

ISSN 0302-9743   ISSN 1611-3349 (electronic)
Lecture Notes in Computer Science
ISBN 978-3-319-28193-3   ISBN 978-3-319-28194-0 (eBook)
DOI 10.1007/978-3-319-28194-0

Library of Congress Control Number: 2015959936

LNCS Sublibrary: SL6 – Image Processing, Computer Vision, Pattern Recognition, and Graphics

Printed on acid-free paper

This Springer imprint is published by SpringerNature
The registered company is Springer International Publishing AG Switzerland

Preface

The First International Workshop on Patch-Based Techniques in Medical Imaging (Patch-MI 2015) was held at Munich, Germany, on October 9, 2015, in conjunction with the 18th International Conference on Medical Image Computing and Computer-Assisted Intervention (MICCAI).

The patch-based technique plays an increasing role in the medical imaging field, with various applications in image segmentation, image denoising, image super-resolution, computer-aided diagnosis, image registration, abnormality detection, and image synthesis. For example, patch-based approaches using the training library of annotated atlases have been the focus of much attention in segmentation and computer-aided diagnosis. It has been shown that the patch-based strategy based on a training library is able to produce an accurate representation of data, while the use of a training library enables one to easily integrate prior knowledge to the model. As an intermediate level between the global image and the localized voxel, patch-based models offer an efficient and flexible way to represent very complex anatomies.

The main aim of the Patch-MI 2015 workshop was to promote methodological advances within the field of patch-based processing in medical imaging. The workshop focused on major trends and challenges in this area, and tried to identify new cutting-edge techniques and their use in medical imaging. We hope the workshop becomes a new platform for translating research from the bench to the bedside. We look for original, high-quality submissions on innovative research and development in the analysis of medical image data using patch-based techniques.

The quality of submissions for this year's meeting was very high. Authors were asked to submit eight-page papers for review. A total of 35 papers were submitted to the workshop in response to the call for papers. Each of the 35 papers underwent a rigorous double-blinded peer-review process, with each paper being reviewed by at least two (typically three) reviewers from the Program Committee, composed of 62 well-known experts in the field. Based on the reviewing scores and critiques, the 25 best papers were accepted for presentation at the workshop and chosen to be included in this volume of *Lecture Notes in Computer Science* published by Springer. A large variety of patch-based techniques applied to medical imaging were well represented at the workshop.

We are grateful to the Program Committee for reviewing the submitted papers and giving constructive comments and critiques, to the authors for submitting high-quality papers, to the presenters for their excellent presentations, and to all the Patch-MI 2015 attendees who came to Munich from all around the world.

October 2015

Pierrick Coupé
Guorong Wu
Yiqiang Zhan
Daniel Rueckert
Brent Munsell

Organization

Program Committee

Paul Aljabar	King's College London, UK
Christian Barillot	IRISA, France
Jérome Boulanger	Curie Institute, France
Weidong Cai	The University of Sydney, Australia
Louis Collins	McConnell Brain Imaging Centre, McGill, Canada
Olivier Colliot	University of Pierre and Marie Curie, France
Olivier Commowick	Inria Rennes – Bretagne Atlantique, France
Maxime Descoteaux	Centre de Recherche CHUS, Canada
Simon Eskildsen	Center of Functionally Integrative Neuroscience, Denmark
Yong Fan	University of Pennsylvania, USA
Vladimir Fonov	McGill University, Canada
Hayit Greenspan	Tel Aviv University, Israel
Ghassan Hamarneh	Simon Fraser University, Canada
Rolf Heckemann	Sahlgrenska University Hospital, Sweden
Mattias Heinrich	Universität Lübeck, Germany
Junzhou Huang	University of Texas at Arlington, USA
Charles Kervrann	Inria Rennes – Bretagne Atlantique, France
Tobias Klinder	Philips Research Europe, Germany
Karim Lekadir	Universitat Pompeu Fabra, Spain
Gang Li	University of North Carolina at Chapel Hill, USA
Shu Liao	Siemens, USA
Jean-Francois Mangin	CEA, France
Jose Manjón	ITACA Institute, Universidad Politecnica de Valencia, Spain
Jerry Prince	Johns Hopkins University, USA
François Rousseau	Telecom Bretagne, France
Mert Sabuncu	Harvard Medical School, USA
Dinggang Shen	University of North Carolina at Chapel Hill, USA
Li Shen	Indiana University, USA
Yonggang Shi	University of South California, USA
Jussi Tohka	Universidad Carlos III de Madrid, Spain
Qian Wang	Shanghai Jiao Tong University, China
Li Wang	University of North Carolina at Chapel Hill, USA
Lin Yang	University of Florida, USA
Shaoting Zhang	University of North Carolina at Charlotte, USA
Guoyan Zheng	University of Bern, Switzerland

Contents

A Multi-level Canonical Correlation Analysis Scheme for Standard-Dose PET Image Estimation

Le An[1], Pei Zhang[1], Ehsan Adeli-Mosabbeb[1], Yan Wang[1,2], Guangkai Ma[1], Feng Shi[1], David S. Lalush[3], Weili Lin[1], and Dinggang Shen[1(✉)]

[1] Department of Radiology and BRIC, University of North Carolina at Chapel Hill, Chapel Hill, USA
dinggang_shen@med.unc.edu
[2] College of Computer Science, Sichuan University, Chengdu, China
[3] Joint UNC-NCSU Department of Biomedical Engineering, North Carolina State University, Raleigh, USA

Abstract. In order to obtain positron emission tomography (PET) image with diagnostic quality, we seek to estimate a standard-dose PET (S-PET) image from its low-dose counterpart (L-PET), instead of obtaining the S-PET image directly by injecting standard-dose radioactive tracer to the patient. Therefore, the risk of radiation exposure can be significantly reduced. To achieve this goal, one possible way is to first map both S-PET and L-PET data into a common space and then perform a patch-based estimation of S-PET from L-PET patches. However, the approach of using all training data to globally learn the common space may not lead to an optimal estimation of a particular target S-PET patch. In this paper, we introduce a data-driven *multi-level Canonical Correlation Analysis* (m-CCA) scheme to tackle this problem. Specifically, a subset of training data that are most useful in estimating a target S-PET patch are identified in each level, and using these selected training data in the subsequent level leads to more accurate common space mapping and improved estimation. In addition, we also leverage multi-modal magnetic resonance (MR) images to provide complementary information to the estimation from L-PET. Validation on a real human brain dataset demonstrates the advantage of our method as compared to other techniques.

1 Introduction

By detecting pairs of gamma rays from the positron-emitting radioactive tracer injected into a live body, the positron emission tomography (PET) scanner creates an image based on the map of radioactivity of the tracer at each voxel. PET images are commonly used in clinical applications such as tumor detection and brain disorder diagnosis [1,10]. In order to obtain a PET image with diagnostic quality, the practical imaging protocol sets the standard tracer dose at a high level, which can be potentially harmful and cause side effects of excessive radiation exposure to the patient. It is thus of great interest to estimate a

© Springer International Publishing Switzerland 2015
G. Wu et al. (Eds.): Patch-MI 2015, LNCS 9467, pp. 1–9, 2015.
DOI: 10.1007/978-3-319-28194-0_1

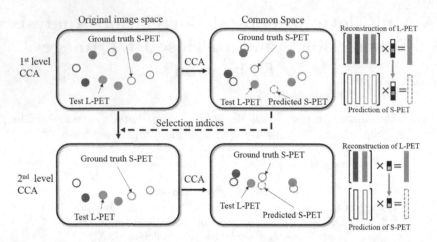

Fig. 1. Illustration of the multi-level CCA scheme (two levels are shown for simplicity). Filled patterns denote L-PET patches and unfilled patterns denote S-PET patches. A pair of L-PET and S-PET patches are indicated by the same color. A coarse reconstruction in the first level is used to select subsets of dictionaries and the estimation in the second level is more accurate thanks to the improved mapping and reconstruction using the refined dictionaries.

standard-dose PET (S-PET) image of desired quality for a patient from another PET image with reduced tracer dose during the image acquisition process. Such image with reduced dose is referred to as low-dose PET (L-PET) image.

There are few works along the line of S-PET image estimation since most of the existing methods focus on the PET imaging process [7,11]. An example can be found in [6], where Kang et al. introduced two different estimation methods: a regression forest (RF) based estimation method and a sparse representation (SR) method. Our proposed method in this paper is inspired by and developed based on the latter. To estimate a target S-PET patch, its corresponding low-dose PET (L-PET) patch is first sparsely represented by an L-PET dictionary which includes a set of training L-PET patches. The resulting reconstruction coefficients are then directly applied to an S-PET dictionary for estimation, where the S-PET dictionary is composed of a set of S-PET patches, each corresponding to an L-PET patch in the L-PET dictionary. Since the patches in the two dictionaries generally have different distributions (i.e., dissimilar neighborhood structures), it is inappropriate to directly apply the learned coefficients from the L-PET dictionary on the S-PET dictionary for estimation. A better idea is to map both L-PET and S-PET patches to a common space before reconstruction for minimizing their distribution discrepancy.

In this paper, we propose a multi-level Canonical Correlation Analysis (m-CCA) framework for patch-based S-PET estimation. CCA first learns a global mapping with the original coupled L-PET and S-PET dictionaries and maps both kinds of data to their common space. However, a global common space mapping does not necessarily unify the neighborhood structures in the coupled dictionaries that are particularly involved in reconstructing a specific test L-PET

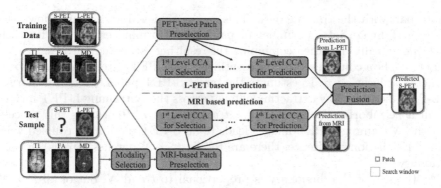

Fig. 2. Our framework for estimating S-PET image from L-PET and MR images. In each level, for a particular test patch, a subset of dictionary atoms are adaptively selected and the refined dictionaries in the original image space are provided to the next level for common space learning and reconstruction.

patch. Thus, the estimation of its corresponding S-PET patch using the same reconstruction coefficients is sub-optimal. We thus introduce a multi-level CCA scheme to resolve this issue. Figure 1 shows a two-level example for simplicity. In the first level, after mapping both L-PET and S-PET data into their common space, a test L-PET patch is reconstructed by the L-PET dictionary and instead of estimating the target S-PET patch in this level, a subset of the L-PET dictionary atoms (e.g., atoms with non-zero coefficients) that are most responsible for reconstructing the test L-PET patch are selected and passed to the next level together with the corresponding S-PET dictionary subset. With this data-driven dictionary refinement, the estimation can be more accurate in the next level. This process can iterate again for further improvement. Besides, modern PET is often integrated with other imaging modalities, such as magnetic resonance imaging (MRI), to provide both metabolic and anatomical information [9]. Thus, in addition to the L-PET-based estimation, we also leverage multi-modal MRI (i.e., T1-weighted and diffusion tensor imaging (DTI)) to generate an MRI-based estimation in a similar way, which is used to complement the L-PET-based estimation in a fusion process.

Below we first elaborate the proposed method in Sect. 2, then show both qualitative and quantitative results in Sect. 3, and finally draw conclusions in Sect. 4.

2 Methodology

Figure 2 shows the framework of our method. In the following, multi-level CCA for L-PET and MRI-based estimation as well as estimation fusion are explained in detail.

2.1 Preselection and Common Space Learning

Suppose we have a training set of N L-PET images and their corresponding S-PET images. Given a test L-PET image, the goal is to estimate its S-PET counterpart with the training data. This can be achieved by breaking down the test L-PET image into a number of patches, performing estimation for each patch individually and then combining the resulting estimated patches.

Let $\mathbf{y}_{L,p}$ be a column vector representing a test L-PET patch of size $m \times m \times m$ extracted at location p. To estimate the target S-PET patch, we first construct an L-PET dictionary by extracting patches across the N training L-PET images within a neighborhood of size $t \times t \times t$ centered at p. Repeating this process with the N training S-PET images leads to an S-PET dictionary coupled with the L-PET dictionary. Hence, there are totally $t^3 \times N$ patches (atoms) in each dictionary.

As the size of the dictionary is proportional to t and N, out of all $t^3 \times N$ patches, we preselect a subset of L-PET patches that are most similar to $\mathbf{y}_{L,p}$ for improved computational efficiency. This is achieved by the strategy in [3] based on the structural similarity (SSIM) [13], and its effectiveness has been shown for patch selection in previous works [3,4]. Let $\mathbf{D}_L = \{\mathbf{d}_{L_i} \in \mathbb{R}^d, i = 1, 2, ..., K\}$ be the L-PET dictionary after preselection and $\mathbf{D}_S = \{\mathbf{d}_{S_i} \in \mathbb{R}^d, i = 1, 2, ..., K\}$ be the corresponding S-PET dictionary, where $d = m \times m \times m$, $\mathbf{d}_{L_i}$ and $\mathbf{d}_{S_i}$ are one pair of L-PET patch and its corresponding S-PET patch. We use CCA to learn the mapping $\mathbf{w}_L, \mathbf{w}_S \in \mathbb{R}^d$ such that after mapping the correlation coefficient between $\mathbf{D}_L$ and $\mathbf{D}_S$ is maximized, i.e.,

$$\arg\max_{\mathbf{w}_L, \mathbf{w}_S} \frac{\mathbf{w}_L^\top \mathbf{C}_{LS} \mathbf{w}_S}{\sqrt{\mathbf{w}_L^\top \mathbf{C}_{LL} \mathbf{w}_L} \sqrt{\mathbf{w}_S^\top \mathbf{C}_{SS} \mathbf{w}_S}}, \tag{1}$$

where the data covariance matrices are computed by $\mathbf{C}_{LL} = E[\mathbf{D}_L \mathbf{D}_L^\top]$, $\mathbf{C}_{SS} = E[\mathbf{D}_S \mathbf{D}_S^\top]$, and $\mathbf{C}_{LS} = E[\mathbf{D}_L \mathbf{D}_S^\top]$, in which $E[\cdot]$ calculates the expectation. The solution of $\mathbf{w}_L$ and $\mathbf{w}_S$ are the eigenvectors of a generalized eigenvalue problem derived from Eq. (1) and the mapping matrices $\mathbf{W}_L$ and $\mathbf{W}_S$ are composed of eigenvectors corresponding to different eigenvalues.

2.2   S-PET Estimation by Multi-level CCA

In the multi-level scheme, we learn CCA mapping in each level and reconstruct the test L-PET patch $\mathbf{y}_{L,p}$ in the common space at all times. Specifically, let $\mathbf{D}_L^1$ and $\mathbf{D}_S^1$ be the L-PET and S-PET dictionaries in the first level and $\mathbf{W}_L^1$ and $\mathbf{W}_S^1$ be the learned mappings. The reconstruction coefficients $\boldsymbol{\alpha}^1$ for $\mathbf{y}_{L,p}$ in this level are determined by

$$\min_{\boldsymbol{\alpha}^1} \|\mathbf{W}_L^{1\top}(\mathbf{y}_{L,p} - \mathbf{D}_L^1 \boldsymbol{\alpha}^1)\|_2^2 + \lambda \|\boldsymbol{\delta} \odot \boldsymbol{\alpha}^1\|_2^2, \quad \text{s.t. } \mathbf{1}^\top \boldsymbol{\alpha}^1 = 1, \tag{2}$$

where $\odot$ is the element-wise multiplication, and each element in $\boldsymbol{\delta}$ is computed from the Euclidean distance between the projected patch $\mathbf{W}_L^\top \mathbf{y}_{L,p}$ and one projected dictionary atom in $\mathbf{W}_L^{1\top} \mathbf{D}_L^1$. Equation (2) is essentially locality-constrained linear coding (LLC) and it has an analytical solution [12]. It is shown in [15] that locality constraint can be more effective than sparsity. Instead of using $\boldsymbol{\alpha}^1$ to estimate the S-PET patch as output, the dictionary atoms in $\mathbf{D}_L^1$ with significant coefficients (e.g., larger than a predefined threshold) in $\boldsymbol{\alpha}^1$ are selected to build a refined L-PET dictionary. The refined L-PET dictionary and the corresponding S-PET dictionary are used for common space learning and reconstruction in the next level.

In the kth level where $k \geq 2$, the reconstruction coefficients $\boldsymbol{\alpha}^k$ are calculated by

$$\min_{\boldsymbol{\alpha}^k} \|\mathbf{W}_L^{k^\top}(\mathbf{y}_{L,p} - \mathbf{D}_L^k\boldsymbol{\alpha}^k)\|_2^2 + \lambda\|\boldsymbol{\delta} \odot \boldsymbol{\alpha}^k\|_2^2 + \gamma\|\mathbf{W}_S^{k^\top}(\mathbf{y}_{S,p}^k - \mathbf{y}_{S,p}^{k-1})\|_2^2,$$
$$\text{s.t. } \mathbf{1}^\top\boldsymbol{\alpha}^k = 1, \tag{3}$$

where $\mathbf{W}_L^k$ and $\mathbf{W}_S^k$ are the CCA mappings for $\mathbf{D}_L^k$ and $\mathbf{D}_S^k$ at the current k^{th} level, $\mathbf{y}_{S,p}^{k-1} = \mathbf{D}_S^{k-1}\boldsymbol{\alpha}^{k-1}$ is the estimated S-PET patch from the previous $k-1^{th}$ level and $\mathbf{y}_{S,p}^k = \mathbf{D}_S^k\boldsymbol{\alpha}^k$ is the estimation in the kth level. The third term of Eq. (3) enforces that the estimation in the kth level does not significantly deviate from the estimation from the $k-1^{th}$ level. This ensures a gradual and smooth refinement in each level.

By repeating the above process, the dictionary atoms that are the most important in reconstructing a test L-PET patch are selected, and therefore the mapping and reconstruction in the subsequent level can be more effective towards the goal of estimating a particular target S-PET patch, thanks to this data-driven adaptive dictionary refinement. In the final level, we obtain the L-PET-based estimation denoted by $\hat{\mathbf{y}}_{S,p}$.

2.3   MRI-Based Estimation and Fusion

As MRI can provide complementary information such as anatomical details, we would like to take this advantage for S-PET estimation. For a given L-PET patch $\mathbf{y}_{L,p}$, we select one MR modality from T1 and DTI (i.e., fractional anisotropy (FA) and mean diffusivity (MD)) such that the normalized correlation between the selected MRI patch $\mathbf{y}_{M,p}$ and $\mathbf{y}_{L,p}$ is the highest, although other advanced methods such as combining all MR modalities can be used. To compute the normalized correlation, the patches are first normalized to have a zero mean and unit variance to eliminate the influence of different intensity scales across different image modalities. The MRI-based estimation $\check{\mathbf{y}}_{S,p}$ is computed similarly as the L-PET-based estimation, $\hat{\mathbf{y}}_{S,p}$, by using the dictionary pair from the MR images of selected modality and the S-PET images in the training set. The final estimation is obtained by

$$\mathbf{y}_{S,p} = \omega_1\hat{\mathbf{y}}_{S,p} + \omega_2\check{\mathbf{y}}_{S,p}. \tag{4}$$

The fusion weights ω_1 and ω_2 are learned adaptively for each target S-PET patch by minimizing the following function

$$\min_{\omega_1, \omega_2} \|\mathbf{W}_L^\top\mathbf{y}_{L,p} - \mathbf{W}_S^\top\mathbf{y}_{S,p}\|_2^2 + \|\mathbf{P}_M^\top\mathbf{y}_{M,p} - \mathbf{P}_S^\top\mathbf{y}_{S,p}\|_2^2,$$
$$\text{s.t. } \mathbf{y}_{S,p} = \omega_1\hat{\mathbf{y}}_{S,p} + \omega_2\check{\mathbf{y}}_{S,p}, \quad \omega_1 + \omega_2 = 1, \quad \omega_1 \geq 0, \quad \omega_2 \geq 0. \tag{5}$$

L-PET   S-PET   T1   DTI (FA)   DTI (MD)

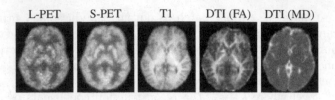

Fig. 3. An example of PET and MR images scanned from one subject.

Table 1. Performance comparisons in terms of PSNR (best results are in bold)

Subject ID	SR [6]	RF [6]	CCA	CCA	CCA	m-CCA	m-CCA	m-CCA
	L+T1	L+T1	L	L+T1	L+T1/DTI	L	L+T1	L+T1/DTI
1	22.7	24.0	25.1	25.4	25.7	25.6	25.9	26.3
2	25.5	26.6	27.0	27.2	27.2	28.0	28.3	28.6
3	23.3	24.8	24.8	25.7	26.2	26.1	26.4	26.7
4	21.7	22.9	23.1	23.6	23.9	23.2	24.0	24.3
5	23.8	25.4	25.6	25.9	26.1	27.1	27.3	27.6
6	21.4	21.3	22.1	22.9	23.3	22.8	22.9	23.2
7	22.1	24.0	25.1	25.4	25.6	25.5	25.9	26.3
8	25.5	26.9	27.4	28.1	28.2	29.3	29.8	30.3
Average	23.3	24.5	25.0	25.5	25.8	26.0	26.3	26.7

where $\mathbf{W}_L$ and $\mathbf{W}_S$ are the mappings in the last level for the L-PET-based estimation, while $\mathbf{P}_M$ and $\mathbf{P}_S$ are the mappings in the last level for MRI-based estimation. This objective function ensures that in their corresponding common spaces, the final output is close to both the test L-PET patch and the test MRI patch. Note that the L-PET-based estimation and the MRI-based estimation can be obtained with different number of levels as described in Sect. 2.2. The solution of ω_1 and ω_2 can be efficiently computed using a recently proposed active-set algorithm [2].

3   Experiments

Our dataset consists of real PET and MR brain images from eight subjects including five females and three males. The mean and the standard deviation of the subjects' ages are 26.4 and 6.2, respectively. For each subject, an L-PET image, an S-PET image as well as three MR images (T1, FA, and MD) were acquired. The tracer dose in L-PET imaging is a quarter of that for obtaining an S-PET image. MR images were rigid aligned to their corresponding PET images, and then all images were affine aligned to the first subject by FLIRT [5]. Each image has a voxel size of $2.09 \times 2.09 \times 2.03\,\text{mm}^3$. Figure 3 shows an example of PET and MR images from one subject.

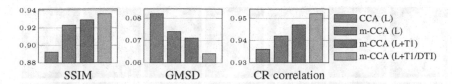

Fig. 4. Quantitative evaluation of our method with intermediate results. Three metrics are considered: SSIM [13] (*higher is better*), GMSD [14], (*lower is better*), and CR [8] correlation (*higher is better*).

To evaluate the proposed method, a *leave-one-out cross-validation* (LOOCV) strategy is adopted. The patch size is set to $m \times m \times m = 5 \times 5 \times 5$ and the neighborhood size for dictionary patch extraction is $t \times t \times t = 15 \times 15 \times 15$. The patches are extracted with a stride of one voxel and the overlapping regions are averaged in constructing the final estimation. During preselection, $K = 1200$ patches are selected. The regularization parameter λ in Eqs. (2) and (3) is set to 0.01 and γ in Eq. (3) is set to 0.1. We use two-level CCA for both L-PET and MRI-based estimation in the experiments, since the use of more levels does not bring significant improvement while increasing the computational time. In the first level, the dictionary atoms with coefficients larger than 0.001 in α^1 are selected for learning common space mappings and reconstruction coefficients α^2 in the second level.

We compare our method with the RF-based and SR-based estimation methods given in [6]. Table 1 shows the results for each subject in terms of peak signal-to-noise ratio (PSNR) by using different methods. Intermediate results in our method are also provided. Specifically, *CCA* means estimation using one-level CCA, *L* indicates that the output is L-PET-based estimation, *L+T1* incorporates both L-PET and MRI-based estimations with T1-weighted MRI as the only source, and *L+T1/DTI* fuses the L-PET and MRI-based estimation using T1 or DTI.

We can see that our method is superior to both the RF-based and SR-based methods even with one-level CCA and L-PET. Incorporating multi-level CCA increases the average PSNR from 25.0 to 26.0. Moreover, fusion with estimation from MRI further improves the output quality. As can be seen from the results, a single level of CCA using L-PET and all MRI modalities achieves an average PSNR of 25.8, which is inferior to the result by m-CCA using L-PET as the only estimation source. A best average PSNR of 26.7 is achieved with the proposed m-CCA using both L-PET and multi-modal MRI. Note that our method does not need the segmentation of brain images into different tissue types as required in the RF-based method [6].

To further evaluate the contribution of each step in our method, we compute the structural similarity (SSIM) [13] and gradient magnitude similarity deviation (GMSD) [14] as additional image quality (IQ) metrics. SSIM considers the perceived change in structural information while GMSD measures how an image is distorted from its undistorted reference. Furthermore, we calculate contrast recovery (CR) which is defined in National Electrical Manufacturers Association

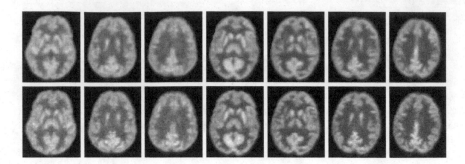

Fig. 5. Estimated S-PET images by our method (*top*) and the ground truth (*bottom*).

(NEMA) IQ protocol and has been used to evaluate PET image quality [8]. The CR is computed as $CR = 1 - \frac{m_{ROI}}{m_{background}}$. In our evaluation, m_{ROI} and $m_{background}$ are the mean voxel intensities of the hippocampus regions and the surrounding background regions. Ideally, in the estimated S-PET image, CR should be the same as that in the ground truth. Thus, we calculate the correlation between the CR scores in the estimated S-PET images and the CR scores in the ground truth S-PET images. A high CR correlation suggests a good estimation.

Figure 4 shows the score comparisons between each combination of the components of our method. Similar to Table 1, each component in our method helps improve the estimation accuracy. The major improvement is from the proposed multi-level CCA scheme, which boosts the quality of the estimations in terms of various quantitative measures. Fusion with MRI-based estimation is also essential and both T1 and DTI are helpful. For qualitative results, some samples of the estimated S-PET images by our method as compared to the ground truth are shown in Fig. 5. As can be seen, the estimated S-PET images are very close to the ground truth S-PET images. The difference between them is that the estimated images are smoother than the ground truth, due to the averaging in constructing the final output from overlapped patches.

4   Conclusions

In this paper, a multi-level CCA scheme has been proposed for estimating standard-dose PET images from low-dose PET and multi-modal MR images. Both quantitative and visual results have validated the efficacy of the proposed method on a real human brain dataset. As compared to state-of-the-art methods, superior performance was achieved by our approach and we have demonstrated that high quality PET images can be estimated from low-dose PET images and MR images, suggesting that the dose of radioactive tracer can be significantly reduced during the PET imaging process while still obtaining high quality PET images. Future work includes larger scale experiments and clinical study of the diagnostic quality of the estimated S-PET images.

References

1. Chen, W.: Clinical applications of PET in brain tumors. J. Nucl. Med. **48**, 1468–1481 (2007)
2. Chen, Y., Mairal, J., Harchaoui, Z.: Fast and robust archetypal analysis for representation learning. In: CVPR, pp. 1478–1485 (2014)
3. Coupé, P., Manjón, J.V., Fonov, V., Pruessner, J., Robles, M., Collins, D.L.: Patch-based segmentation using expert priors: application to hippocampus and ventricle segmentation. NeuroImage **54**, 940–954 (2011)
4. Eskildsen, S.F., Coupé, P., Fonov, V., Manjón, J.V., Leung, K.K., Guizard, N., Wassef, S.N., Østergaard, L.R., Collins, D.L.: BEaST: Brain extraction based on nonlocal segmentation technique. NeuroImage **59**(3), 2362–2373 (2012)
5. Fischer, B., Modersitzki, J.: FLIRT: A flexible image registration toolbox. In: Gee, J.C., Maintz, J.B.A., Vannier, M.W. (eds.) WBIR 2003. LNCS, vol. 2717, pp. 261–270. Springer, Heidelberg (2003)
6. Kang, J., Gao, Y., Wu, Y., Ma, G., Shi, F., Lin, W., Shen, D.: Prediction of standard-dose PET image by low-dose PET and MRI images. In: Wu, G., Zhang, D., Zhou, L. (eds.) MLMI 2014. LNCS, vol. 8679, pp. 280–288. Springer, Heidelberg (2014)
7. Nguyen, V.G., Lee, S.J.: Incorporating anatomical side information into PET reconstruction using nonlocal regularization. IEEE TIP **22**, 3961–3973 (2013)
8. Oehmigen, M., Ziegler, S., Jakoby, B.W., Georgi, J.C., Paulus, D.H., Quick, H.H.: Radiotracer dose reduction in integrated PET/MR: Implications from national electrical manufacturers association phantom studies. J. Nucl. Med. **55**, 1361–1367 (2014)
9. Pichler, B.J., Kolb, A., Nägele, T., Schlemmer, H.P.: PET/MRI: Paving the way for the next generation of clinical multimodality imaging applications. J. Nucl. Med. **51**, 333–336 (2010)
10. Quigley, H., Colloby, S.J., O'Brien, J.T.: PET imaging of brain amyloid in dementia: a review. Int. J. Geriatr. Psychiatry **26**, 991–999 (2011)
11. Wang, G., Qi, J.: PET image reconstruction using kernel method. IEEE TMI **34**, 61–71 (2015)
12. Wang, J., Yang, J., Yu, K., Lv, F., Huang, T., Gong, Y.: Locality-constrained linear coding for image classification. In: CVPR, pp. 3360–3367 (2010)
13. Wang, Z., Bovik, A., Sheikh, H., Simoncelli, E.: Image quality assessment: from error visibility to structural similarity. IEEE TIP **13**, 600–612 (2004)
14. Xue, W., Zhang, L., Mou, X., Bovik, A.: Gradient magnitude similarity deviation: a highly efficient perceptual image quality index. IEEE TIP **23**, 684–695 (2014)
15. Yu, K., Zhang, T., Gong, Y.: Nonlinear learning using local coordinate coding. In: NIPS, pp. 2223–2231 (2009)

Image Super-Resolution by Supervised Adaption of Patchwise Self-similarity from High-Resolution Image

Guorong Wu[1(✉)], Xiaofeng Zhu[1], Qian Wang[2], and Dinggang Shen[1]

[1] Department of Radiology and BRIC,
University of North Carolina at Chapel Hill, Chapel Hill, USA
guorong_wu@med.unc.edu
[2] Med-X Research Institute of Shanghai Jiao Tong University, Shanghai, China

Abstract. Image super-resolution is of great interest in medical imaging field. However, different from natural images studied in computer vision field, the low-resolution (LR) medical imaging data is often a stack of high-resolution (HR) 2D slices with large slice thickness. Consequently, the goal of super-resolution for medical imaging data is to reconstruct the missing slice(s) between any two consecutive slices. Since some modalities (e.g., T1-weighted MR image) are often acquired with high-resolution (HR) image, it is intuitive to harness the prior self-similarity information in the HR image for guiding the super-resolution of LR image (e.g., T2-weighted MR image). The conventional way is to find the profile of patchwise self-similarity in the HR image and then use it to reconstruct the missing information at the same location of LR image. However, the local morphological patterns could vary significantly across the LR and HR images, due to the use of different imaging protocols. Therefore, such direct (un-supervised) adaption of self-similarity profile from HR image is often not effective in revealing the actual information in the LR image. To this end, we propose to employ the existing image information in the LR image to supervise the estimation of self-similarity profile by requiring it *not only* being optimal in representing patches in the HR image, *but also* producing less reconstruction errors for the existing image information in the LR image. Moreover, to make the anatomical structures spatially consistent in the reconstructed image, we simultaneously estimate the self-similarity profiles for a stack of patches across consecutive slices by solving a group sparse patch representation problem. We have evaluated our proposed super-resolution method on both simulated brain MR images and real patient images with multiple sclerosis lesion, achieving promising results with more anatomical details and sharpness.

1 Introduction

In most imaging-based studies and clinical diagnosis, image resolution is important to reveal disease-specific imaging markers and quantify the structure/functional difference across individual subjects. However, a high-resolution 3D image is not always available due to consideration of radiation dose or scanning time, thus leading to a compromised low-resolution image (i.e., a stack of high in-plane resolution 2D slices with

© Springer International Publishing Switzerland 2015
G. Wu et al. (Eds.): Patch-MI 2015, LNCS 9467, pp. 10–18, 2015.
DOI: 10.1007/978-3-319-28194-0_2

large slice thickness). Hence, the key to resolution enhancement in medical imaging is to reconstruct the missing slices between any adjacent HR 2D slices.

So far, various image super-resolution (SR) methods have been proposed by using *either* single LR image *or* multiple LR images. In contrast, Rousseau [1] attempted to use both LR and HR images of the same subject for SR in magnetic resonance (MR) imaging. As an HR 3D T1-weighted MR image is often scanned, it is very attractive to enhance an LR image (e.g., T2-weighted MR image) by learning some prior from its corresponding HR T1 image. A possible choice of such prior is the patchwise self-similarity profile, which describes the representation of an image patch by a set of surrounding patches in the HR image. The underlying assumption is that: if the LR (T2) image and its HR (T1) image lie in the same space, their corresponding points should have a similar self-similarity profile. Thus, the LR (T2) image point can borrow the self-similarity profile computed from the HR (T1) image to recover the missing intensity value by a weighted average of existing intensity values in the LR (T2) image.

Since different imaging modalities measure different tissue properties, the above assumption could fail. For example, the imaging pattern of multiple sclerosis (MS) lesion is clearly visible in the T2-weighted image, but not in the T1-weightd image. Hence, Rousseau [1] proposed to transfer the self-similarity profiles from the HR image to the LR image according to the correlation between the self-similarity profiles separately estimated in the HR and LR images, where the latter has to be estimated from certain initialization. Due to the lack of clear guidance in adapting the self-similarity profiles from HR image, it is still limited in revealing the actual appearances in the LR image. In addition, most of the existing super-resolution methods estimate self-similarity profile at each image point independently, thus leading to inconsistency along the structure boundaries due to the independent estimations.

To overcome all the above limitations, we propose to use the existing image information in the LR image to guide the adaption of self-similarity profile from the HR image. Specifically, we require the estimated patchwise self-similarity profile should satisfy the following conditions: (1) it should best represent each image patch by its nearby patches in the HR image; (2) it should produce the lowest reconstruction error between the existing image appearance in the LR image and the predicted image appearance by adapting the self-similarity profile from HR image; (3) it should be consistent across neighboring slices; and (4) it should be free of initialization. We accordingly propose a novel SR method for jointly recovering all missing intensities for a stack of patches across consecutive slices by solving a group sparse patch representation problem.

We have extensively evaluated our novel SR method on both simulated brain MR images (from Brainweb) and the clinical images with MS lesion. Promising results are achieved, with significant improvement on structural details and image sharpness.

2   Method

Super-Resolution Model in Medical Imaging Scenario. The SR model, widely used in computer vision, assumes that an LR image is a degraded version of the to-be-estimated HR image. Various regularization terms are used to constrain the space of solutions, which inevitably alters the existing intensity values in LR image. In medical imaging field, the task is slightly different since the LR image is usually a stack of HR 2D images. The goal of SR is mainly to increase the resolution across slices. Meanwhile, the estimated HR image is required to preserve the existing intensity values since they are critical in diagnosis and investigation.

In light of this, our proposed SR method is fully data-driven, aiming to achieve M-times SR by reconstructing the $M - 1$ missing slices between every two consecutive slices L_t^0 and L_{t+1}^0 in the LR image $L = \left[L_1^0, \ldots, L_t^0, \ldots, L_N^0\right]$, which has N 2D slices. Hence, the enhanced HR image H is constructed as $H = [[H_1], \ldots, [H_t] \ldots, [H_N]]$, where each slice bundle $[H_t] = \left[L_t^0, H_t^1, \ldots, H_t^{M-1}\right]$ starts with one original slice L_t^0, followed by $M - 1$ recovered slices $\left\{H_t^m | m = 1, \ldots, M - 1\right\}$. In our method, there is an HR prior image $Y = [[Y_1], \ldots, [Y_t], \ldots, [Y_N]]$ that can be used to guide the SR, where $[Y_t] = \left[Y_t^0, \ldots, Y_t^{M-1}\right]$ denotes a particular slice bundle of HR prior image. As the HR prior image is acquired from the same subject, it is not difficult to obtain good registration between Y and L.

Unsupervised Self-similarity Adaption. Assume that the space of a 2D plane has been divided into the overlapped patches. For an arbitrary patch centered at $v \in \mathbb{R}^2$ in the 2D plane, we use $y_t^m(v)$, a column vector (green solid box in Fig. 1), to denote the intensity values within the patch from slice Y_t^m in the HR prior image. Next, we can estimate the self-similarity profile for $y_t^m(v)$ by using the image patches extracted from a search neighborhood $n(v)$ in slices Y_t^0 and Y_{t+1}^0, which form the HR patch dictionary $D = \{y_{t+\varepsilon}^0(u) | u \in n(v), \varepsilon = 0, 1\}$. Note that we only collect the image patches from the HR prior image at slices Y_t^0 and Y_{t+1}^0, since we will reconstruct the missing intensity values by only using the existing imaging data in slices L_t^0 and L_{t+1}^0 of LR image. Similarly, we can construct another dictionary E by replacing each column in D with the corresponding patch from the LR image. Since the SR procedure is the same at every location v, we drop off the variable v in $y_t^m(v)$ for clarity. Non-local mean technique is used in [1] to determine the self-similarity of each atom in D w.r.t. the target y_t^m. In order to suppress the noisy patches, we go one step further to solve the self-similarity profile w_t^m (a column vector) with sparsity constraint [2, 3] as:

$$\hat{w}_t^m = \arg \min_{w_t^m} \left\| y_t^m - Dw_t^m \right\|_2^2 + \lambda \left\| w_t^m \right\|_1, \tag{1}$$

where large value in the weighting vector $\hat{w}_t^m$ suggests high self-similarity between particular atom in D and y_t^m. Since the HR prior image Y is aligned with the LR image L, the unsupervised way to recover the image patch h_t^m in LR image domain is to directly apply the self-similarity profile $\hat{w}_t^m$ to the dictionary E by $\hat{h}_t^m = E\hat{w}_t^m$.

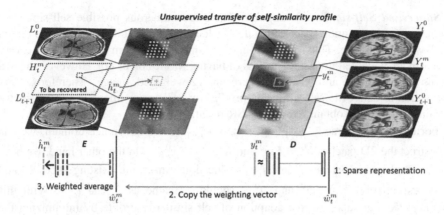

Fig. 1. Unsupervised adaptation of the self-similarity profile from HR image Y to LR image L (Color figure online).

As shown in Fig. 1, dots in the middle right and middle left are the centers of the atoms in D and E, respectively. Due to the sparsity constraint in (1), only a few atoms in D have the non-zero weights (i.e., those red dots), and the rest have zero weights (i.e., yellow dots). The unsupervised adaption of self-similarity profile is to simply copy and apply the weighting vector to E, as shown in the bottom of Fig. 1.

Supervised Self-similarity Adaption by Group Sparse Patch Representation. To overcome the limitations of unsupervised self-similarity adaption, we propose our new supervised approach with the following improvements.

A. Concurrent Self-similarity Profile Computation. Instead of computing the self-similarity profile for each patch independently, we simultaneously determine the self-similarity profiles for a stack of 2D image patches $\boldsymbol{\Psi} = \left[y_t^0, y_t^1 \ldots, y_t^{M-1}, y_{t+1}^0\right]$, where they have the same centers in the 2D plane but in consecutive slices. The goal is to jointly estimate the stack of the missing patches $[h_t^m]_{m=1,\ldots M-1}$ between the two existing LR slices L_t^0 and L_{t+1}^0. It is apparent that the patches between two consecutive LR slices L_t^0 and L_{t+1}^0 have similar appearances, although the slice thickness might be large. Thus, it is reasonable to require their self-similarity profiles should be similar as well. Thus, by placing all self-similarity profiles into a weighting matrix $\boldsymbol{W} = \left[w_t^0, w_t^1 \ldots, w_t^{M-1}, w_{t+1}^0\right]$, the joint sparse patch representation can be formulated by introducing the $L_{2,1}$-norm [4] for requiring each weighting vector in $\boldsymbol{W}$ to have a similar sparsity pattern:

$$\hat{w} = \arg\ \min_{\boldsymbol{W}} \|\boldsymbol{\Psi} - \boldsymbol{DW}\|_2^2 + \lambda_1 \|\boldsymbol{W}\|_1 + \lambda_2 \|\boldsymbol{W}\|_{2,1} \qquad (2)$$

where λ_1 and λ_2 are the coefficients balancing the strength of sparsity and the consistency of sparsity pattern.

B. Supervised Self-similarity Adaption. There are numerous possible self-similarity profiles w_t^m in the solution space of (2) if y_t^m is located in the white matter (WM) region of T1-weighted image. This is because most of the patches from WM region are very similar in T1-weighted image, regardless of having MS lesion or not. However, the MS lesions have unique and visible pattern in T2-weighted image. Therefore, clear supervision to adapt the self-similarity profile from HR prior image to the LR image domain is the key to obtain reasonable SR result.

Fortunately, by directly adapting w_t^0 and w_{t+1}^0 to the LR image domain, we can reconstruct the 2D patches $\widehat{h}_t^0 = E w_t^0$ and $\widehat{h}_{t+1}^0 = E w_{t+1}^0$. On the other hand, we have the observed image patches l_t^0 and l_{t+1}^0 at location v from the existing slices L_t^0 and L_{t+1}^0, respectively. Thus, $\widehat{h}_t^0$ and $\widehat{h}_{t+1}^0$ should be same as l_t^0 and l_{t+1}^0. With this guidance, we can supervise the adaption of self-similarity profile by minimizing the residuals, e.g., $\left\| l_t^0 - E w_t^0 \right\|_2^2$ and $\left\| l_{t+1}^0 - E w_{t+1}^0 \right\|_2^2$. Since we use the $L_{2,1}$-norm to enforce each column vector in W having the similar sparsity pattern, the adaption of w_t^0 and w_{t+1}^0 can be propagated to other self-similarity profiles w_t^m. Hence, we further extend the objective function of joint self-similarity profiles estimation in (2) to the supervised adaption as below:

$$\hat{w} = \arg\ \min_W \| \mathbf{\Psi} - D w \|_2^2 + \lambda_1 \| W \|_1 + \lambda_2 \| W \|_{2,1} + \lambda_3 \sum\nolimits_{\varepsilon=0}^{1} \left\| l_{t+\varepsilon}^0 - E w_{t+\varepsilon}^0 \right\|_2^2, \quad (3)$$

where λ_3 is a coefficient to control the strength of supervision. To optimize (3), we use the $L_{2,1}$ regularized Euclidian projection method in [4, 5].

Figure 2 illustrates $2\times$ super resolution scenario ($M = 2$) of our supervised self-similarity profile adaption. The pink solid boxes denote the patches from the HR prior image, while the pink dash boxes denote the corresponding patches in the LR image. We jointly optimize the self-similarity profiles for the image patches on the HR prior image (pink and green boxes in the right panel of Fig. 2) via the $L_{2,1}$-norm sparse patch representation. Meanwhile, we steer the adaption of the self-similarity profiles towards the LR image domain by minimizing the residuals between the existing and reconstructed image patches (black dash arrows in the bottom of Fig. 2). After we repeat the same procedure to all locations with missing intensity values, we can obtain the resolution enhanced image H from the LR image L.

3   Experiments

We evaluate the performance of our new SR method on simulated MR brain image (from Brainweb) and real patient image with MS lesion, using PSNR (Peak Signal-to-Noise Ratio) and SSIM (Structural Similarity Index) [6] as quantitative measures. We compare the SR performance with both cubic and B-spline interpolations. In addition, we evaluate the role of supervised self-similarity profile adaption by comparing our full method (with the supervision term in Eq. 3) with the degraded method (only using the group sparsity term in Eq. 2).

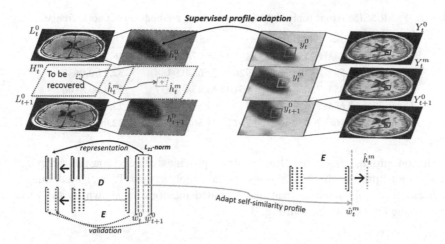

Fig. 2. Overview of the supervised self-similarity adaption (Color figure online).

3.1   Simulated MR Brain Image from Brainweb

Brainweb provides a simulated brain database, which is often used as gold standard for evaluating image enhancement performance. In this experiment, we use the HR T1-weighted image of $181 \times 217 \times 180$ voxels (voxel resolution $1 \times 1 \times 1\,\mathrm{mm}^3$) as the HR prior image. And, the HR T2-weigthed image ($181 \times 217 \times 180$ voxles, with voxel resolution $1 \times 1 \times 1\,\mathrm{mm}^3$) is used as the ground truth to compute the PSNR and SSIM measures. Table 1 shows the PSNR and SSIM scores on the noise free normal images, by cubic interpolation, B-spline interpolation, our degraded method (without supervised self-similarity profile adaption), and our full method. In order to specifically evaluate the advantage of *supervised self-similarity profile adaption* in our method, Table 2 shows the PSNR/SSIM scores computed only in the MS regions (i.e., the blue boxes shown in Fig. 3), instead of the entire brain. In both normal and MS cases, our supervised SR method achieves the highest PSNR and SSIM scores.

Table 1. PSNR/SSIM scores of SR methods on the noise free *normal* images.

Thickness	Cubic	B-spline	Degraded method	Our full method
2 mm	27.26/0.9380	27.35/0.9388	36.23/0.9682	**36.96/0.9802**
3 mm	22.21/0.8945	22.74/0.9015	30.18/0.9518	**32.83/0.9735**
5 mm	20.68/0.7692	20.93/0.7699	26.13/0.8126	**26.54/0.8163**
7 mm	18.31/0.7292	18.41/0.7305	24.36/0.7584	**24.89/0.7589**
9 mm	16.96/0.7024	17.11/0.7040	22.41/0.7306	**22.77/0.7353**

The reconstructed HR images by four methods are displayed in Fig. 3, with the normal image shown in the top panel while the MS images shown in the bottom panel. It is obvious that our method reveals more anatomical details than all other three methods, as indicated by the red arrows in normal image group and the blue boxes in

Table 2. PSNR/SSIM scores (only in MS region) of SR methods on the noise free *MS* images.

Thickness	Cubic	B-spline	Degraded method	Our full method
2 mm	26.74/0.8945	26.83/0.8949	35.97/0.9635	**36.25/0.9662**
3 mm	21.59/0.8831	27.36/0.9262	29.65/0.9438	**32.17/0.9637**
5 mm	20.05/0.7506	20.15/0.7510	25.43/0.8037	**25.83/0.8100**
7 mm	17.68/0.7161	17.83/0.7167	23.54/0.7416	**23.81/0.7422**
9 mm	16.16/0.7005	16.26/0.7011	21.86/0.7264	**22.05/0.7304**

MS lesion group. Since our full method provides supervision on adaption of self-similarity profile, the MS regions in the reconstructed T2-weighted image are much closer to gold standard than our degraded methods, as shown by the zoom-in views in the blue dash boxes in Fig. 3.

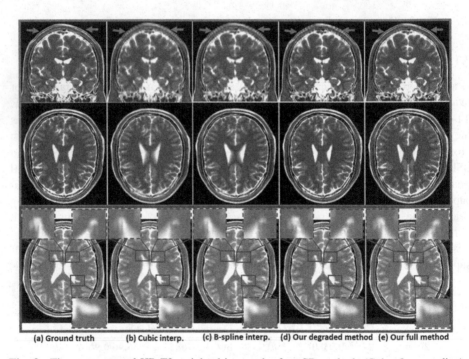

(a) Ground truth   (b) Cubic interp.   (c) B-spline interp.   (d) Our degraded method   (e) Our full method

Fig. 3. The reconstructed HR T2-weighted images by four SR methods (Color figure online)

3.2 Real Patient MR Brain Image with MS Lesion

We repeat the experiment on 12 T2-weighted MR images of MS patients with slice thickness 3 mm. The T1-wighted prior image for each patient reaches 1 mm slice thickness. To quantitatively evaluate the SR performance, we first generate the low-resolution images from 3 mm to 6 mm thickness by discarding the odd number slices. Then we apply 2× super resolution using four different SR methods to reconstruct back to 3 mm thickness. Table 3 shows the averaged PSNR and SSIM scores

Table 3. Performance (PSNR/SSIM) of SR methods on MS patients.

6 mm → 3 mm	Cubic	B-spline	Degraded method	Our full method
Whole brain	15.25/0.6532	15.49/0.6539	19.35/0.7116	**20.77/0.7206**
MS region only	17.43/0.7069	17.53/0.7077	22.16/0.7328	**23.26/0.7416**

(in whole brain and MS regions, respectively) by cubic interpolation, B-spline interpolation, our degraded method, and our full method.

Second, we enhance the original T2-weighted image from 3 mm to 1 mm. The reconstructed HR images by four SR methods are shown in Fig. 4. Through visual inspection, the reconstructed images by our full SR method have better image quality (i.e., anatomical details and sharpness) than other three methods.

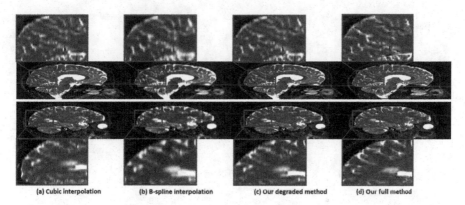

(a) Cubic interpolation   (b) B-spline interpolation   (c) Our degraded method   (d) Our full method

Fig. 4. Visualization of resolution enhancement on MS patient data by four SR methods.

4 Conclusion

We have developed a novel super-resolution method that can reconstruct the missing slices of a given image for resolution enhancement. This is achieved by adapting the self-similarity profiles from the HR prior image, using the LR image to supervise the adaption procedure via group sparse patch representation. Promising super resolution results have been achieved on both simulated and real patient data, which demonstrate its wide possible applications in various clinical studies.

References

1. Rousseau, F.: A non-local approach for image super-resolution using intermodality priors. Med. Image Anal. **14**, 594–605 (2010)
2. Tong, T., Wolz, R., Coupé, P., Hajnal, J., Rueckert, D.: Segmentation of MR images via discriminative dictionary learning and sparse coding: application to hippocampus labeling. NeuroImage **76**, 11–23 (2013)

3. Tibshirani, R.: Regression shrinkage and selection via the lasso. J. R. Stat. Soc. Ser. B **58**(1), 267–288 (1996)
4. Liu, J., Ji, S., Ye, J.: Multi-task feature learning via efficient L2,1-norm minimization. In: Proceeding of the 25th Conference on Uncertainty in Artificial Intelligence, Montreal, Canada (2012)
5. Liu, J., Ji, S., Ye, J.: SLEP: sparse learning with efficient projections. Arizona State University (2009)
6. Wang, Z., Bovik, A.C., Sheikh, H.R., Simoncelli, E.P.: Image quality assessment: from error visibility to structural similarity. IEEE Trans. Image Process. **13**, 600–612 (2004)

Automatic Hippocampus Labeling Using the Hierarchy of Sub-region Random Forests

Lichi Zhang[1], Qian Wang[1], Yaozong Gao[2,3], Guorong Wu[3], and Dinggang Shen[3(✉)]

[1] School of Biomedical Engineering, Med-X Research Institute,
Shanghai Jiao Tong University, Shanghai, China
{lichizhang,wang.qian}@sjtu.edu.cn
[2] Department of Computer Science,
University of North Carolina at Chapel Hill, Chapel Hill, USA
yzgao@cs.unc.edu
[3] Department of Radiology and BRIC,
University of North Carolina at Chapel Hill, Chapel Hill, USA
{grwu,dgshen}@med.unc.edu

Abstract. In this paper, we propose a multi-atlas-based framework for labeling hippocampus regions in the MR images. Our work aims at extending the random forests techniques for better performance, which contains two novel contributions: *First*, we design a novel strategy for training forests, to ensure that each forest is specialized in labeling the certain sub-region of the hippocampus in the images. In the testing stage, a novel approach is also presented for automatically finding the forests relevant to the corresponding sub-regions of the test image. *Second*, we present a novel localized registration strategy, which further reduces the shape variations of the hippocampus region in each atlas. This can provide better support for the proposed sub-region random forest approach. We validate the proposed framework on the ADNI dataset, in which atlases from NC, MCI and AD subjects are randomly selected for the experiments. The estimations demonstrated the validity of the proposed framework, showing that it yields better performances than the conventional random forests techniques.

1 Introduction

Accurate hippocampus labeling in the Magnetic Resonance (MR) brain images is a task of pivotal importance to the researches of many neural diseases including the Alzheimer's disease, schizophrenia and epilepsy [1]. The approaches are highly demanded, since it is infeasible to manually label a large set of 3D MR images. The main challenge in the segmentation of the hippocampus is that its grey intensity has close similarity to the surrounding region-of-interests (ROIs), such as amygdala, caudate nucleus, and thalamus [2]. Recent developments in this field concentrate on utilizing the information of manually labeled atlas images for the estimation of the test image. Currently a popular way among those techniques is the multi-atlas label propagation (MALP),

© Springer International Publishing Switzerland 2015
G. Wu et al. (Eds.): Patch-MI 2015, LNCS 9467, pp. 19–27, 2015.
DOI: 10.1007/978-3-319-28194-0_3

because of its robustness and simplicity for brain image labeling. Basically, there are two steps in the MALP approaches: (1) implement image registration to spatially align all images, and (2) use manual labels of the atlases to label the test image following certain label fusion strategies. There are many efforts aiming at improving the two steps. The detailed literature can be found in [3–6].

Random forest [7, 8] has been proven as a robust and fast multi-class classifier, which has been widely applied in many applications. A major contribution of the random forest is its bagging strategy, which adds randomness when training the classifiers. Zikic et al. [9] developed an "atlas forest" approach, which encodes each individual atlas and its corresponding label map via random forest. In the testing stage, atlas forests produce individual probabilistic labeling maps for the test image, the average of which is then regarded as the final labeling. Lombaert et al. [10] introduced Laplacian forests, in which the training images are re-organized and embedded into a low-dimensional manifold. Images having close similarities are grouped together. In the training stage, each tree is learned using only specific group of similar atlases following a guided bagging approach. The strategy concerning tree selection for the given test image is also proposed. The method is demonstrated experimentally to yield higher training efficiency and segmentation accuracy.

In this paper, we focus on the high variation across individual sub-regions in the ROI, and present a novel hierarchical learning framework to further improve the labeling performance. In the training stage, we develop a set of random forests, in which each forest is trained for a specific sub-region of the ROI. The random forests are placed into a hierarchical structure, which is derived from the registration-based auto-context technique. Specifically, for a higher level in the hierarchy, the random forests are trained with the context features that are extracted from the outputs of the lower level. Moreover, the lower-level outputs also guide all atlas and test images to be better registered for the higher level. In the testing stage, we select optimal forests for individual sub-regions of the test image. Therefore, the labeling results can be gradually improved by the hierarchy of random forests.

2 Method

In this section, we present the detailed description of the hierarchical learning framework, which consists of the training and the testing stages. The random forests implemented in this work are trained following a novel sub-region labeling strategy, while as in the testing stage a corresponding forest selection approach is applied for predicting the labeling information of the test image. In Sect. 2.1 we elaborate the strategy of sub-region random forests along with the forest selection method. Following the registration-based auto-context strategy, the method of sub-region random forest is extended as a hierarchical structure, in which each level contains a set of forests for image labeling. In Sect. 2.2, we describe the registration-based auto-context model, while as in Sect. 2.3 we present the methodologies of the proposed framework in the training and testing stages, respectively.

2.1 Sub-region Random Forest

The main idea of the sub-region random forest for labeling, as presented in Fig. 1, is that individual sub-regions should be trained and tested with the most suitable classifiers, as the variation across individual sub-regions can be high. In the training stage, we commence by randomly extracting numerous patches from the training images. Note that there is a higher priority of choosing patches in the boundary parts of the hippocampus. Suppose there are m patches selected, the set of 3D cubic patches is denoted as $P = \{p_1, p_2, \ldots, p_m\}$.

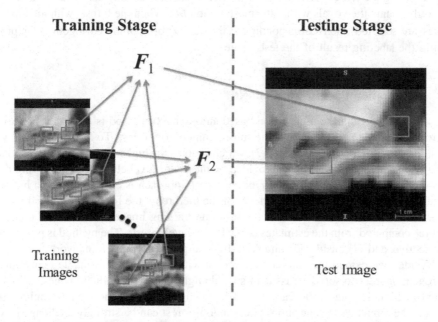

Fig. 1. The process of training and testing sub-region random forests. F_i is the trained forest specialized for labeling the corresponding sub-region in the test image.

Next, we cluster the selected patches based on their intensity similarities, which are measured by the mean of squared intensity differences between each pair of patches, given as: $S(p_i, p_j) = \sum_{x=1}^{r} \sum_{y=1}^{r} \sum_{z=1}^{r} [p_i(x,y) - p_j(x,y)]^2 / r^3$, where r is the patch length. The similarity measures are then utilized by the affinity propagation method [11] for clustering. When similar patches are grouped together, each cluster has its own forest to be trained, which can be used for predicting the labeling result of the corresponding sub-regions in test images.

In the testing stage, we follow the forest selection strategy to find the appropriate classifiers for labeling each voxel in the test image. It is implemented by utilizing a labeling prior (i.e., from tentative labeling output) as the reference. The estimation of the prior is presented in Sect. 2.3. Denoting the test image as I', and the prior as D', the i-th trained forest in the k-th level as F_i^k with their corresponding estimate D_i^k, we also obtain the overall mask information M_i in each cluster, which is the union of all regions that the patches in that cluster have ever covered. Denote the set of patches in the i-th cluster as $P^i = \{p_1^i, p_2^i, \ldots, p_{m_i}^i\}$, we have: $M_i = \bigcup_{j=1}^{m_i} R(p_j^i)$, where $R(p_j^i)$ is the region for p_j^i. The novel metric for the testing image is given as follows:

$$W\left(I', F_i^k\right) = DSC\left(D', D_i^k, M_i\right), \tag{1}$$

where $W\left(I', F_i^k\right)$ is the score for the forest selection. $DSC\left(D', D_i^k, M_i\right)$ is the function for measuring the Dice overlapping ratio between the two labeling estimates D' and D_i^k, as it only counts the voxels within the mask region M_i. When the forests with the top W scores are selected, their corresponding estimates D_i^k are combined together for producing the labeling result of the test image.

2.2 Registration-Based Auto-Context

Our aim in proposing the registration-based auto-context method is to further improve the robustness and performance of the sub-region random forest. To fulfill this goal, we consider the auto-context model in [13], which enables the higher-level forests to encode more comprehensive information provided by the lower-level classifiers. Following the auto-context model, the sub-region random forest approach is extended to be a hierarchical structure framework. In each level of the hierarchy, the forests are trained using *not only* the image appearance features from the training images, *but also* the context features computed from the estimates of the lower-level forests. The method is proved to be effective, and is considered suitable to be incorporated in this framework.

Besides, we extend the auto-context model with the aid of deformable registration approach, in order to solve the issue of spatial alignment in individual images, as mentioned in Sect. 1. Due to the variation of hippocampus across individual training/test images, the robustness of the sub-region random forest can be strongly challenged. As only the patches within a certain sub-region are provided for training the classifier, the forest would certainly give poor labeling predictions when it was applied to other mis-aligned sub-regions in test images. Therefore, the labeling performances can be greatly reduced.

In this paper, the tool of the diffeomorphic Demons [12] is applied to reduce the shape variations of the ROIs in the training/test images[1]. The conventional process of deformable registration is to align the intensity images into the template space that could be arbitrarily chosen, and then apply the computed warps to their corresponding label maps. However, the global registration process is ineffective in experiments, as the hippocampus is too small compared with the whole brain MR images.

---

[1] Settings for the diffeomorphic demons are: 15, 10 and 5 iterations in low, middle and high resolution. The smoothing kernel size is set as 2.0.

Therefore, we decide to implement a localized deformable registration in this work, which only focuses on aligning the ROI of hippocampus instead. This novel strategy is incorporated with the auto-context model, which is regarded as the registration-based auto-context method in this paper. The detailed methodology is given as follows:

(1) In the bottom level, we commence by initializing the context feature by averaging the initially-aligned label maps of all training atlases. It is shown in the experimental section that this strategy is proved valid when labeling the hippocampus region in the brain MR images. Since the shape and location variations of different atlases are stable, the average information of all label maps can be basically considered as the initial context feature for training the classifiers. The deformable registration in this level is also implemented following the traditional way, by registering whole intensity images directly.

(2) In the higher level, we first perform the localized registration to the training and test images. Since the labeling information for the test image is unknown, we use the estimated label maps in the lower level instead, to align with the label maps in the training images. In order to avoid the potential registration error, the label maps are smoothed by a Gaussian filter with $\sigma = 1$ mm. We then register the smoothed label maps to the template space, and apply the obtained warp information to the intensity images.

(3) Since the quality of registration is gradually improved when approaching the topmost of the hierarchy, the training and testing for individual levels of the hierarchy of random forests actually happen in different image spaces. Therefore, the estimated labeling is first warped back to the original image space using the inverted warp information in the lower level, and then registered to the template space in the higher level. Therefore, the tentative labeling results will get updated automatically through the increased levels of the hierarchy, enabling the higher-level forests to generate more robust and accurate labeling results.

2.3   Hierarchical Learning Framework

The methodologies in the training and testing stages for the proposed hierarchical learning framework are presented as follows:

Training Stage

(1) In the bottom level, we initialize the context feature and perform deformable registration by following the strategy of the registration-based auto-context method. Also note that since the localized registration strategy is not implemented in the bottom level as described in Sect. 2.2, the sub-region random forest is therefore not eligible to be applied in this level. Hence we instead apply the conventional random forest approach to the training images, where the bagging procedure is applied by the uniform sampling of the whole region in all training images.

(2) In the higher level, the estimates in the lower level are utilized for the deformable registration. Their corresponding probability label estimates for each hippocampus region are aligned to the template space using the computed warp information, and then considered as the context feature for training the forests in the higher level.

(3) Process of patch extraction and clustering is implemented, following the strategies introduced in Sect. 2.1. The procedure of the forest clustering and re-training is therefore implemented iteratively for completing the hierarchical structure of the forests in the end.

Testing Stage

(1) Given a new test image, we also commence by obtaining the context feature and implementing the registration following the same strategy as the training stage. In the bottom level, the forest selection strategy is not implemented, since the sub-region corresponds to the whole ROI and only one forest is available in this level, and the selection strategy requires prior labeling information.

(2) In the second and higher levels, the labeling estimate in the lower level is considered as the prior for the selection strategy, and also the source of the context features in the hierarchy. Using the introduced fusion strategy, iteratively the labeling results will be further refined, which is ended when reaching the top-most level in the hierarchy.

3   Experimental Results

In this section, we evaluate the proposed framework for labeling hippocampus in MR brain images. The dataset employed is the Alzheimer's Disease Neuroimaging Initiative (ADNI) dataset[2] [14], which provides a large number of adult brain MR images acquired from 1.5T MR scanners, along with the annotated left and right hippocampi.

We have randomly selected 101 ADNI images from the Normal Control (NC), Mild Cognitive Impairment (MCI) and Alzheimer's Disease (AD) subjects, in which one atlas containing the closest label map similarity in overall with the rest is considered as the template for the registration process. The template itself is excluded from subsequent training and testing. We used the standard preprocessing procedures following the works introduced in [6] to ensure the validity of the estimation. Besides, the ITK-based histogram matching program was also applied to all the ADNI images for the experiments, which were then rescaled to the intensity range [0 255]. Next, we implemented the FLIRT program in the FSL library [15] for affine registration to bring all images into the template space.

We implemented 10-fold cross-validation experiments for demonstrating the validity of the proposed methods. State succinctly, the 100 images are equally divided into 10 folds. In each fold, we select one fold for testing, and the rest for training.

---

[2] http://adni.loni.ucla.edu.

Table 1. Quantitative comparison of performances in different configurations when labeling the left and the right hippocampi.

DSC	Bottom level	Second level
Left Hippo.	81.82 % ± 0.89 %	82.31 % ± 0.90 %
Right Hippo.	82.08 % ± 0.60 %	82.33 % ± 0.60 %
Overall	**81.95 % ± 0.66 %**	**82.32 % ± 0.67 %**

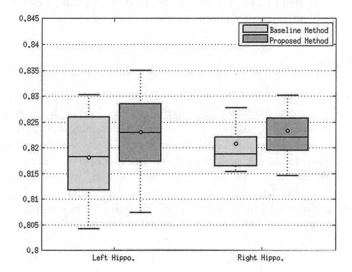

Fig. 2. The box plot for the labeling accuracies of different configurations on the left (left panel) and the right (right panel) hippocampi.

It is also noted that the same settings and parameters were used in all the experiments. Their values are decided by considering both aspects of computation costs and estimation performance. The maximum depth of each tree is 20, and each leaf node has a minimum of 8 samples. Each node chooses Haar-like features from a pool at the size of 1000. The Haar-like features are calculated from the 3D patches with the maximal size of 10 mm × 10 mm × 10 mm.

In this paper we construct a two-level hierarchical structure in the training stage for efficient computation. In the bottom level, one single random forest is trained using the conventional approach, which has 720 trees since the number of training atlases is large. In the second level, 20 patches with size of 15 × 15 × 15 are extracted in each training image. The number of forests are decided by the clustering process using affinity propagation based on the default settings, and each forest has 15 trees.

Our goal in this section is to demonstrate the improvements of the performance when the novel strategies are applied in the second level. Table 1 shows the comparison results between the labeling estimates and the groundtruth using the Dice ratio. Figure 2 presents the box plots that visualize the performances of the two levels. The left and the right panels show the information of the left and the right hippocampi, respectively. It can be observed that in both hippocampi, the DSC scores of the second level are better than that in the bottom level, which represent the performances of the conventional random forest technique. It is also worth noting that the p-value in the two-tailed paired t-test between any two levels for both left and right hippocampi is lower than 0.05, indicating that the proposed strategies can significantly improve the labeling accuracy when applied to MR brain images. The average runtime of the labeling process is around 10 min using a standard computer (Intel Core i7-4770 K 3.50 GHz, 16 GB RAM), which is affordable in the applications of medical image analysis. It is also noted that in the future work, more levels will be developed in the current hierarchical structure of random forests.

4   Conclusion

In this paper, we present a novel framework using the random forests and several other techniques. While the conventional methods train the forests using whole region information, each forest obtained following the proposed training strategy is focused on *only* the specific sub-regions of the ROI. We also provide the novel registration-based auto-context method to aid our work, and also a forest selection strategy for choosing the most suitable classifiers. In the experimental section, we apply the proposed framework to the ADNI dataset, in which we observe some significant improvements in the labeling performance. In the future work, we will seek possibilities of applying the proposed frameworks to labeling of other ROIs in the brain images.

References

1. Van Leemput, K., Bakkour, A., Benner, T., Wiggins, G., Wald, L.L., Augustinack, J., Dickerson, B.C., Golland, P., Fischl, B.: Automated segmentation of hippocampal subfields from ultra high resolution in vivo MRI. Hippocampus **19**, 549–557 (2009)
2. Fischl, B., Salat, D.H., Busa, E., Albert, M., Dieterich, M., Haselgrove, C., Van Der Kouwe, A., Killiany, R., Kennedy, D., Klaveness, S.: Whole brain segmentation: automated labeling of neuroanatomical structures in the human brain. Neuron **33**, 341–355 (2002)
3. Jia, H., Yap, P.-T., Shen, D.: Iterative multi-atlas-based multi-image segmentation with tree-based registration. NeuroImage **59**, 422–430 (2012)
4. Warfield, S.K., Zou, K.H., Wells, W.M.: Simultaneous truth and performance level estimation (STAPLE): an algorithm for the validation of image segmentation. IEEE Trans. Med. Imaging **23**, 903–921 (2004)
5. Wu, G., Wang, Q., Zhang, D., Nie, F., Huang, H., Shen, D.: A generative probability model of joint label fusion for multi-atlas based brain segmentation. Med. Image Anal. **18**, 881–890 (2013)
6. Coupé, P., Manjón, J.V., Fonov, V., Pruessner, J., Robles, M., Collins, D.L.: Patch-based segmentation using expert priors: application to hippocampus and ventricle segmentation. NeuroImage **54**, 940–954 (2011)
7. Breiman, L.: Random forests. Mach. Learn. **45**(1), 5–32 (2001). Springer
8. Criminisi, A., Shotton, J., Konukoglu, E.: Decision forests: A unified framework for classification, regression, density estimation, manifold learning and semi-supervised learning. Found. Trends® Comput. Graph. Vis. **7**, 81–227 (2012)

9. Zikic, D., Glocker, B., Criminisi, A.: Atlas encoding by randomized forests for efficient label propagation. In: Mori, K., Sakuma, I., Sato, Y., Barillot, C., Navab, N. (eds.) MICCAI 2013, Part III. LNCS, vol. 8151, pp. 66–73. Springer, Heidelberg (2013)

10. Lombaert, H., Zikic, D., Criminisi, A., Ayache, N.: Laplacian forests: semantic image segmentation by guided bagging. In: Golland, P., Hata, N., Barillot, C., Hornegger, J., Howe, R. (eds.) MICCAI 2014, Part II. LNCS, vol. 8674, pp. 496–504. Springer, Heidelberg (2014)

11. Frey, B.J., Dueck, D.: Clustering by passing messages between data points. Science **315**, 972–976 (2007)

12. Vercauteren, T., Pennec, X., Perchant, A., Ayache, N.: Diffeomorphic demons: efficient non-parametric image registration. NeuroImage **45**, S61–S72 (2009)

13. Tu, Z., Bai, X.: Auto-context and its application to high-level vision tasks and 3D brain image segmentation. IEEE Trans. Pattern Anal. Mach. Intell. **32**, 1744–1757 (2010)

14. Mueller, S.G., Weiner, M.W., Thal, L.J., Petersen, R.C., Jack, C., Jagust, W., Trojanowski, J.Q., Toga, A.W., Beckett, L.: The Alzheimer's disease neuroimaging initiative. Neuroimaging Clin. N. Am. **15**, 869–877 (2005)

15. Jenkinson, M., Beckmann, C.F., Behrens, T.E., Woolrich, M.W., Smith, S.M.: Fsl. Neuroimage **62**, 782–790 (2012)

Isointense Infant Brain Segmentation by Stacked Kernel Canonical Correlation Analysis

Li Wang[1], Feng Shi[1], Yaozong Gao[1,2],
Gang Li[1], Weili Lin[3], and Dinggang Shen[1(✉)]

[1] IDEA Lab, Department of Radiology and BRIC,
University of North Carolina at Chapel Hill, Chapel Hill, NC, USA
dinggang_shen@med.unc.edu

[2] Department of Computer Science, University of North Carolina at Chapel Hill,
Chapel Hill, NC, USA

[3] MRI Lab, Department of Radiology and BRIC,
University of North Carolina at Chapel Hill, Chapel Hill, NC, USA

Abstract. Segmentation of isointense infant brain (at ∼ 6-month-old) MR images is challenging due to the ongoing maturation and myelination process in the first year of life. In particular, signal contrast between white and gray matters inverses around 6 months of age, where brain tissues appear isointense and hence exhibit extremely low tissue contrast, thus posing significant challenges for automated segmentation. In this paper, we propose a novel segmentation method to address the above-mentioned challenges based on stacked kernel canonical correlation analysis (KCCA). Our main idea is to utilize the 12-month-old brain image with high tissue contrast to guide the segmentation of 6-month-old brain images with extremely low contrast. Specifically, we use KCCA to learn the common feature representations for both 6-month-old and the subsequent 12-month-old brain images of same subjects to make their features comparable in the common space. Note that the longitudinal 12-month-old brain images are not required in the testing stage, and they are required only in the KCCA based training stage to provide a set of longitudinal 6- and 12-month-old image pairs for training. Moreover, for optimizing the common feature representations, we propose a stacked KCCA mapping, instead of using only the conventional one-step of KCCA mapping. In this way, we can better use the 12-month-old brain images as multiple atlases to guide the segmentation of isointense brain images. Specifically, sparse patch-based multi-atlas labeling is used to propagate tissue labels in the (12-month-old) atlases and segment isointense brain images by measuring patch similarity between testing and atlas images with their learned common features. The proposed method was evaluated on 20 isointense brain images via leave-one-out cross-validation, showing much better performance than the state-of-the-art methods.

1 Introduction

The first year of life is the most dynamic phase of postnatal human brain development, with the rapid tissue growth and development of a wide range of cognitive and motor functions. To accurately measure the early brain development, one critical step is to

© Springer International Publishing Switzerland 2015
G. Wu et al. (Eds.): Patch-MI 2015, LNCS 9467, pp. 28–36, 2015.
DOI: 10.1007/978-3-319-28194-0_4

segment the infant brain image into different regions of interest (ROIs), e.g., white matter (WM), gray matter (GM), and cerebrospinal fluid (CSF). It is well-known that the segmentation of infant brain MRI is considerably more difficult than that of the adult brain MRI [1], due to reduced tissue contrast [2], increased noise, severe partial volume effect [3], and ongoing white matter myelination [2, 4]. In fact, as shown in Fig. 1, there are three distinct phases in the first-year brain MR images, with each phase having quite different white-gray matter contrast patterns (in chronological order) [5]: (1) the infantile phase (≤ 5 months), in which GM shows higher signal intensity than WM in the T1 MR images, as shown in Fig. 1(a); (2) the isointense phase (6–8 months), in which the signal intensity of WM is increasing during the development due to the myelination and maturation process; in this phase, GM has the lowest signal difference from WM, resulting in the lowest

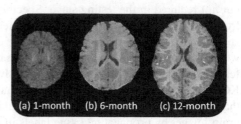

(a) 1-month   (b) 6-month   (c) 12-month

Fig. 1. Illustration of three distinct phases in infant brain development, with each phase having quite different WM/GM contrast patterns in the T1 MR images: (a) infantile, (b) isointense, and (c) early adult-like phases. The tissue contrast in the isointense phase (b) is the lowest, resulting in significant difficulty for tissue segmentation.

tissue contrast and hence significant difficulty for tissue segmentation; (3) the early adult-like phase (≥ 12 months), where GM intensity is much lower than that of WM in the T1 MR images, and this pattern is similar with that of the adult MR images.

Although many methods have been proposed for infant brain image segmentation, most of them focused either on segmentation of the infantile-phase images (≤ 5 months) or early adult-like images (≥ 12 months) [3, 4, 6, 7], which demonstrate a relatively good contrast between white matter and gray matter. **There is limited work that could effectively address the difficulties in segmentation of the isointense infant images.** Shi *et al.* [8] first proposed a 4D joint registration and segmentation framework for the segmentation of infant MR images in the first year of life. In this method, longitudinal images in both infantile and early adult-like phases were used to guide the segmentation of images in the isointense phase. The major limitation of these methods is that they fully depend on the availability of longitudinal images. On the other side, Wang *et al.* [9] proposed a sparse patch-based labeling method, which employs a number of isointense atlases with T1, T2 and FA (calculated from diffusion tensor imaging) for guiding the segmentation of isointense infant images. However, requirement of using three modality images (T1, T2 and FA) limits its application for subjects with no longitudinal images. *Moreover, the reliability of manual segmentation for the isointense atlases is also limited due to the extremely low tissue contrast in the isointense phase.*

In this paper, we propose a novel segmentation method to address the above-mentioned difficulties, by using stacked kernel canonical correlation analysis (KCCA) to learn common features for different time-point brain images. Our main motivation is to use the brain images with high tissue contrast (e.g., 12-month brain images) to guide the segmentation of 6-month-old brain images with low tissue contrast. Since the intensity appearances between them are dramatically different, it is not appropriate to directly utilize intensity appearance as features. To this end, we propose to employ KCCA to learn the common feature representations for the 6-month-old and the follow-up 12-month-old images of same subjects in the training stage. Note that the follow-up 12-month-old images are required only in the KCCA based training stage, but not required in the testing stage. Specifically, we consider image patches extracted from those pairs of training images as raw features, and then project them to a common space by KCCA. Also, instead of using the conventional one step of KCCA mapping, which is often not sufficient to capture those highly non-linear correlations between raw features, we iteratively project the previously mapped features and thus form a stacked KCCA mapping to seek an optimal common space for feature representation. After that, we employ a sparse patch-based multi-atlas labeling [9] to segment isointense brain images by propagating tissue labels in the training 12-month-old images (used as atlases), where patch similarity between testing (6-month-old) and atlas (12-month-old) images is measured by the learned common features. In experiments, we have comprehensively validated our method on 20 isointense brain images, obtaining much better results than the counterpart state-of-the-art methods.

2   Method

Our dataset consists of 20 infant subjects scanned at 6 months and 12 months of age. T1-weighted images were acquired for 144 sagittal slices with resolution of $1 \times 1 \times 1$ mm^3 on a Siemens head-only 3T scanners. During the scan, infants were asleep, unsedated, fitted with ear protection, and their heads were secured in a vacuum-fixation device. For image preprocessing, each 6-month-old image was non-rigidly registered to their corresponding 12-month-old image. Afterwards, standard image preprocessing steps were performed before segmentation, including skull stripping, intensity inhomogeneity correction [10], histogram matching, and removal of the cerebellum and brain stem by using in-house tools. To generate ground-truth segmentations of 12-month-old images, we first generated an initial reasonable segmentation by FreeSurfer [11], and then performed manual editing by an experienced rater to correct segmentation errors.

2.1   Stacked Kernel Canonical Correlation Analysis

Given a set of aligned 6-month-old and follow-up 12-month-old images, we randomly selected N pairs of image patches from 6-month-old and corresponding 12-month-old images, which are denoted as $\{x_n\}_{n=1}^N \in \mathbb{R}^{D \times N}$ and $\{y_n\}_{n=1}^N \in \mathbb{R}^D$, respectively. Here, x_n and y_n are D-dimensional column vectors. For simplicity, let $X = [x_1, \ldots, x_n, \ldots, x_N] \in \mathbb{R}^{D \times N}$, $Y = [y_1, \ldots, y_n, \ldots, y_N] \in \mathbb{R}^{D \times N}$. The aim of canonical correlation analysis (CCA) is to find a pair of linear projections ($w_x \in \mathbb{R}^D$ and $w_y \in \mathbb{R}^D$) to maximize the correlation between $w_x^T X$ and $w_y^T Y$ [12]. However, CCA is limited to linear transformation, which is often not sufficient to capture the highly non-linear relationship between X and Y. KCCA offers an alternative solution by first projecting the data (i.e., X) into a high dimensional feature space $\mathcal{H}_x$ via a mapping ϕ_x such that data in the feature space become $\Phi_X = [\phi_x(x_1) \cdots \phi_x(x_N)] \in \mathbb{R}^{\mathcal{N}_x \times N}$, where $\mathcal{N}_x$ is the dimension of feature space $\mathcal{H}_x$ that can be very high or even infinite. The mapping ϕ_x from input data to the feature space $\mathcal{H}_x$ is performed implicitly by considering a positive definite kernel function k_x satisfying $k_x(x_1, x_2) = \phi_x(x_1), \phi_x(x_2)$, where $\langle \cdot, \cdot \rangle$ is an inner product in $\mathcal{H}_x$, rather than by giving the coordinates of ϕ_x explicitly. Here, we choose k_x as a Gaussian kernel: $k_x(x_1, x_2) = \exp\left(-x_1 - x_2^2/(2\sigma_x^2)\right)$. Similarly, we can project Y into a feature space $\mathcal{H}_y$ associated with a Gaussian kernel k_y through function ϕ_y such that $\Phi_Y = [\phi_y(y_1) \ldots \phi_y(y_N)] \in \mathbb{R}^{\mathcal{N}_y G \times N}$. Thus, after mapping X to Φ_X and Y to Φ_Y, we then can apply the ordinary linear CCA to the data pair (Φ_X, Φ_Y). Let $K_X = \langle \Phi_X, \Phi_X \rangle \in \mathbb{R}^{N \times N}$ and $K_Y = \langle \Phi_Y, \Phi_Y \rangle \in \mathbb{R}^{N \times N}$ be *kernel matrices*. KCCA seeks linear transformation in the Reproducing Kernel Hilbert Space by expressing the projections as linear combinations of the training data, i.e., $w_x = \Phi_X \alpha = \sum_{n=1}^{N} \alpha_n \phi_x(x_n)$, $w_y = \Phi_Y \beta = \sum_{n=1}^{N} \beta_n \phi_y(y_n)$ where $\alpha, \beta \in \mathbb{R}^N$ are called *dual vectors*. The first pair of *dual vectors* can be determined by solving the following optimization problem:

$$\{\alpha_1, \beta_1\} = \arg\max_{\alpha \in \mathbb{R}^N, \beta \in \mathbb{R}^N} \frac{\alpha^T K_X K_Y \beta}{\sqrt{(\alpha^T K_X K_X \alpha) \cdot (\beta^T K_Y K_Y \beta)}} \tag{1}$$

which is often regularized as the following optimization problem to overcome the risk of over-fitting problem [12, 13],

$$\{\alpha_1, \beta_1\} = \arg\max_{\alpha \in \mathbb{R}^N, \beta \in \mathbb{R}^N} \frac{\alpha^T K_X K_Y \beta}{\sqrt{(\alpha^T K_X K_X \alpha + r_x \alpha^T K_X \alpha) \cdot (\beta^T K_Y K_Y \beta + r_y \beta^T K_Y \beta)}}. \tag{2}$$

where r_x and r_y are the positive regularization constants. The subsequent *dual vectors* $\{\alpha_j, \beta_j\}$ are found iteratively by solving (2) with the constraints that $\{\alpha_j, \beta_j\}$ should be orthogonal to all previous *dual vectors*. Specifically, let $A = [\alpha_1 \cdots \alpha_l]$ and $B = [\beta_1 \cdots \beta_l]$ be the sets of *dual vectors* for X and Y, respectively, where

---

Algorithm 1. Stacked Kernel CCA Mapping

Input: Training data $X \in \mathbb{R}^{D \times N}$, $Y \in \mathbb{R}^{D \times N}$

Repeat

    Construct and center kernel matrices K_X, K_Y

    Compute *dual vectors* A, B in Eq. (2)

    Set $X \leftarrow A^T K_X$, $Y \leftarrow B^T K_Y$

Until reaching the maximum number of iterations

Output: Stacked KCCA projected X, Y

$l = \min(\text{rank}(K_X), \text{rank}(K_Y))$. Therefore, the projections of the training data X and new testing X^{test} from their respective original spaces to the common space can be given by $\mathbf{X} = A^T K_X$ and $\hat{X}^{test} = A^T K_X^{test}$, where $\left[K_X^{test}\right]_{mn} = k_x\left(x_m, x_n^{test}\right)$. Similarly, the projections of the training data Y is computed as $\mathbf{Y} = B^T K_Y$.

Due to the highly non-linear relationship between native image features X and Y, one step of KCCA is often not sufficient since the error between projections of X and Y, defined as $\left\|A^T K_X - B^T K_Y\right\|^2$ may still be large [13]. To reduce this error and seek the optimal common feature space, we can further apply KCCA on the previously projected $\hat{X}$ and $\hat{Y}$. By iteratively finding projecting functions via the KCCA, we can then obtain a sequence of projections for a stacked mapping. The stacked KCCA mapping algorithm is given in Algorithm 1. The advantage of stacked mapping is demonstrated in Fig. 2, where we use the Euclidian distance between projected features as similarity measure. Specifically, Fig. 2(a) and (b) show a testing 6-month-old image and an atlas of 12-month-old image. The similarity map is computed by comparing the respective projected features of the reference point (indicated by red cross) w.r.t. all other points in the atlas. Figure 2(c) and (d) show the respective similarity maps by one step KCCA and the two steps KCCA. It can be clearly seen that the learned common features by two steps KCCA are more distinctive than those by one step KCCA mapping.

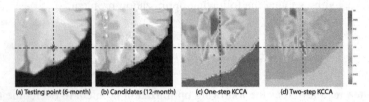

(a) Testing point (6-month)   (b) Candidates (12-month)   (c) One-step KCCA   (d) Two-step KCCA

Fig. 2. Similarity maps between (a) a point (indicated by red cross) in the testing (6-month-old) image and (b) all points in the atlas (12-month-old) image, by (c) one-step KCCA mapping and (d) two-step KCCA mapping, respectively. Dotted lines are placed in the same location in different images (Color figure online).

2.2 Sparse Patch-Based Labeling

Given a new 6-month-old testing image, we use the 12-month-old training images (of other subjects) with tissue labels as multiple atlases to guide the segmentation. Let C be the total number of atlases. Before labeling, all the atlases are first affine aligned to the testing image space. Based on the learned projections for the common feature representation, we can project each testing image patch and each atlas image patch into the common space. Since the projected features are comparable in the common space, we can perform labeling based on sparse patch-based representation. Specifically, for each point p in the testing 6-month-old image, its patch can be rearranged as a column vector x_p^{test} and its projected features as $\hat{x}_p^{test} = A^T K_{x_p}^{test}$, where $K_{x_p}^{test} \in \mathbb{R}^N$ is a N-demensional column vector with n-th entry as $k_x\left(x_n, x_p^{test}\right)$. Similarly, for each point q in the search neighborhood $\mathcal{N}(p)$ of the c-th aligned atlases, its patch y_q^c is projected as $\hat{y}_q^c = B^T K_{y_q}^c$, where $K_{y_q}^c \in \mathbb{R}^N$ is a N-demensional column vector with n-th entry as $k_y\left(y_n, y_q^c\right)$. Thus, a dictionary can be defined as $D_p \stackrel{def}{=} \left\{\hat{y}_q^c, c = 1, \ldots, C, \forall q \in \mathcal{N}(p)\right\}$. Then, the label fusion can be formulated as a sparse representation problem:

$$\min_{\substack{\theta \\ \theta \geq 0}} \frac{1}{2} \left\| \hat{x}_p^{test} - D_p\theta \right\|_2^2 + \lambda_1 \|\theta\|_1 + \frac{\lambda_2}{2} \|\theta\|_2^2 \tag{3}$$

In the above formulation, the first term is the data fitting term, and the second term is the $l1$ regularization term for enforcing the sparse constraint on the reconstruction coefficient θ, and the last term is the $l2$ smoothness term for enforcing similar coefficients for similar elements in D_p. The parameters λ_1 and λ_2 are the positive constants. Equation (3) is a convex combination of $l1$ lasso [14] and $l2$ ridge penalty, which encourages a grouping effect while keeping a similar sparsity of representation [15]. Each element of the sparse coefficient vector θ, i.e., θ_q^c, reflects the similarity between the testing patch $\hat{x}_p^{test}$ and each atlas patch $\hat{y}_q^c$ in the patch dictionary. Based on the assumption that similar patches should share similar tissue labels, we use the estimated sparse coefficients θ to compute the probability of the voxel p belonging to the j-th tissue, $j \in \{WM, GM, CSF\}$, i.e., $P_p(j) = \Sigma_c \Sigma_q \theta_q^c$, if $L_q^c == j$, where L_q^c is the tissue label (WM, GM, or CSF) for voxel q in the c-th atlas.

3 Experimental Results and Analysis

We validate the proposed method on 20 infant subjects via a leave-one-out strategy, where each subject contains 6-month-old and 12-month-old MR T1 images. Specifically, we learn common feature representations based on 19 subjects with aligned 6-month-old and 12-month-old images via stacked KCCA and then use 19 12-month-old images with tissue labels as multiple atlases to guide the segmentation of 6-month-old image of the remaining testing subject. In our implementation, we randomly selected 10,000 pair of patches with size of $11 \times 11 \times 11$ as the original features from each pair of 6-month-old and corresponding 12-month-old images of 19 training subjects. We set the regularization parameters $r_x = r_y = 0.5$, and Gaussian kernel parameters $\sigma_x = \sigma_y = 2.5$ for each KCCA mapping. In our study, we found two-step KCCA mapping is sufficient.

We first perform qualitative comparisons with **(1)** majority voting (MV), **(2)** conventional patch-based method (CPM) [16], and **(3)** patch-based labeling based on sparse representation (SR) [9], as shown in Fig. 3(a). Specifically, MV assigns the tissue label by obtaining the most votes (from the aligned atlases) to each voxel, with result shown in Fig. 3(b). CPM employs the Sum of the Squared Difference (SSD) to measure the similarity between the original image patches of the testing image and the atlas images, while SR employs the estimated sparse coefficients as similarities. Since both CPM and SR directly employ image patches as features, these two methods are not able to produce reasonable segmentation results, due to large appearance difference between 6-month-old testing image and 12-month-old atlases. For fair comparison with these two methods, we use 19 6-month-old training images (with tissue labels) as multiple atlases to guide the segmentation in these two methods. Results of these two comparison methods are shown in Fig. 3(c–d). It can be seen that these two comparison methods still cannot achieve satisfactory results due to the extremely low tissue contrast in the 6-month-old testing image. Figure 3(e) shows segmentation results obtained by the proposed method with one step of KCCA mapping. It can be seen that the estimated probabilities are more accurate than those by all comparison methods. After a stacked KCCA mapping, the correlation between 6-month-old and 12-month-old images are further increased, thus the estimated probabilities are further improved, as shown in Fig. 3(f). Figure 3(g) shows the ground-truth. To better compare the results of these different methods, the zoomed probabilities are also presented in the bottom row. Figure 4 shows the WM/GM surfaces obtained by different methods. The zoomed views are also provided in the bottom row for better comparison. It can be observed that the result with stacked KCCA is more consistent with the ground truth.

We then quantitatively evaluate the performance of different methods by employing Dice ratio. The average Dice ratio of each method on segmentation of isointense brain images, tested with 20 leave-one-out validations, is reported in Table 1. Our proposed method with stacked KCCA achieves significantly better results than other methods (p-value < 0.05). Besides

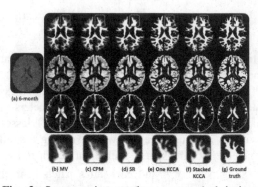

Fig. 3. Segmentation results on a typical isointense brain image (a). Results by comparison methods: (b) Majority voting (MV), (c) conventional patch-based method (CPM) [16], and (d) patch-based sparse representation (SR) [9]. Results by proposed methods: (e) with *one step KCCA*, and (f) *stacked KCCA*. (g) shows the ground truth. In each column, we show the estimated probability maps of WM, GM and CSF, along with the zoomed WM probability map, by different method.

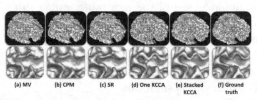

Fig. 4. WM/GM surfaces obtained by (a) majority voting (MV), (b) conventional patch-based method (CPM), (c) patch-based sparse representation (SR), (d) the proposed method with *one step KCCA*, (e) *stacked KCCA*, and (f) ground-truth segmentation.

using Dice ratio, we also measure the mean surface distance error between the automatically estimated WM/GM (GM/CSF) surfaces and the ground-truth surfaces, as shown in Table 1, further demonstrating the advantage of our method.

Table 1. Segmentation performances of five different methods on isointense brain images, tested by 20 leave-one-out validations.

Method		MV	CPM [16]	SR [9]	One KCCA	Stacked KCCA
Dice ratio (%)	WM	73.95 ± 3.41	73.80 ± 2.33	73.65 ± 1.45	80.25 ± 1.22	**82.34 ± 0.68**
	GM	72.96 ± 2.48	74.47 ± 1.98	75.25 ± 1.38	78.95 ± 1.12	**81.57 ± 1.00**
	CSF	70.32 ± 0.95	73.94 ± 1.34	75.26 ± 1.01	76.25 ± 0.77	**78.80 ± 0.59**
Mean surface distance (in *mm*)	WM/GM	3.06 ± 0.58	2.98 ± 0.66	2.75 ± 0.55	2.33 ± 0.33	**1.90 ± 0.34**
	GM/CSF	5.84 ± 0.71	5.47 ± 0.88	5.25 ± 0.57	3.12 ± 0.41	**2.65 ± 0.29**

4 Discussion and Conclusion

In this paper, we have proposed a novel method for segmentation of isointense infant brain images. Our main motivation is to employ the 12-month-old brain images with high image contrast as multiple atlases to guide the segmentation of 6-month-old brain images with low image contrast. We particularly employ a stacked KCCA mapping to seek the common feature representations so that the extracted features from 6-month-old and 12-month-old images are comparable. The proposed method was evaluated on 20 6-month-old brain images using leave-one-out cross-validation, showing much better results than the state-of-the-art methods. It is worth noting that the common feature representations learned by stacked KCCA can also be applied to other applications, such as registration of 6-month-old and 12-month-old brain images. In the future, we will extend the stacked KCCA mapping from two time-points, i.e., 6-month-old and 12-month-old, to multiple time-points in the first year of life [12].

References

1. Išgum, I., Benders, M.J.N.L., Avants, B., et al.: Evaluation of automatic neonatal brain segmentation algorithms: the NeoBrainS12 challenge. Med. Image Anal. **20**, 135–151 (2015)
2. Weisenfeld, N.I., Warfield, S.K.: Automatic segmentation of newborn brain MRI. Neuroimage **47**, 564–572 (2009)
3. Xue, H., Srinivasan, L., Jiang, S., et al.: Automatic segmentation and reconstruction of the cortex from neonatal MRI. Neuroimage **38**, 461–477 (2007)
4. Gui, L., Lisowski, R., Faundez, T., et al.: Morphology-driven automatic segmentation of MR images of the neonatal brain. Med. Image Anal. **16**, 1565–1579 (2012)
5. Paus, T., Collins, D.L., Evans, A.C., et al.: Maturation of white matter in the human brain: a review of magnetic resonance studies. Brain Res. Bull. **54**, 255–266 (2001)
6. Prastawa, M., Gilmore, J.H., Lin, W., et al.: Automatic segmentation of MR images of the developing newborn brain. Med. Image Anal. **9**, 457–466 (2005)
7. Warfield, S.K., Kaus, M., Jolesz, F.A., et al.: Adaptive, template moderated, spatially varying statistical classification. Med. Image Anal. **4**, 43–55 (2000)

8. Shi, F., Yap, P.T., Shen, D., Lin, W., Gilmore, J.H.: Spatial-temporal constraint for Segmentation of serial infant brain MR images. In: Liao, H., Eddie Edwards, P.J., Pan, X., Fan, Y., Yang, G.Z. (eds.) MIAR 2010. LNCS, vol. 6326, pp. 42–50. Springer, Heidelberg (2010)

9. Wang, L., Lin, W., Gilmore, J.H., Shi, F., Li, G., Shen, D.: Integration of sparse multi-modality representation and geometrical constraint for isointense infant brain segmentation. In: Mori, K., Sakuma, I., Sato, Y., Barillot, C., Navab, N. (eds.) MICCAI 2013, Part I. LNCS, vol. 8149, pp. 703–710. Springer, Heidelberg (2013)

10. Sled, J.G., Zijdenbos, A.P., Evans, A.C.: A nonparametric method for automatic correction of intensity nonuniformity in MRI data. IEEE Trans. Med. Imaging 17, 87–97 (1998)

11. Dale, A.M., Fischl, B., Sereno, M.I.: Cortical surface-based analysis: I segmentation and surface reconstruction. NeuroImage 9, 179–194 (1999)

12. Hardoon, D.R., Szedmak, S., Shawe-Taylor, J.: Canonical correlation analysis: an overview with application to learning methods. Neuroal Comput. 16, 2639–2664 (2004)

13. Hardoon, D., Shawe-Taylor, J.: Convergence analysis of kernel canonical correlation analysis: theory and practice. Mach. Learn. 74, 23–38 (2009)

14. Tibshirani, R.J.: Regression shrinkage and selection via the lasso. J. R. Stat. Soc. Ser. B 58, 267–288 (1996)

15. Zou, H., Hastie, T.: Regularization and variable selection via the Elastic Net. J. R. Stat. Soc. Ser. B 67, 301–320 (2005)

16. Coupé, P., Manjón, J., Fonov, V., et al.: Patch-based segmentation using expert priors: Application to hippocampus and ventricle segmentation. NeuroImage 54, 940–954 (2011)

Improving Accuracy of Automatic Hippocampus Segmentation in Routine MRI by Features Learned from Ultra-High Field MRI

Shuyu Li[1,2], Feng Shi[2], Guangkai Ma[2], Minjeong Kim[2],
and Dinggang Shen[2(✉)]

[1] School of Biological Science and Medical Engineering,
Beihang University, Beijing, China
[2] Department of Radiology and BRIC,
University of North Carolina at Chapel Hill,
Chapel Hill, NC, USA
{fengshi,minjeong_kim,dinggang_shen}@med.unc.edu,
{shuyu.syli,maguangkai}@gmail.com

Abstract. Ultra-high field MR imaging (e.g., 7T) provides unprecedented spatial resolution and superior signal-to-noise ratio, compared to the routine MR imaging (e.g., 1.5T and 3T). It allows precise depiction of small anatomical structures such as hippocampus and further benefits diagnosis of neurodegenerative diseases. However, the routine MR imaging is still mainly used in research and clinical studies, where accurate hippocampus segmentation is desired. In this paper, we present an automatic method for segmenting hippocampus from the routine MR images by learning 7T-like features from the training 7T MR images. Our main idea is to map features of the routine MR image to be similar to 7T image features, thus increasing their discriminability in hippocampus segmentation. Specifically, we propose a patch-based mapping method to map image patches of the routine MR images to the space of image patches of the 7T MR images. Thus, for each patch in the routine MR image, we can generate a new mapped patch with 7T-like pattern. Then, using those mapped patches, we can use a random forest to train a sequence of classifiers for hippocampus segmentation based on the appearance, texture, and contexture features of those mapped patches. Finally, hippocampi in the test image can be segmented by applying the learned image patch mapping and trained classifiers. Experimental results show that the accuracy of hippocampus segmentation can be significantly improved by using our learned 7T-like image features, in comparison to the direct use of features extracted from the routine MR images.

1 Introduction

Hippocampus is an anatomical structure located in medial temporal lobe, and plays important roles in the consolidation of information from short-term memory to long-term memory and also spatial navigation [1]. It becomes of major interest due to its implications in multiple psychiatric disorders and neurodegenerative diseases, e.g.,

© Springer International Publishing Switzerland 2015
G. Wu et al. (Eds.): Patch-MI 2015, LNCS 9467, pp. 37–45, 2015.
DOI: 10.1007/978-3-319-28194-0_5

Alzheimer's disease (AD). Specifically, hippocampal volume and morphological characteristics have been proven as valuable biomarkers for diagnosis and tracking of brain diseases [2]. Therefore, a reliable and accurate way for segmenting hippocampus is necessary to better quantify subtle structural changes in the brain.

Manual delineation by trained raters has been considered as the gold standard in hippocampus segmentation, but the process is tedious and time consuming. Thus, it would be extremely valuable to develop an automated hippocampus segmentation method with high accuracy. Recently, many automatic methods have been developed for hippocampus segmentation, which generally can be divided into two categories. The first category is the atlas-based segmentation methods, which propagate the pre-defined labels in an atlas image to a subject image (under segmentation) by building their spatial correspondences using deformable image registration. Multi-atlases-based methods [3] can mediate the inter-subject variability and produce better segmentation results through label fusion from multiple atlases. The second category is the learning-based segmentation methods. Based on the image features extracted from both hippocampus and non-hippocampus areas in the training images, machine learning techniques can be used to train a classifier to discriminate the hippocampus from the background. Note that, regardless of the atlas-based methods or learning-based approaches, most existing methods have been developed for the routine MR images, i.e., 1.5T or 3T MR images.

With the advance development of MR imaging techniques, 7T MRI offers unprecedent spatial resolution as well as superior tissue contrast, which allows clear depiction of small anatomical details. Previous studies [4] have demonstrated fine details of *in vivo* hippocampal structure using 7T MRI, including the boundary of hippocampus as well as the visualization of individual subfields within the hippocampus. Although hippocampus segmentation methods using ultra-high field MRIs have achieved higher accuracy over the routine MR images [5], they are still limited to a small cohort of normal subjects. This is because 7T imaging is now still mainly used for research purpose, not clinical applications, due to practical issues during image acquisition, e.g., lack of a standard protocol and the long imaging time. Therefore, there is still a long way to go before we can use 7T scanner to investigate a large population of diseased brains.

On the other hand, in machine learning area, recent studies have proposed to map raw features to another feature space for increasing their discriminative power. For example, kernel-based methods can make linear models work in the nonlinear settings by mapping the data to the higher dimensions where the mapped data exhibits linear patterns [6]. This domain transfer approach aims to learn a new feature representation for the input features by linear or nonlinear mapping, in order to enlarge the dis-criminations of mapped features in the new feature space and then eventually improve the classification performance. Accordingly, we are motivated to map features of the routine MR images to the space of features of the 7T images, where the hippocampus and surrounding tissues are better separable.

In this paper, we propose a learning-based method for segmenting hippocampus in the routine MR images, guided by features learned from 7T MR images. In particular, based on the feature mapping between the routine MR and 7T MR images, we can make the image patches of routine MR images similar to 7T image patches, thus allowing better separation of hippocampus from surrounding tissues. Then, we use random forest to train a sequence of classifiers based on the features (i.e., appearance, texture and context features) of those mapped patches. In the application stage, when given a new test image, we can first map each of its image patches to be 7T-like. Then, we can apply a sequence of trained classifiers to the features of those mapped image patches for obtaining a hippocampus probability map. Experimental results show that our proposed method can significantly improve the segmentation accuracy, compared to the conventional approach.

2 Method

Our goal is to improve the segmentation performance in routine MR images by mapping the features extracted from routine MR images to the space of 7T image features, where the hippocampus and surrounding tissues are better separable. The overview of our proposed framework is shown in Fig. 1. In the *training* stage, we determine the relationships between patches from the routine MR and 7T MR images by using a patch-based mapping approach. Then, the random forest is used to construct a sequence of classifiers based on multiple types of features, i.e., appearance, texture and context features, extracted from the mapped image patches of routine MR images. In the *testing* stage, for a new test image under segmentation, its mapped version of 7T-like image is first reconstructed using the learned mapping function. Then, the hippocampus in the test image can be segmented by applying a sequence of trained classifiers to the mapped 7T-like patches of the test image.

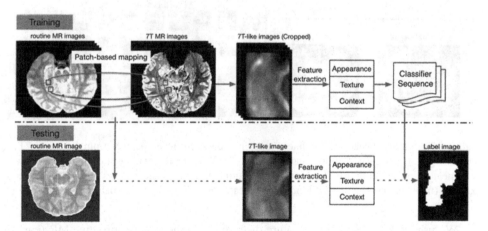

Fig. 1. The flowchart of our proposed hippocampus segmentation framework, including a training stage (top) and a testing stage (bottom).

2.1 Patch-Based Mapping

Our main contribution is to use a patch-based mapping approach to learn the relationships between the patches from routine MR images and the patches from 7T MR images. First, the linear mapping is built based on the principal component analysis (PCA) models built on the patches from the routine MR images and 7T MR images separately, thus allowing the mapping of their distributions in high dimensional space. In this way, we can obtain the initially mapped patch in 7T space for each patch in the routine MR images. Second, a nonlinear mapping is further employed for each image patch of routine MR images to seek for its correspondence by searching 7T image patches within the closest Euclidean distance from its initially mapped version by the above linear mapping.

Specifically, we define searching windows (as shown by orange boxes in Fig. 2A) at the same location in both the routine MR image and 7T MR image spaces. Then, we extract a number of patches centered at the voxels within the searching windows while allowing the overlap between the extracted patches (as shown by blue and yellow boxes in Fig. 2A). We use the intensity of each voxel as feature, thus each patch can be represented by a column vector $x \in R^{p \times 1}$, where p is the size of feature dimension. Each patch x is regarded as a feature point in the high dimensional feature space (with p-dimensions). Note that the routine MR images and 7T MR images have their respective feature distributions in their own spaces, as shown by the schematic illustrations in the top of Fig. 2A.

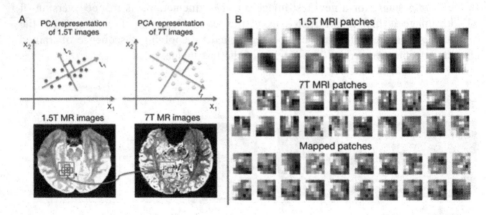

Fig. 2. Patch-based linear and nonlinear mappings between image patches from 1.5T and 7T MR images. (A) Linear mapping can be done by PCA representations (top), followed by nonlinear mapping (bottom). (B) Examples of original 1.5T image patches (top), 7T image patches (middle), and mapped 1.5T image patches in the 7T space (bottom).

We use PCA to describe the feature distribution in the spaces of routine MR (e.g., 1.5T) and 7T MR images, respectively:

$$X_{1.5T}^T = U_{1.5T} \sum\nolimits_{1.5T} W_{1.5T}^T \text{ and } X_{7T}^T = U_{7T} \sum\nolimits_{7T} W_{7T}^T \tag{1}$$

Where X is the data matrix $(x_1, x_2,..., x_n)$, and n is the number of patches within each searching window. $\sum$ is a $n \times p$ rectangular diagonal matrix, containing the singular values of X, and U is a $p \times n$ matrix, whose columns are orthogonal unit vectors of length p. W is a $p \times p$ matrix $(t_1, t_2, \ldots, t_p)$, whose columns, t_i, $i = 1, \cdots p$, are orthogonal unit vectors of length p. By using PCA, each eigenvector represents the direction of data distribution, while all eigenvectors are independent to each other. The eigenvalue $\lambda(i)$ represents the variance of data along the direction of the i-th eigenvector. We build the mapping relationships among the patches from the routine MR and 7T MR images by linearly aligning their distributions as shown in Eq. 2 below. The patch in routine MR space is first centered, and then rotated and scaled to match the distribution in the 7T space, thus getting the mapped patch.

$$x_{map}^T = (x_{1.5T}^T - \bar{x}_{1.5T}^T) \cdot W_{1.5T} \cdot A \cdot P \cdot W_{1.5T}^T + \bar{x}_{7T}^T \qquad (2)$$

where $\bar{x} = \frac{1}{N}\sum_{i=1}^{N} x_i$. Here, $A = W_{1.5T}^T \cdot W_{7T}$ is the matrix representing the rotation from the feature space of routine MR patches to the feature space of 7T MR patches, and P is the scale matrix. Note that, P is a diagonal matrix defined in Eq. 3, while the diagonal elements are the ratios of eigenvalues from the two distributions:

$$P = \begin{bmatrix} \lambda_{7T}(1)/\lambda_{1.5T}(1) & \cdots & 0 \\ \vdots & \ddots & \vdots \\ 0 & \cdots & \lambda_{7T}(p)/\lambda_{1.5T}(p) \end{bmatrix} \qquad (3)$$

In this way, for each patch $x_{1.5T}$ in the routine MR space, we can get its mapped patch x_{map} in 7T space as shown in Fig. 2B.

For the j-th mapped patch $x_{map}(j)$ from routine MR images (shown in pink box in Fig. 2A), we further compute its Euclidean distances to all 7T patches (shown in yellow boxes in Fig. 2A) within the searching window $SW(j)$ of the j-th location in 7T MR images to find a 7T image patch with the closest Euclidean distance (as shown by red box in Fig. 2A) as its corresponding 7T image patch $\hat{x}_{7T}(j)$.

$$\hat{x}_{7T}(j) = \min_{k \in SW(j)} \left\| x_{map}(j) - x_{7T}(k) \right\|^2 \qquad (4)$$

For each patch in the routine MR image, we get a new mapped patch with 7T-like appearance. Then, we reconstruct a new 7T-like image for each training routine MR image by weighted averaging of these mapped patches.

2.2 Learning-Based Segmentation

In this section, we describe the details on how to train classifier (random forest) with features extracted from 7T-like images and their corresponding labels (i.e., hippocampus or non-hippocampus) as defined in the original 1.5T MR training images.

Feature Extraction. Three types of features, i.e., image appearance, texture, and context features, are extracted from the 7T-like training images.

Image appearance features include intensity, spatial location, and Haar-like features at different scales [7]. For each voxel, we further extract *texture features*, e.g., the first-order difference filters, the second-order difference filters, 3D Hyperplane filters, 3D Sobel filters, Laplacian filters, and Range difference filters.

By using image appearance and texture features to train classifier, the initial probability map for hippocampus label can be obtained by the trained random forest, where a higher value denotes the higher probability of the respective voxel belonging to hippocampus. Then, we can use this probability map to extract *context features* [8]. By combining context features with the previous appearance and texture features, we can train next classifier, which can also use for producing a new probability map. By iteratively extracting contexture features and training new classifier, we can finally obtain a sequence of trained classifiers [9], which can be used to iteratively segment hippocampus for test image in the testing stage.

Training of Random Forest. From each image in a training dataset, consisting of a number of mapped 7T-like images, we randomly select half of hippocampus voxels from the training images as positive samples, and also the same size of voxels from the exterior region around the hippocampal boundary as negative samples. Then, the features, i.e., image appearance, texture, context, are extracted from image patches centered at those selected voxels. Finally, we use random forest [10] to train the classifier. Note that random forest is an ensemble learning method, which can construct a set of decision trees at training time and then perform classification at the application time by combining the outcomes of all decision trees.

Testing. For a new test image to be segmented, we first reconstruct its 7T-like image based on the mapping steps described in Sect. 2.1. Then, various features, i.e., image appearance, texture and context, are extracted for each voxel in the mapped 7T-like version of the test image. Afterwards, the trained classifiers are sequentially applied to the competed features for generating a sequence of probability maps. Finally, the binary segmentation result of hippocampus is obtained by applying the level-set algorithm on the final obtained probability map.

3   Experiments

3.1   Data

We incorporated two datasets in this study, (1) a 1.5T MR dataset for segmentation and (2) a 7T MR dataset for helping learn 7T-like features for the 1.5T MR images.

1.5T MR dataset: 20 normal subjects were selected from IXI dataset (http://brain-development.org), including 10 females and 10 males with the age of 31.55 ± 9.70 years. MRI scans were obtained on the 1.5T GE Signa Echo speed scanner. T1 weighted 3D volume was acquired with 124 coronal slices at the resolution of $0.9375 \times 0.9375 \times 1.5$ mm^3.

7T MR dataset: 7T MR images also include 20 normal subjects, consisting of 6 males and 14 females with the age of 28.92 ± 16.51 years. The images were acquired using a 3D fast low-angle shot (Spoiled FLASH) sequence with 60 slices at the resolution of $0.35 \times 0.35 \times 0.35$ mm^3. The image plane was set parallel to the longest axis running through the hippocampus.

All images were pre-processed using the following steps: (1) skull stripping, (2) inhomogeneity correction, (3) intensity normalization for making image contrast and luminance consistent across all subjects, and (4) rotation to make the coronal slice orthogonal to the long axis of hippocampus. For 7T MRI data, all images were affine aligned to a template. For 1.5T MRI data, all images were upsampled with the same resolution as 7T MR images by using trilinear interpolation and then affine registered to the 7T template. Lastly, all images were cropped using a small rectangle box for covering left and right hippocampi separately, in order to reduce the computational burden.

3.2 Experimental Setting

A leave-one-out cross-validation strategy (i.e., one subject used as testing data, and other 19 subjects used as training set) was adopted and repeated 20 times. The parameters in our method were set as follows: patch size $7 \times 7 \times 7$, and searching window $21 \times 21 \times 21$. 500 Haar-like features and 376 texture features were used. Specifically, the number of trees was set as 20 in the random forest, with the depth of each tree as 20. We iterated the program 4 times, where context features were updated in each iteration. In all experiments, we used same parameter settings.

We compared the hippocampus segmentation results using IXI 1.5T data by our proposed method (i.e., with patch-based 7T-like feature mapping) and by the baseline method (i.e., without any mapping procedure). To quantitatively evaluate the performance of our proposed method, Dice similarity coefficient $Dice(S1, S2) = 2V(S1 \cap S2)/(V(S1) + V(S2))$ was used between the manual label $S1$ and automatic segmentation $S2$, where $V(S)$ is the volume of a segmentation S. Note that, a higher Dice ratio indicates better segmentation in the range of [0, 1].

3.3 Experimental Results

Visual Inspection. We show the segmentation results by our proposed method and the baseline method in Fig. 3. It can be observed that our segmented hippocampus (Fig. 3B) has more similar shape with manual segmentation (more obviously in the zoom-in views) than the result by the baseline method (Fig. 3C).

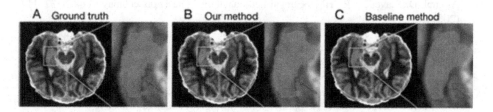

Fig. 3. Comparison of segmentation results by our method (B) and baseline method (C), as well as the ground truth (A).

Quantitative Results. The comparison of averaged Dice overlap ratio of hippocampus segmentation results by our proposed method and the baseline method w.r.t. ground truths is provided in Table 1, separately for left and right hippocampi. Our proposed method by employing the features from the 7T-like images achieves much higher segmentation accuracy than the baseline method directly using the features from the original 1.5T images. Our method also achieves much higher segmentation accuracy in the comparison with the two existing algorithms [11, 12]. Note that, the results by the two algorithms are directly referred as reported in the papers, where individual results on left and right hippocampi are not available.

Table 1. The comparison of hippocampal segmentation by proposed method (with patch-based 7T-like feature mapping procedure), baseline method (without the mapping procedure), and two existing methods using IXI dataset.

Method	Dice (left)	Dice (right)	Dice (left + right)
Proposed method	**0.881 ± 0.018**	**0.874 ± 0.029**	**0.878**
Baseline method	0.855 ± 0.039	0.840 ± 0.024	0.848
Chupin 2007	–	–	0.840
Wu 2015	–	–	0.846

4 Conclusion

We presented a new automatic hippocampus segmentation method for the routine MR images by learning features from high-field 7T MR images. Our method is built on the patch-based mapping approach, which aimed to find the most similar patch from high-field MR images for each patch in the routine MR image by statistical mapping. Using the features acquired from the mapped 7T-like images, we achieved significant improvement for hippocampus segmentation. It is worth indicating that our approach can also be used to improve segmentation accuracy for other anatomical structures in the low-resolution images by learning features from high-resolution images.

References

1. Amaral, D., Lavenex, P.: Hippocampal neuroanatomy. The Hippocampus Book 1, 37–114 (2007)
2. Akhondi-Asl, A., Jafari-Khouzani, K., Elisevich, K., Soltanian-Zadeh, H.: Hippocampal volumetry for lateralization of temporal lobe epilepsy: automated versus manual methods. NeuroImage 54, S218–S226 (2011)
3. Chupin, M., et al.: Fully automatic segmentation of the hippocampus and the amygdala from MRI using hybrid prior knowledge. In: Ayache, N., Ourselin, S., Maeder, A. (eds.) MICCAI 2007, Part I. LNCS, vol. 4791, pp. 875–882. Springer, Heidelberg (2007)
4. Cho, Z.H., Han, J.Y., Hwang, S.I., Kim, D.S., Kim, K.N., Kim, N.B., Kim, S.J., Chi, J.G., Park, C.W., Kim, Y.B.: Quantitative analysis of the hippocampus using images obtained from 7.0 T MRI. NeuroImage 49, 2134–2140 (2010)

5. Kim, M., Wu, G., Li, W., Wang, L., Son, Y.D., Cho, Z.H., Shen, D.: Automatic hippocampus segmentation of 7.0 Tesla MR images by combining multiple atlases and auto-context models. NeuroImage **83**, 335–345 (2013)
6. Muller, K.R., Mika, S., Ratsch, G., Tsuda, K., Scholkopf, B.: An introduction to kernel-based learning algorithms. IEEET Neural Netw. **12**, 181–201 (2001)
7. Viola, P., Jones, M.J.: Robust real-time face detection. Int. J. Comput. Vision **57**, 137–154 (2004)
8. Tu, Z.W., Bai, X.A.: Auto-context and its application to high-level vision tasks and 3D brain image segmentation. IEEET Pattern Anal. **32**, 1744–1757 (2010)
9. Wang, L., Gao, Y.Z., Shi, F., Li, G., Gilmore, J.H., Lin, W.L., Shen, D.G.: LINKS: Learning-based multi-source IntegratioN frameworK for segmentation of infant brain images. NeuroImage **108**, 160–172 (2015)
10. Breiman, L.: Random forests. Mach. Learn. **45**, 5–32 (2001)
11. Chupin, M., Mukuna-Bantumbakulu, A.R., Hasboun, D., Bardinet, E., Baillet, S., Kinkingnehun, S., Lemieux, L., Dubois, B., Garnero, L.: Anatomically constrained region deformation for the automated segmentation of the hippocampus and the amygdala: method and validation on controls and patients with Alzheimer's disease. NeuroImage **34**, 996–1019 (2007)
12. Wu, G.R., Kim, M.J., Sanroma, G., Wang, Q., Munsell, B.C., Shen, D.G.: Hierarchical multi-atlas label fusion with multi-scale feature representation and label-specific patch partition. NeuroImage **106**, 34–46 (2015)

Dual-Layer ℓ_1-Graph Embedding
for Semi-supervised Image Labeling

Qian Wang[1]($^\boxtimes$), Guorong Wu[2], and Dinggang Shen[2]

[1] Med-X Research Institute, Shanghai Jiao Tong University, Shanghai, China
wang.qian@sjtu.edu.cn
[2] Department of Radiology and BRIC, University of North Carolina at Chapel Hill,
Chapel Hill, USA

Abstract. In non-local patch-based (NLPB) labeling, a target voxel can fuse its label from the manual labels of the atlas voxels in accordance to the patch-based voxel similarities. Although state-of-the-art NLPB method mainly focuses on labeling a single target image by many atlases, we propose a novel semi-supervised strategy to address the realistic case of only a few atlases yet many unlabeled targets. Specifically, we create an ℓ_1-graph of voxels, such that each target voxel can fuse its label from not only atlas voxels but also other target voxels. Meanwhile, each atlas voxel can utilize the feedbacks from the graph to check whether its expert labeling needs to be corrected. The ℓ_1-graph is built by applying (dual-layer) sparsity learning to all target and atlas voxels represented by their surrounding patches. By embedding the voxel labels to the graph, the target voxels can jointly compute their labels. In the experiment, our method with the capabilities of (1) joint labeling and (2) atlas label correction has enhanced the accuracy of NLPB labeling significantly.

1 Introduction

Medical image labeling aims to parcellate each target image under consideration into individual anatomical structures, thus enabling region-based quantitative analyses within and across images. The technique has drawn intense attention from the community of medical image computing in recent years due to its importance to imaging-based clinical studies. Though manual labeling is still regarded as one of the most promising ways to generate the "ground truth", automatic methods are emerging as competitive solutions rapidly. In particular, automatic labeling has demonstrated its advantages of low cost and high efficiency in processing a huge number of images. The scales of related studies can thus become much larger, leading to more statistical powers of their findings.

Multi-atlas strategy has proven its effectiveness for automatic labeling of medical images. The strategy can be divided into three steps in general. *First*, a few atlases need to be manually delineated by human experts. *Then*, The expert labeling information is transferred to the unlabeled target images [1–3]. *Finally*, the contributions from the atlases are fused to label the target images [4–10]. In the simple *majority voting* (MV) method, for instance, all atlas and target

© Springer International Publishing Switzerland 2015
G. Wu et al. (Eds.): Patch-MI 2015, LNCS 9467, pp. 46–53, 2015.
DOI: 10.1007/978-3-319-28194-0_6

images are spatially normalized. Given each target voxel, the probability of its label can then be computed by counting the frequencies of the labels occurring at the same locations of all registered atlases.

A key notion for multi-atlas image labeling is that visually similar voxels in different images should have similar anatomical labels [6]. The *non-local patch-based* (NLPB) method [5] is a typical implementation bearing this notion. Specifically, all voxels can signify their visual appearances by their surrounding image patches for the computation of voxel similarity. Each target voxel may incorporate contributions from the non-local atlas voxels within a certain neighborhood. The contributions of the atlas voxels are adaptively fused regarding their visual similarities to the target voxel. The NLPB method, as well as its many variants, is widely applied to medical image labeling nowadays.

The NLPB method asks for as many atlases as possible, and handles the target images in a sequential order. However, this *many-to-one* scheme may not always function well in real clinical studies, as people tend to provide minimal yet high-cost expert labeling of the atlases. For example, researchers often manually label only a few healthy subjects as the atlases, and expect to further label other normal/pathological images automatically. In this scenario, we argue that a sophisticated *few-to-many* scheme can be better, since the introduction of more target images may contribute to labeling each other [1].

Motived by the above, we propose a novel *semi-supervised* strategy for the *few-to-many* NLPB labeling. Our method is capable of (1) jointly labeling all target images and (2) compensating for possible incorrect expert labeling of the atlases. Specifically, we create an ℓ_1-graph of voxels, such that each target voxel can fuse its label from the atlas voxels and other target voxels. At the same time, the atlas voxels can also utilize the feedbacks from the graph to check whether their expert labeling needs to be adjusted. The ℓ_1-graph is built by applying (dual-layer) sparsity learning to capture the similarities within all target and atlas voxels under consideration. By embedding the labels of all voxels to the ℓ_1-graph, the target voxels can compute their labels jointly.

2   Method

In NLPB labeling, each target voxel calculates the probability of its possible label based on the expert labeling transferred from the non-local atlas voxels. For convenience, we define a set of unlabeled target voxels (i.e., at the same locations of different target images) as $\mathcal{U}$ and a set of labeled atlas voxels (i.e., with potential contributions to $\mathcal{U}$) as $\mathcal{L}$ throughout this paper. Given $i \in \mathcal{U}$ and $j \in \mathcal{L}$, their appearances are signified by $\mathbf{x}_i$ and $\mathbf{x}_j$, respectively. In particular, $\mathbf{x}_i$ and $\mathbf{x}_j$ are often the vectorized image patches surrounding corresponding voxels (i.e., i and j). The length of $\mathbf{x}_i$ or $\mathbf{x}_j$ thus equals the size of the image patch. We further denote the probabilities of the labels of the voxels i and j as $\mathbf{y}_i$ and $\mathbf{y}_j$, respectively. The length of $\mathbf{y}_i$ or $\mathbf{y}_j$ is the same with the number of possible labels including the background. The task of NLPB labeling is then to estimate $\{\mathbf{y}_i, i \in \mathcal{U}\}$, given $\{\mathbf{x}_i, i \in \mathcal{U}\}$, $\{\mathbf{x}_j, j \in \mathcal{L}\}$, and $\{\tilde{\mathbf{y}}_j, j \in \mathcal{L}\}$.

Note that we deliberately use $\tilde{\mathbf{y}}_j$, instead of $\mathbf{y}_j$, to indicate that the labels of the atlas voxels are already known.

2.1   NLPB Labeling and Graph Embedding

Since similar voxels should have similar labels, we can compute the similarity between voxels based on their surrounding image patches and gauge the contributions from individual atlas voxels for determining the labels of the target voxels. Typically, we calculate the similarity between $\mathbf{x}_i$ and $\mathbf{x}_j$ following

$$w_{ij} = \exp\left(-\frac{\|\mathbf{x}_i - \mathbf{x}_j\|^2}{2\sigma^2}\right), \quad \forall i \in \mathcal{U}, \forall j \in \mathcal{N}_i \subseteq \mathcal{L}. \tag{1}$$

The label probability of the target voxel, namely $\mathbf{y}_i$, can then be fused by

$$\mathbf{y}_i = \frac{\sum_{j \in \mathcal{N}_i \subseteq \mathcal{L}} w_{ij}\tilde{\mathbf{y}}_j}{\sum_{j \in \mathcal{N}_i \subseteq \mathcal{L}} w_{ij}}, \quad \forall i \in \mathcal{U}. \tag{2}$$

The term $\mathcal{N}_i$ often qualifies the contributions from the non-local atlas voxels located within the neighborhood of each target voxel only. The NLPB model combining (1) and (2) can be reduced to MV by increasing σ to infinity and reducing the size of $\mathcal{N}_i$ to minimum. Meanwhile, we note that the labeling of individual target voxels are independent of each other as in the above.

We further interpret the NLPB labeling through the theory of graph embedding. For the target voxel $i \in \mathcal{U}$ specifically, it is contributed and connected by the atlas voxel $j \in \mathcal{N}_i$. The edge between them represents the contribution from j to i, and is assigned with the similarity measure w_{ij}. Then, the task of NLPB labeling is to embed the labels of all voxels in accordance to the graph that is derived from the similarities of image patches, following

$$\mathbf{y}_i = \arg\min_{\mathbf{y}_i} \sum_{j \in \mathcal{N}_i \subseteq \mathcal{L}} w_{ij}\|\mathbf{y}_i - \tilde{\mathbf{y}}_j\|^2, \quad \forall i \in \mathcal{U}. \tag{3}$$

It is easy to derive the solution that is exactly the same with (2). An illustration of the graph embedding process for NLPB labeling can be found in Fig. 1(a).

We aim to introduce the semi-supervised strategy for NLPB labeling. To this end, we re-write (3) to (4) as a summary of the proposed method, which is featured by:

1. All target voxels in $\mathcal{U}$ are jointly labeled. For a certain target voxel, the contributions to determine its label may come from not only the atlas voxels but also its connected target voxels in the graph (c.f. the first term in (4)).
2. The atlas voxels can deviate from their expert labeling adaptively (c.f. the second term in (4)), in order to alleviate the influences of possibly incorrect contributions from the atlases.

$$\{\mathbf{y}_i\}_{i \in \mathcal{U}} = \arg\min_{\{\mathbf{y}_i\}_{i \in \mathcal{U}}} \sum_{m \in \{\mathcal{U} \cup \mathcal{L}\}} \sum_{n \in \{\mathcal{U} \cup \mathcal{L}\}} w_{mn}\|\mathbf{y}_m - \mathbf{y}_n\|^2 + \alpha \sum_{j \in \mathcal{L}} \|\mathbf{y}_j - \tilde{\mathbf{y}}_j\|^2. \tag{4}$$

We will detail our solution to (4) in the form of graph embedding in the next.

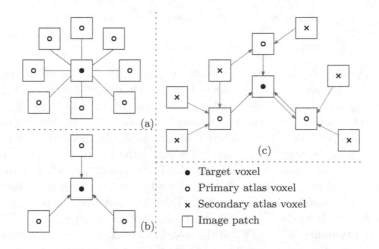

Fig. 1. NLPB labeling can be solved through graph embedding by: (a) the conventional method (e.g., [5]); (b) using the ℓ_1-graph; (c) the proposed method. Note that only a single target voxel is used for simplicity in this figure (Color figure online).

2.2 Laplacian-Based Embedding of ℓ_1-Graph

Graph Laplacian can help us solve (3) as well as (4). Specifically, we create an augmented matrix $\mathbf{Y} = \left[\mathbf{Y}^U, \tilde{\mathbf{Y}}^L \right]$, such that $\mathbf{y}_i$ ($i \in \mathcal{U}$) and $\tilde{\mathbf{y}}_j$ ($j \in \mathcal{L}$) are ordered as individual column vectors in $\mathbf{Y}^U$ and $\tilde{\mathbf{Y}}^L$, respectively. The adjacency matrix $\mathbf{W}$, which is filled in by w_{ij}, records the similarity between each pair of voxels. We then define the graph Laplacian of $\mathbf{W}$ as $\boldsymbol{\Delta} = \mathbf{D} - \mathbf{W}$. $\mathbf{D}$ is the diagonal degree matrix, where each diagonal entry is the sum of the corresponding row in $\mathbf{W}$. If the similarity is calculated by (1), both $\mathbf{W}$ and $\boldsymbol{\Delta}$ are symmetric. Thus, the problem in (3) is equivalent to minimize $\mathbf{Y}'\boldsymbol{\Delta}\mathbf{Y}$, as

$$\mathbf{Y}^U = -\tilde{\mathbf{Y}}^L \boldsymbol{\Delta}^{UL} \left(\boldsymbol{\Delta}^{UU} \right)^{-1}, \quad \boldsymbol{\Delta} = \begin{bmatrix} \boldsymbol{\Delta}^{UU} & \boldsymbol{\Delta}^{UL} \\ \boldsymbol{\Delta}^{LU} & \boldsymbol{\Delta}^{LL} \end{bmatrix}. \quad (5)$$

Our proposed method utilizes the ℓ_1-norm-based sparsity learning to estimate voxel similarity and thus build an ℓ_1-graph of voxels. An illustration of the ℓ_1-graph is available in Fig. 1(b). In the ℓ_1-graph, each target voxel only needs to consider the contributions from a limited number of most similar atlas/target voxels. By discarding many other redundant and confusing contributions, the labeling results can be more accurate [10]. Meanwhile, since the number of edges of the ℓ_1-graph is reduced due to sparsity constraint, the computation burden (i.e., regarding (5)) can be saved significantly.

In order to build the ℓ_1-graph, we first create a dictionary matrix $\mathbf{X} = \{\cdots, \mathbf{x}_m, \cdots\}$. Without loss of generality, the index m denotes all target and non-local atlas voxels under consideration. Then, the sparse representation of $\mathbf{x}_m$, regarding all other column vectors in $\mathbf{X}$, can be acquired through

$$\mathbf{w}_m = \arg\min_{\mathbf{w}_m} \|\mathbf{x}_m - \mathbf{X}\mathbf{w}_m\|^2 + \beta\|\mathbf{w}_m\|_{\ell_1},$$

$$\text{s.t.} \quad w_{mn} \geq 0, w_{mm} = 0. \tag{6}$$

The n-th entry in the coefficient vector $\mathbf{w}_m$, namely w_{mn}, is often perceived as the similarity from $\mathbf{x}_n$ to $\mathbf{x}_m$. Due to the ℓ_1-norm constraint controlled by β, there are only a few edges associated with each target voxel in the ℓ_1-graph.

It is worth noting that the embedding solution in (5) cannot be directly applied to the ℓ_1-graph. The reason is that the similarity measure derived from (6) is directional, leading to: (1) directed edges in the ℓ_1-graph (c.f. blue arrows in Fig. 1(b)); (2) asymmetry of $\mathbf{W}$ and $\mathbf{\Delta}$. To this end, we define a diagonal matrix $\mathbf{D}^*$, in addition to $\mathbf{D}$, as each diagonal entry in $\mathbf{D}^*$ is the sum of the corresponding column of $\mathbf{W}$. Then, $\mathbf{\Delta}^* = \mathbf{D}^* - \mathbf{W}'$ is defined to be the column graph Laplacian. It is shown by [11] that the optimization problem in (3) can be converted to minimize $\mathbf{Y}'\mathbf{C}\mathbf{Y}$, as the matrix $\mathbf{C} = \mathbf{\Delta} + \mathbf{\Delta}^*$ is symmetric. The labels of all target voxels can thus be jointly computed following

$$\mathbf{Y}^U = -\tilde{\mathbf{Y}}^L \mathbf{C}^{UL} \left(\mathbf{C}^{UU}\right)^{-1}, \quad \mathbf{C} = \begin{bmatrix} \mathbf{C}^{UU} & \mathbf{C}^{UL} \\ \mathbf{C}^{LU} & \mathbf{C}^{LL} \end{bmatrix}. \tag{7}$$

2.3 Dual-Layer Sparsity Learning

It is possible that certain atlas labeling is incorrect. Therefore, we allow the atlas voxels to deviate from their original labels in the proposed method (c.f. the second term in (4)). That is, the ℓ_1-graph not only transfers the labeling information from the atlases to the targets, but also provides feedbacks to individual atlases at the same time. Since the edges in the ℓ_1-graph are directed, we need to compute the inward edges for the atlas voxels. Specifically, we use the dual-layer sparsity learning approach as follows.

1. For each target voxel, we apply the first-layer sparsity learning (c.f. (6)). The target voxel is thus connected from the *primary* atlas voxels (i.e., in the set $\mathcal{P} \subseteq \mathcal{L}$) and other target voxels (i.e., in $\mathcal{U}$).
2. For each primary atlas voxel, the second-layer sparsity learning is applied. More *secondary* atlas voxels (i.e., in the set $\mathcal{S} \subseteq \mathcal{L}\backslash\mathcal{P}$) are incorporated into the graph. Note that the secondary atlas voxels are directly connected to the primary atlas voxels only, rather than the target voxels.

The dual-layer sparsity learning is illustrated by Fig. 1(c), where the edges of the first layer and the second layer are colored in blue and red, respectively. Other atlas voxels (in $\mathcal{L}\backslash\{\mathcal{P}\cup\mathcal{S}\}$) are inactive and thus excluded from the graph. In general, the ℓ_1-graph allows us to (1) compute the labels of the target voxels jointly and (2) adjust the expert labeling of the primary atlas voxels at the same time. Specifically, the objective function in (4) can be converted to minimize

$$\begin{bmatrix} \mathbf{Y}^U & \mathbf{Y}^P & \tilde{\mathbf{Y}}^S \end{bmatrix}' \begin{bmatrix} C^{UU} & C^{UP} & C^{US} \\ C^{PU} & C^{PP} & C^{PS} \\ C^{SU} & C^{SP} & C^{SS} \end{bmatrix} \begin{bmatrix} \mathbf{Y}^U & \mathbf{Y}^P & \tilde{\mathbf{Y}}^S \end{bmatrix} + \alpha\|\mathbf{Y}^P - \tilde{\mathbf{Y}}^P\|^2. \tag{8}$$

The closed-form solution to the above is

$$\mathbf{Y}^U = -\left(\alpha \tilde{\mathbf{Y}}^P - \tilde{\mathbf{Y}}^S \mathbf{C}^{SP}\right) \cdot \left(\mathbf{C}^{PP} + \alpha \mathbf{I}\right)^{-1} \cdot \mathbf{C}^{PU}$$
$$\cdot \left(\mathbf{C}^{UU} - \mathbf{C}^{UP}\left(\mathbf{C}^{PP} + \alpha \mathbf{I}\right)^{-1}\mathbf{C}^{PU}\right)^{-1} \tag{9}$$

Note that (9) is equivalent to (5) and (7) when α is set to infinity. Therefore, our method can be regarded as a generalized form of the NLPB labeling.

2.4 Summary

We briefly summarize the proposed method as follows:

1. For a certain location, we extract all image patches regarding $\mathcal{U}$ and $\mathcal{L}$;
2. We apply sparsity learning to $\mathcal{U}$ and acquire the first layer of the ℓ_1-graph;
3. Sparsity learning is further applied to reveal the second layer of the graph;
4. The labels of all target voxels are jointly embedded following (9).

3 Experimental Results

In order to demonstrate the capability of the proposed method, we apply it to hippocampus labeling of brain MR images. In particular, we randomly select 10 atlas and 60 target images from the Alzheimer's Disease Neuroimaging Initiative (ADNI) database. All atlas images are from healthy subjects. The target images can be divided into three equally-sized sub-groups, corresponding to the subjects of health control (HC), mild cognitive impairment (MCI), and the Alzhermer's disease (AD), respectively. It is worth noting that MCI is typically regarded as a transitional stage between HC and AD. Meanwhile, abnormal atrophy of the hippocampus is closely related to AD, making the morphology of the hippocampus an important bio-marker to AD diagnosis and treatment [12].

After standard pre-processing (i.e., bias correction, skull-stripping, histogram matching, and affine registration), we utilize the 10 HC atlases to label the 60 targets by the proposed method (designated as "Proposed III" in Table 1) and four alternatives. In addition to the well-known "MV" and "NLPB" [5] methods, "Sparse-NLPB" computes the similarities between the target and the non-local atlas voxels via sparsity learning. "Joint-NLPB" [10], a latest NLPB variant, allows each atlas voxel to estimate the confidence of its contribution by interacting with other atlas voxels through a generative probability model. Note that all four existing methods label individual target voxels sequentially, in contrary to the joint labeling style in our method.

We evaluate the Dice ratio, a widely accepted metric, as the indicator of the labeling quality. The Dice ratio measures the overlapping between the multi-atlas labeling result and the expert labeling in the ADNI database, as higher Dice ratio often implies more accurate labeling. The Dice ratios of individual methods are compared in Table 1. The scores are averaged over the left/right hippocampus across target images already. For fair comparison, all voxels are signified by $5 \times 5 \times 5$ image patches. The size of the non-local search neighborhood is $9 \times 9 \times 9$. We set β to 0.1 for the fist-layer sparsity learning of our method and for Sparse/Joint-NLPB as recommended by [10]. In the second layer of our method, however, we increase β to 0.2 for selecting fewer secondary atlas voxels and also less computation. The parameter α is arbitrarily set to 5.

Table 1. The Dice ratios of hippocampus labeling through different methods.

Method	HC	MCI	AD	Overall
MV	0.591 ± 0.078	0.589 ± 0.089	0.566 ± 0.111	0.582 ± 0.093
NLPB	0.682 ± 0.042	0.675 ± 0.040	0.660 ± 0.061	0.672 ± 0.048
Sparse-NLPB	0.729 ± 0.035	0.704 ± 0.039	0.684 ± 0.048	0.706 ± 0.041
Joint-NLPB	0.755 ± 0.027	0.733 ± 0.038	0.719 ± 0.046	0.736 ± 0.037
Proposed I	0.742 ± 0.027	0.720 ± 0.044	0.691 ± 0.050	0.718 ± 0.040
Proposed II	0.741 ± 0.028	0.728 ± 0.041	0.716 ± 0.045	0.728 ± 0.038
Proposed III	$\mathbf{0.756 \pm 0.025}$	$\mathbf{0.750 \pm 0.040}$	$\mathbf{0.744 \pm 0.041}$	$\mathbf{0.750 \pm 0.035}$

As in Tabel 1, our method (Proposed III) yields significantly higher Dice ratio in overall, compared to the four existing methods. We note that the performances of our method and Joint-NLPB are close for the target images of HC. However, regarding MCI and AD where hippocampus labeling is more difficult in general, our method owns a large margin ahead. We attribute this improvement to the introduction of the semi-supervised strategy, which enables (1) joint labeling of all target voxels and (2) adaptive label correction for primary atlas voxels.

We design two degraded cases of our method for further evaluation. In "Proposed I", each HC/MCI/AD sub-group of 20 target images is jointly labeled. In "Proposed II", all three sub-groups of 60 target images are jointly labeled. The parameter β is set to infinity for both Proposed I and II, such that the primary atlas voxels follow their expert labeling strictly. Comparing Proposed I to (Sparse-)NLPB, the joint labeling strategy has shown its advantages in all three sub-groups. Comparing Proposed II to I, we conclude that the introduction of more target images leads to better labeling quality, especially for the MCI/AD target images whose appearances are less similar to the atlases. Comparing Proposed III to II, we conclude that the primary atlas voxels can effectively correct their original labels and thus improve their contributions to the target voxels, once the secondary atlas voxels are incorporated.

4 Discussion

We have proposed a semi-supervised patch-based labeling method, and applied it to hippocampus labeling for brain MR images. Specially, we build a dual-layer ℓ_1-graph of voxles, and jointly label all target voxels through graph embedding.

The dual-layer graph topology is "deeper" than the flat design of most state-of-the-art methods, where atlas voxels are directly connected to the target voxels only. In our method, however, the primary atlas voxels can interact with the graph to adjust its original expert labeling. In this way, the contributions of the atlas voxels can become much more accurate.

Our method well fits the clinical studies in which a few atlas images are expected to label many targets. To this end, we have shown that it is necessary to incorporate all target images for the joint labeling. It is also worth noting that the accuracy of multi-atlas labeling is strongly dependent on the number and the composition of the atlases. To this end, we will investigate a possible way to select the minimal number of optimal atlases in future. We will also work on to improve the speed performance of our method.

References

1. Wolz, R., Aljabar, P., Hajnal, J.V., Hammers, A., Rueckert, D., Initiative, A.D.N., et al.: Leap: learning embeddings for atlas propagation. NeuroImage **49**(2), 1316–1325 (2010)
2. Jia, H., Yap, P.T., Shen, D.: Iterative multi-atlas-based multi-image segmentation with tree-based registration. Neuroimage **59**(1), 422–430 (2012)
3. Zikic, D., Glocker, B., Criminisi, A.: Encoding atlases by randomized classification forests for efficient multi-atlas label propagation. Med. Image Anal. **18**(8), 1262–1273 (2014)
4. Sabuncu, M.R., Yeo, B.T., Van Leemput, K., Fischl, B., Golland, P.: A generative model for image segmentation based on label fusion. IEEE Trans. Med. Imaging **29**(10), 1714–1729 (2010)
5. Coupé, P., Manjón, J.V., Fonov, V., Pruessner, J., Robles, M., Collins, D.L.: Patch-based segmentation using expert priors: application to hippocampus and ventricle segmentation. NeuroImage **54**(2), 940–954 (2011)
6. Rousseau, F., Habas, P.A., Studholme, C.: A supervised patch-based approach for human brain labeling. IEEE Trans. Med. Imaging **30**(10), 1852–1862 (2011)
7. Asman, A.J., Landman, B.A.: Non-local STAPLE: an intensity-driven multi-atlas rater model. In: Ayache, N., Delingette, H., Golland, P., Mori, K. (eds.) MICCAI 2012, Part III. LNCS, vol. 7512, pp. 426–434. Springer, Heidelberg (2012)
8. Wachinger, C., Golland, P.: Spectral label fusion. In: Ayache, N., Delingette, H., Golland, P., Mori, K. (eds.) MICCAI 2012, Part III. LNCS, vol. 7512, pp. 410–417. Springer, Heidelberg (2012)
9. Wang, H., Suh, J.W., Das, S.R., Pluta, J.B., Craige, C., Yushkevich, P.A.: Multi-atlas segmentation with joint label fusion. IEEE Trans. Pattern Anal. Mach. Intell. **35**(3), 611–623 (2013)
10. Wu, G., Wang, Q., Zhang, D., Nie, F., Huang, H., Shen, D.: A generative probability model of joint label fusion for multi-atlas based brain segmentation. Med. Image Anal. **18**(6), 881–890 (2014)
11. Yan, S., Wang, H.: Semi-supervised learning by sparse representation. In: SDM, pp. 792–801. SIAM (2009)
12. Thompson, P.M., Hayashi, K.M., de Zubicaray, G.I., Janke, A.L., Rose, S.E., Semple, J., Hong, M.S., Herman, D.H., Gravano, D., Doddrell, D.M., et al.: Mapping hippocampal and ventricular change in alzheimer disease. Neuroimage **22**(4), 1754–1766 (2004)

Automatic Liver Tumor Segmentation in Follow-Up CT Scans: Preliminary Method and Results

Refael Vivanti[1(✉)], Ariel Ephrat[1], Leo Joskowicz[1],
Naama Lev-Cohain[2], Onur A. Karaaslan[2], and Jacob Sosna[2]

[1] The Rachel and Selim Benin School of Computer Science and Engineering,
The Hebrew University of Jerusalem, Jerusalem, Israel
Refael.vivanti@mail.huji.ac.il
[2] Department of Radiology,
Hadassah Hebrew University Medical Center, Jerusalem, Israel

Abstract. We present a new, fully automatic algorithm for liver tumors segmentation in follow-up CT studies. The inputs are a baseline CT scan and a delineation of the tumors in it and a follow-up scan; the outputs are the tumors delineations in the follow-up CT scan. The algorithm starts by defining a region of interest using a deformable registration of the baseline scan and tumors delineations to the follow-up CT scan and automatic liver segmentation. Then, it constructs a voxel classifier by training a Convolutional Neural Network (CNN). Finally, it segments the tumor in the follow-up study with the learned classifier. The main novelty of our method is the combination of follow-up based detection with CNN-based segmentation. Our experimental results on 67 tumors from 21 patients with ground-truth segmentations approved by a radiologist yield a success rate of 95.4 % and an average overlap error of 16.3 % (std = 10.3).

1 Introduction

Radiological follow-up of tumors is essential liver tumor therapy. The analysis of Tumor volume changes in longitudinal CT scans is required for treatment evaluation. Today, most radiologists estimate the tumor size with linear measurements methods such as RECIST [1]. It is well known that this estimate can be off by as much as 50 %, especially for tumors with irregular shapes. Previous research shows that true volumetric measurements are the most accurate information for tumor monitoring [2].

Tumor delineation is the main bottleneck of tumor volume computation. Manual delineation is time-consuming, is user-dependent, and requires expert knowledge. Semi-automatic segmentation methods, e.g., live wire, region growing, and level sets also require user interaction and may lead to significant intra- and inter- observer variability. Automatic tumor segmentation poses significant challenges and is not part of the clinical workflow, with the exception of a few tumor types. Model-based methods are also limited, as they require the construction of generic tumor priors for the segmentation. Moreover, most methods process each follow-up scan independently without taking advantage of the availability of the previous scans of the same patient.

© Springer International Publishing Switzerland 2015
G. Wu et al. (Eds.): Patch-MI 2015, LNCS 9467, pp. 54–61, 2015.
DOI: 10.1007/978-3-319-28194-0_7

In the past decade, researchers have developed a variety of methods for semi-automatic and automatic segmentation of liver tumors. Bourquain et al. [3] describe an interactive region-growing method for the vessels and tumors. Li et al. [4] use a machine learning technique to classify the intensity profiles of the liver tumors. The method is biased to blob-like tumors, so it is less accurate for tumors with irregular borders. Both methods require many seeds per CT slice and are thus of limited clinical use. Other methods use machine learning for liver tumors segmentation. However, the features that they use for the classification are hand-crafted and different for each method. Freiman et al. [5] use an SVM classifier to automatically produce many seeds for a graph based liver tumor segmentation. The hand-crafted features were the mean, std, minimum and maximum value in a 5x5x5 window. Zhou et al. [6] also use an SVM classifier, with the area median and the voxel value as features. Liver tumors segmentation was the subject of the 2008 MICCAI 3D Liver Tumors Segmentation Challenge Workshop. It consisted of 14 groups describing interactive, semi-automatic, and automatic liver tumors segmentation algorithms [7].

Recent works directly address the follow-up tumor segmentation task. In these works, the tumor delineation of the baseline scan serves as a patient-specific prior for the automatic tumor segmentation of the follow-up scan [8–10]. They show that the robustness and accuracy of the tumor volume and tumor volume difference measures significantly improve when the patient-specific tumor delineation from the baseline is used. Weizman et al. [8] uses a prior from the baseline MRI scan for Optic Path Gliomas segmentation. Vivanti et al. [9] use a similar method for lung tumors.

Only a few works address the follow-up of liver tumors. Cohen et al. [10] use the baseline tumor delineation after affine registration between the two scans to initialize 2D region-growing segmentation for each scan slice. Their work is limited to liver metastases. Moltz et al. [11] segment sphere-shaped liver metastases based on rigid registration between the scans. Militzer et al. [12] perform follow-up liver tumors segmentation with a pre-computed generative growth model created with Probabilistic Boosting Trees from many follow-up cases. To the best of our knowledge, [12] is the only work that does not assume spherical liver tumors in the follow-up framework.

Among the various machine learning techniques currently in use, Convolutional Neural Networks (CNN) [13] were brought to their full potential by making them both large and deep. They have proved their effectiveness in a wide variety of tasks, ranging from handwritten character recognition to neuronal structures segmentation [14]. One of the advantages of CNN over SVM methods is that of automatically learns the features, thus obviating the need to customize hand-crafted features.

In this paper we present a new automatic algorithm for liver tumor segmentation in follow-up CT studies. The inputs are the baseline scan and the tumors delineation, and a follow-up scan; the outputs are the tumors delineations in the follow-up CT scan. The algorithm consists of four steps: (1) deformable registration of the baseline scan and tumors delineations to the follow-up CT scan; (2) automatic segmentation of the liver; (3) construction of a voxel classifier by training a Convolutional Neural Network (CNN) on all baseline scans and; (4) final segmentation of the tumor in the follow-up study with the learned classifier. The main novelty of our method is the combination of follow-up based detection with CNN-based segmentation.

The advantages of our method are: (1) it is fully automatic; (2) it addresses a wide variety of liver tumors and metastases; (3) it performs local deformable registration to model more accurately the tumor transformation; and (4) it uses CNN to simultaneously learn features and builds a classifier based on them.

2   Method

The basic premise of our method is that the radiologist-validated tumor delineation in the baseline scan is a high-quality prior for the tumor location and size in the follow-up scan. The tumor location and size prior is automatically constructed by registration of the baseline and follow-up scans, thus allowing us to handle a large variety of tumors sizes (Fig. 1), and to obviate the need for detection method.

2.1   Registration

The first step is to automatically compute a liver mask using the stand-alone liver segmentation method in [15]. The method relies on Bayesian classification, adaptive morphological operations, and active contours for liver segmentation. We perform this segmentation for both the baseline and the follow-up scans. Although not always accurate, this mask provides an adequate coarse Region of Interest (ROI).

The next step is to define a ROI that contains the follow-up tumor with high probability. This ROI is obtained by registering the baseline scan and its tumors delineations to the follow-up scan. The registration between the baseline and the follow-up scan is performed in two steps. The first is a global deformable registration between the baseline and follow-up scans in the liver ROI automatically computed in the baseline scan using the liver mask. The liver global ROI deformable registration consists of a rigid affine registration followed by a deformable registration with B-Splines.

The second step is a separate local deformable registration for each baseline tumor delineation. The baseline tumor delineation is enclosed in an axis-aligned bounding box that defines the local tumor ROI. The local registration is performed for each baseline tumor in three stages: (1) pure translation registration; (2) rigid affine registration, and; (3) deformable registration by Mutual Information. The baseline delineation is transferred to the follow-up scan using the concatenation of the resulting transformations, and bounded in an axis-aligned 3D bounding box. This local registration step allows modeling more accurately the tumors changes.

Finally, the follow-up tumor ROI is doubled in each direction to account for possible tumor growth of up to eightfold in volume and to compensate for residual registration errors. The registration stage obviates the need for a separate detection step.

2.2   Deep Learning

We use a Convolutional Neural Network (CNN) to classify each voxel as being either 'tumor' or 'healthy'. The classification is based on voxel intensities in an axis-aligned

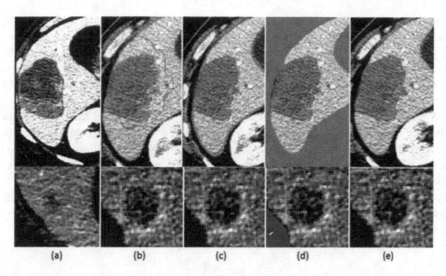

Fig. 1. Illustration of the main steps of the segmentation process on two tumors (top and bottom row): (a) baseline tumor with delineation (red) on which the CNN is trained; (b) follow-up tumor with transformed baseline delineation superimposed on it. The deformable registration between the baseline and the follow-up scans is used to set the ROI that contains the follow-up tumor; (c) tumor voxel classification based on the CNN; (d) liver mask for the removal of false positives, and; (e) final segmentation after segmentation leaks removal (Color figure online).

square centered at the voxel. The liver mask is used to exclude the voxels from the baseline set that are outside the liver.

We define first an Artificial Neural Network (ANN) as a directed weighted graph whose computation units are the graph vertices and whose arcs are weighted. In a feed-forward computation, for each vertex v_i, the values from each input vertex v_j is multiplied by the weight of the connecting edge w_j. The output of v_i is a function of the sum $\sum_j w_j v_j$, e.g., the Rectified Linear Unit function $\mathrm{ReLU}(x) = \max(0, x)$.

In the training step, the ANN is discriminatively trained by determining its edge weights with the standard back-propagation algorithm. The weights are updated by stochastic gradient descent with the equation:

$$\Delta w_{ij}(t+1) = \Delta w_{ij}(t) + \eta \frac{\partial C}{\partial w_{ij}}$$

where η is the learning rate and C is the cost function. At iteration t, a single tagged training example is used to adjust the weights by back propagation. After each epoch – a one-time pass over the entire training set – the learning rate η is reduced to allow finer weights adjustment in the following epochs.

In a CNN, one or more layer is convolutional: the nodes are grouped in kernels, and the weights of the input edges to these nodes are the values of this kernel. When feed-forwarding through each node, the computation of the sum $\sum_j w_j v_j$ is also the convolution of one kernel element and the input values. The actual values of the kernels, together with all other edge's weights are determined by back propagation. The convolution layer replaces the correlation with manually-determined kernels in the feature-extraction step in other machine learning methods. The advantage of CNN is that it can simultaneously learn both the appropriate kernels for feature extraction and a voxel-classifier based on those features.

We use a CNN with seven hidden layers (Fig. 2). The input layer has one node for each pixel a the 35x35 patch. The first hidden layer is convolutional, with 48 kernels. Each kernel computes a convolution of the input with a 4x4 kernel followed by a ReLU function and a 2x2 pooling layer. Layers three and five are convolutional, with 48 5x5 kernels followed by a ReLU function and a 2x2 pooling layer. Layer seven is fully-connected with 200 nodes followed by a ReLU function. The output layer is the classification layer with two fully connected output nodes based on the softmax function:

$$p_j = \frac{\exp(x_j)}{\sum_k \exp(x_k)}$$

where p_j is the probability to be in a class, and x_j and x_k are the total inputs from nodes j and k in the former layer, respectively. The number of kernels, nodes, and their functions were determined experimentally after several trial runs.

To separate between training and test sets, we train our network on the baseline scans, and test it on the follow-up tumors. The training set is derived from the baseline tumor in four stages: (1) remove non-liver voxels from the baseline scans using the liver mask; (2) normalize the baseline tumor ROI to compensate for different contrast agent doses so its mean and std intensity values are equal to those of the follow-up tumor ROI; (3) remove from the training set examples from the larger class, so the 'tumor' and 'healthy' classes are of equal size, and; (4) shuffle the training set. We then train the CNN with this training set for many epochs until convergence, using dropout (randomly zeroing) of half of the edges after each epoch to avoid over-fitting.

2.3 Segmentation

Once the CNN is trained, the follow-up tumor ROI is segmented by classifying all of its voxels in four steps: (1) run the trained CNN in feed-forward to classify each patch; (2) classify non-liver voxels as healthy tissue with the liver mask of the follow-up scan; (3) remove the remaining segmentation leaks with the method described in [8], and; (4) remove small holes and "islands" with morphological operations.

3 Experimental Results

We evaluate our method on 67 tumors from pairs of CT scans from 21 patients. The scans were acquired on a 64-row CT scanner (Phillips Brilliance 64) and are of size $512 \times 512 \times 350 - 500$ voxels, $0.6 - 1.0 \times 0.6 - 1.0 \times 0.7 - 3$ mm, with contrast agent.

The cases were carefully chosen from the hospital archive to represent the variety of patient ages, conditions, and pathologies. The tumors include hypodense, mixed tumors, and metastases of varying sizes and shapes with volume >1 cc. The mean time difference between the baseline and the follow-up scans is 3.78 months (std = 2.44), in a time range of 1.03–11.2 months. The tumor volumes range is 1.1–4477.86 cc. The mean volumetric change is 126.48 cc (std = 224.05). An expert radiologist approved the tumors ground-truth delineations in both the baseline and the follow-up scans.

We quantify the follow-up tumor segmentation error with the DICE volumetric overlap error (VOE) and the average symmetric surface distance (ASSD) over the entire liver. A VOE >70 % is considered as failure and not included in the mean.

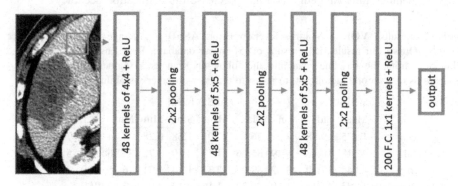

Fig. 2. Illustration of the CNN as a voxel classifier: nine layers, of which 7 are hidden layers, **Input**: 35x35 voxel-centered patch. **F.C.** – Fully Connected. **Output**: voxel classification as 'tumor' or 'healthy'

We compare our results to Freiman et al. [5] since their code is available to us, report good stand-alone segmentation results [7] and use machine learning with hand-crafted features. We use the liver tumor ground truth center of mass as a seed for their method. Note that our validation data set is significantly larger and diverse than that of [7].

We have implemented our method with the following settings. For registration, we use the Elastix registration toolbox [16] with the gradient descent optimizer with up to 200 iterations. For B-Spline registration, we set the grid spacing to 12 mm. For CNN, we use the Caffe deep learning framework with GPU acceleration [17]. In each epoch, a batch of 100 examples is processed simultaneously. We stop the convergence after 6,000 epochs. All computations were performed on an Intel® Core™ i7-4930 K CPU @3.40 GHz, 3701 MHz, 6 Cores, 32 GB RAM running Windows 7 x64 operating system and NVIDIA GeForce GTX TITAN GPU.

Table 1 summarizes the results. Our method achieves a VOE of 16.75 % (std = 9.88), a significant improvement of 60.29 % in comparison to the tumor stand-alone segmentation in [5]. The ASSD is 2.05 mm (std = 1.68), an improvement of 81.65 %. The success rate was improved by 89.98 %. The minimum and maximum values were also improved. The running time of our method was less than 5 min for all cases.

To quantify the contribution of the segmentation step, we compute the accuracy of the patient-specific prior to the registration step. The VOE and ASSD without the segmentation step are 42.46 % (std = 17.1) and 3.32 mm (std = 1.74) respectively. To quantify the inter-observer delineation variability, we asked a second radiologist to delineate 10 datasets. The mean VOE and ASSD between the delineations are 11.83 % (std = 11.12) and 1.16 mm (std = 1.12) respectively.

We conclude that the follow-up framework effectively focuses the segmentation on the tumor ROI using the baseline tumor delineation and contributes to the robustness and accuracy of the follow-up segmentation. This is achieved by providing a strong prior for the follow-up tumor segmentation. Stand-alone methods such as that in [5] must detect the tumor ROI in the entire image base on weak or non-existent priors, which sometimes fails altogether and may decrease the delineation accuracy.

Table 1. Results: **VOE** – Volume Overlap Error. **ASSD** – Average Symmetric Surface Distance. **Ours** - our results, [5] - results of [5] on our database, **Reg.** - using the transformed delineation from the baseline scan into the follow-up scan as a segmentation. **2nd obs.** - delineations of a second radiologist, to measure the inter-observer variability.

	VOE [%]				ASSD [mm]				Success %
	Mean	Std	Min	Max	Mean	Std	Min	Max	
Ours	16.75	9.88	4.53	36.10	2.05	1.68	0.28	5.14	90.47
[5]	42.18	19.43	8.49	65.06	11.17	7.89	3.72	28.96	42.85
Reg.	42.46	17.10	18.02	69.05	3.32	1.74	1.21	6.35	100
2nd obs.	11.83	11.12	1.29	29.32	1.16	1.12	0.07	3.52	100

4   Conclusions

We have presented a new automatic liver tumor segmentation method for follow-up CT studies. The inputs to the method are baseline CT scan of the liver, the delineation of the tumor in it and the follow-up scan. The output is the delineation of the tumor in the follow-up scan. Our method uses a cascade of registration methods to define a well-fitted tumor ROI on the follow-up scan based on the baseline delineation. A Convolutional Neural Network is trained on all baseline liver masking to classify tumor and healthy voxels. The CNN is used as a voxel classifier to produce the follow-up tumor segmentation. The segmentation leaks in the resulting tumor segmentation are then removed to produce the final result.

The novelty of our work is in the use of CNN with automatic features learning – in contrast with previous work that use various hand-crafted features. Importantly, the follow-up framework obviates the need for tumor detection step, significantly increasing robustness and accuracy as compared to stand-alone segmentation methods. Our method yields an overlap error of 16.75 %, an improvement of 60.29 % in comparison to [5]. Our registration approach includes an additional local step that focuses on the tracked tumor and helps refine the ROI. Our results on 67 tumors pairs from 21 patients show a considerable improvement over stand-alone SVM based methods and may provide relevant clinical measurements for liver tumors. We plan to apply our method to other organs' tumors, and to additional imaging modalities, e.g. MRI.

References

1. Eisenhauer, E., Therasse, P., et al.: New response evaluation criteria in solid tumours: revised RECIST guideline (version 1.1). Eu. J. Cancer **45**(2), 228–247 (2009)
2. Miller, A.B., Hoogstraten, B., Staquet, M., Winkler, A.: Reporting results of cancer treatment. Cancer **47**(1), 207–214 (2011)
3. Bourquain, H., Schenk, A., Link, F., Preim, B., Peitgen, O.H.: Hepavision2a software assistant for preoperative planning in living related liver transplantation and oncologic liver surgery. In: Proceedings of the 16th Conference on Computer Assisted Radiology and Surgery, pp. 341–346 (2002)
4. Li, Y., Hara, S., Shimura, K.: A machine learning approach for locating boundaries of liver tumors in ct images. In: Proceedings of the 18th International Conference on Pattern Recognition, pp. 400–403 (2006)
5. Freiman, M., Cooper, O., Lischinski, D., Joskowicz, L.: Liver tumors segmentation from CTA images using voxels classification and affinity constraint propagation. Int. J. Comput. Assist. Radiol. Surg. **6**(2), 247–255 (2010)
6. Zhou, J., Xiong, W., Tian, Q., Qi, Y., Liu, J., Leow, W. K., Han, T., Venkatesh, S.K., Wang, S.C.: Semi-automatic segmentation of 3D liver tumors from CT scans using voxel classification and propagational learning. In: MICCAI Workshop, vol. 41, p. 43 (2008)
7. Deng, X., Du, G.: Proceedings of the 3D Segmentation in the Clinic: grand challenge II - Liver Tumor Segmentation (2008). www.grand-challenge2008.bigr.nl/proceedings/liver/articles
8. Weizman, L., Ben-Sira, L., Joskowicz, L., Precel, R., Constantini, S., Ben-Bashat, D.: Automatic segmentation and components classification of optic pathway gliomas in MRI. In: Jiang, T., Navab, N., Pluim, J.P., Viergever, M.A. (eds.) MICCAI 2010, Part I. LNCS, vol. 6361, pp. 103–110. Springer, Heidelberg (2010)
9. Vivanti, R., Joskowicz, L., Karaaslan, O.A., Sosna, J.: Automatic lung tumor segmentation with leaks removal in follow-up CT studies. Int. J. Comp. Assist. Radiol. Surgery (2015) (to appear). 10.1007/s11548-015-1150-0
10. Cohen, A.B., Diamant, I., et al.: Automatic detection and segmentation of liver metastatic lesions on serial CT examinations. In: Proceedings of the SPIE Medical Imaging Conference, pp. 903519–903527 (2014)
11. Moltz, J.H., Schwier, M., Peitgen, H.O.: A general framework for automatic detection of matching lesions in follow-up CT. In: Proceedings of the IEEE International Symposium on Biomedical Imaging, pp. 843–846 (2009)
12. Militzer, A., Tietjen, C., Hornegger, J.: Learning a prior model for automatic liver lesion segmentation in follow-up CT images. Dept Informatik Technical Reports, CS-2013-03, ISSN 2191-5008 (2013)
13. Fukushima, K.: Neocognitron: A self-organizing neural network for a mechanism of pattern recognition unaffected by shift in position. Bio. Cybern. **36**(4), 193–202 (2011)
14. Ji, S., Xu, W., Yang, M., Yu, K.: 3D convolutional neural networks for human action recognition. IEEE Trans. Pattern Anal. Mach. Intel. **35**(1), 221–231 (2013)
15. Freiman, M., Eliassaf, O., et al.: An iterative Bayesian approach for nearly automatic liver segmentation: algorithm and validation. Int. J. Comp. Aided Rad. Surg. **3**, 439–446 (2008)
16. Klein, S., Staring, M., Murphy, K., Viergever, M.A., Pluim, J.P.: Elastix: a toolbox for intensity-based medical image registration. Trans. Med. Imaging **29**(1), 196–205 (2010)
17. Jia, Y.: Caffe: An open source convolutional architecture for fast feature embedding (2013). http://caffe.berkeleyvision.org

Block-Based Statistics for Robust Non-parametric Morphometry

Geng Chen[1,3], Pei Zhang[3], Ke Li[2], Chong-Yaw Wee[3], Yafeng Wu[1], Dinggang Shen[3], and Pew-Thian Yap[3(✉)]

[1] Data Processing Center, Northwestern Polytechnical University, Xi'an, China
[2] Fundamental Science on Ergonomics and Environment Control Laboratory, Beihang University, Beijing, China
[3] Department of Radiology and BRIC, UNC Chapel Hill, Chapel Hill, NC, USA
ptyap@med.unc.edu

Abstract. Automated algorithms designed for comparison of medical images are generally dependent on a sufficiently large dataset and highly accurate registration as they implicitly assume that the comparison is being made across a set of images with locally matching structures. However, very often sample size is limited and registration methods are not perfect and may be prone to errors due to noise, artifacts, and complex variations of brain topology. In this paper, we propose a novel statistical group comparison algorithm, called *block-based statistics* (BBS), which reformulates the conventional comparison framework from a non-local means perspective in order to learn what the statistics would have been, given perfect correspondence. Through this formulation, BBS (1) explicitly considers image registration errors to reduce reliance on high-quality registrations, (2) increases the number of samples for statistical estimation by collapsing measurements from similar signal distributions, and (3) diminishes the need for large image sets. BBS is based on permutation test and hence no assumption, such as Gaussianity, is imposed on the distribution. Experimental results indicate that BBS yields markedly improved lesion detection accuracy especially with limited sample size, is more robust to sample imbalance, and converges faster to results expected for large sample size.

1 Introduction

Magnetic resonance imaging (MRI) is a powerful tool for *in vivo* detection of structural differences associated with diseases. A common approach taken by traditional voxel-based morphometry (VBM) [1] is to compare two sets of images, typically images from the patient population and the healthy population, voxel-by-voxel. Such comparison can either be done at a group level or at an individual level. The former aims at characterizing the overall cause of a disease whereas the latter focuses on detecting its early signs and, possibly, its future evolution.

To correct for structural variations between individuals, many MRI data comparison methods depend on large-scale, high-quality registrations. In fact,

---

This work was supported in part by a UNC BRIC-Radiology start-up fund and NIH grants (EB006733, EB009634, AG041721, and MH100217).

© Springer International Publishing Switzerland 2015
G. Wu et al. (Eds.): Patch-MI 2015, LNCS 9467, pp. 62–70, 2015.
DOI: 10.1007/978-3-319-28194-0_8

many methods inherently assume perfect alignment between images, which is seldom possible in real practice. Registration methods are not perfect and may be prone to errors due to noise, artifacts, and complex variations of brain topology. Registration error reduces the reliability of statistical comparison outcomes since detections and misdetections might be due to comparisons between mismatched structures. This stringent requirement on registration can be somehow relaxed by smoothing the images, e.g., by a Gaussian kernel, prior to comparison. This will however eliminate subtle details in the images and finer pathologies are hence elusive and might not be detected. Increasing sample size might help suppress random misalignment errors, but will at the same time reduce the possibility of detecting pathologies associated with systematically misaligned structures. The appropriate modeling of misalignment errors in statistical comparison methods is not only important for more accurate comparisons, but is also important to make full use of available samples and improve the statistical power in detecting fine-grained abnormalities associated with diseases.

Statistical comparison of MRI data usually relies on parametric or permutation statistical tests, which often require large databases to produce reliable outcomes. However, in medical imaging studies, a large sample size is often difficult to obtain due to low disease prevalence, recruitment difficulties, and data matching issues. To simplify the task of estimating the distribution of a static of interest, very often the distribution is assumed to be Gaussian and the task of distribution estimation is hence reduced to the estimation of model parameters. This Gaussianity assumption, however, often does not hold, especially for higher-order non-linear quantities whose distributions have unknown forms and are too complex to be modeled by simple Gaussians.

In this paper, we will introduce a robust technique, called block-based statistics (BBS), for group comparisons using small noisy databases. BBS unites the strengths of permutation test [2] and non-local estimation [3]. Permutation test makes little assumption about the distribution of a test statistic and allows a non-parametric determination of group differences. Non-local estimation uses a block matching mechanism to locate similar realizations of similar signal processes to significantly boost estimation efficacy. Through our evaluations using synthetic data and real data, we found that such combination allows accurate detection of group differences with a markedly smaller number of samples, allows greater robustness to sample imbalance, and improves speed of convergence to results expected for large sample size.

2 Approach

BBS entails a block matching component, which corrects for alignment errors, and a permutation testing component, where matching blocks are used for effective non-parametric statistical inference.

2.1 Block Matching

To deal with misalignment, block matching is used to determine similar structures for comparison purposes. Restricting statistical comparisons to only

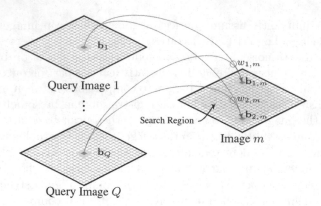

Fig. 1. Block Matching. Block matching is performed based on a set of query images. Each block $\mathbf{b}_{i,m}$ within the search region in an image m is compared with block set $\{\mathbf{b}_q | q = 1, 2, \ldots, Q\}$. The weight $w_{i,m}$ indicates the degree of similarity between $\mathbf{b}_{i,m}$ and $\{\mathbf{b}_q\}$.

matched blocks will encourage comparison of similar and not mismatched information (e.g., due to structural misalignment). For group comparison, block matching is facilitated by a set of query images that are representative of each group. This is to avoid the bias involved in only using any single image from each group as the reference for block matching. When the group size is small, the query set consists of all images in each group. When the group size is large, a small number of query images representing different cluster centers can be selected with the help of a clustering algorithm. For any image in the group, blocking matching is performed with respect to the query images (see Fig. 1). That is, at each location in the common space of the query images, a set of blocks are concurrently compared with a block in the image.

We assume that two groups of images (i.e., M_1 images $I^{[1]}_{m_1 \in \{1, \ldots, M_1\}}$ in the first group and M_2 images $I^{[2]}_{m_2 \in \{1, \ldots, M_2\}}$ in the second group), which can be vector-valued, have been registered to the common space. We are interested in comparing voxel-by-voxel images in the first group with the images in the second group. For each point $\mathbf{x} \in \mathbb{R}^3$ in the common space defined by the query images of the two groups, we define a common block neighborhood $\mathcal{N}(\mathbf{x})$ and arrange the elements (e.g., intensity values) of the voxels in this block neighborhood lexicographically as two sets of vectors $\{\mathbf{b}^{[1]}_{q_1} \in \mathbb{R}^d | q_1 = 1, 2, \ldots, Q_1\}$ and $\{\mathbf{b}^{[2]}_{q_2} \in \mathbb{R}^d | q_2 = 1, 2, \ldots, Q_2\}$, where Q_g is the number of query images in group $g \in \{1, 2\}$. Block matching is then performed as follows:

1. For each image $I^{[1]}_{m_1}$, search for blocks $\{\mathbf{b}^{[1]}_{i_1, m_1} | i_1 = 1, 2, \ldots\}$ that are similar to block set $\{\mathbf{b}^{[1]}_{q_1}\}$. Do the same for each $I^{[2]}_{m_2}$ using $\{\mathbf{b}^{[2]}_{q_2}\}$ as the reference to obtain blocks $\{\mathbf{b}^{[2]}_{i_2, m_2} | i_2 = 1, 2, \ldots\}$.

2. Assign a weight $w^{[1]}_{i_1, m_1}$ to the central voxel $\mathbf{p}^{[1]}_{i_1, m_1}$ of each block $\mathbf{b}^{[1]}_{i_1, m_1}$, depending on the similarity between $\mathbf{b}^{[1]}_{i_1, m_1}$ and $\{\mathbf{b}^{[1]}_{q_1}\}$. Similarly, assign a weight $w^{[2]}_{i_2, m_2}$ to the central voxel $\mathbf{p}^{[2]}_{i_2, m_2}$ of each block $\mathbf{b}^{[2]}_{i_2, m_2}$.

3. Utilize the set of weighted samples $\{(w_{i_1,m_1}^{[1]}, \mathbf{P}_{i_1,m_1}^{[1]})|i_1 = 1, 2, \ldots; m_1 = 1, 2, \ldots, M_1\}$ and $\{(w_{i_2,m_2}^{[2]}, \mathbf{P}_{i_2,m_2}^{[2]})|i_2 = 1, 2, \ldots; m_2 = 1, 2, \ldots M_2\}$ to infer the differences between $\{I_{m_1}^{[1]}|m_1 = 1, 2, \ldots, M_1\}$ and $\{I_{m_2}^{[2]}|m_2 = 1, 2, \ldots, M_2\}$.

The weight is defined as

$$
w_{i_g,m_g}^{[g]} = \left[\prod_{q_g=1}^{Q_g} K_{\mathbf{H}} \left(\begin{bmatrix} \mathbf{b}_{i_g,m_g}^{[g]} \\ \mathbf{x}_i \end{bmatrix} - \begin{bmatrix} \mathbf{b}_{q_g}^{[g]} \\ \mathbf{x} \end{bmatrix} \right) \right]^{\frac{1}{Q_g}}, \tag{1}
$$

where $K_{\mathbf{H}}(\cdot) = |\mathbf{H}|^{-1} K(\mathbf{H}^{-1} \cdot)$ is a multivariate kernel function with symmetric positive-definite bandwidth matrix $\mathbf{H}$ [4,5]. The weight indicates the similarity between a pair of blocks in a $(d + 3)$-dimensional space. This framework has several advantages: it can help correct for potential registration errors between images, and it can significantly increase the number of samples required for performing voxel-wise comparison. Statistical power can also be improved since the confounding variability due to misalignment can be reduced.

2.2   Permutation Test

We assume that the weighted samples $\mathbf{Z}^{[1]} = \{(w_{i_1,m_1}^{[1]}, \mathbf{P}_{i_1,m_1}^{[1]})\}$ and $\mathbf{Z}^{[2]} = \{(w_{i_2,m_2}^{[2]}, \mathbf{P}_{i_2,m_2}^{[2]})\}$ determined previously are independent random samples drawn from two possibly different probability distributions $F^{[1]}$ and $F^{[2]}$. Our goal is to test the null hypothesis H_0 of no difference between $F^{[1]}$ and $F^{[2]}$, i.e., $H_0 : F^{[1]} = F^{[2]}$. A hypothesis test is carried out to decide whether or not the data decisively reject H_0. This requires a test statistic $\hat{\theta} = s(\mathbf{Z}^{[1]}, \mathbf{Z}^{[2]})$, such as the difference of means. In this case, the larger value of the statistic, the stronger is the evidence against H_0. If the null hypothesis H_0 is not true, we expect to observe larger values of $\hat{\theta}$ than if H_0 is true. The hypothesis test of H_0 consists of computing the achieved significance level (ASL) of the test, and seeing if it is too small according to certain conventional thresholds. Having observed $\hat{\theta}$, the ASL is defined to be the probability of observing at least that large a value when the null hypothesis is true: ASL $= \text{Prob}_{H_0}\{\hat{\theta}^* \geq \hat{\theta}\}$. The smaller the value of ASL, the stronger the evidence against H_0.

   The permutation test assumes that under null hypothesis $F^{[1]} = F^{[2]}$, the samples in both groups could have come equally well from either of the distributions. In other words, the labels of the samples are exchangeable. Therefore the null hypothesis distribution can be estimated by combining all the $N_1 + N_2$ samples from both groups into a pool and then repeating the following process for a large number of times B:

1. Take N_1 samples without replacement to form the first group, i.e., $\mathbf{Z}^{*[1]}$, and leave the remaining N_2 samples to form the second group, i.e., $\mathbf{Z}^{*[2]}$.
2. Compute a *permutation replication* of $\hat{\theta}$, i.e., $\hat{\theta}^* = s(\mathbf{Z}^{*[1]}, \mathbf{Z}^{*[2]})$.

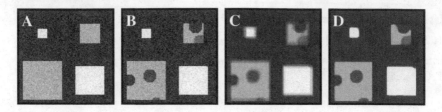

Fig. 2. Synthetic Data. Noisy reference images with (A) normal structures (squares) and (B) lesions (circles). (C) Average image of 10 perturbed versions of (B). (D) Average image after block-matching correction.

The null hypothesis distribution is approximated by assigning equal probability on each permutation replication. The ASL is then computed as the fraction of the number of $\hat{\theta}^*$ that exceeds θ: $\text{ASL} = \#\{\hat{\theta}^* \geq \hat{\theta}\}/B$.

2.3 Choice of Kernel

A variety of kernel functions are possible in general [6]. Consistent with non-local means [3], we use a Gaussian kernel, i.e., $K(\mathbf{u}) = \alpha \exp\left(-\frac{1}{2}\mathbf{u}^T\mathbf{u}\right)$, and hence $K_{\mathbf{H}}(\mathbf{u}) = |\mathbf{H}|^{-1}K(\mathbf{H}^{-1}\mathbf{u}) = \frac{\alpha}{|\mathbf{H}|} \exp\left(-\frac{1}{2}\mathbf{u}^T\mathbf{H}^{-2}\mathbf{u}\right)$, where α is a constant to ensure unit integral. The choice of $\mathbf{H}$ is dependent on the application. For simplicity, we set $\mathbf{H} = \text{diag}(h_1^{[b]}, \ldots, h_d^{[b]}, h_1^{[x]}, \ldots, h_3^{[x]})$ with $h_k^{[b]} = \sigma\sqrt{d}$. The noise level σ can be estimated by the method outlined in [7]. We set $h_k^{[x]}$ to be half the value of the search radius.

3 Experiments

We evaluated the effectiveness of BBS in detecting group differences using synthetic and real *in vivo* diffusion MRI data. The standard permutation test [2] was used as the comparison baseline. Group comparison was performed voxel-wise by the sum of squared differences (SSD) of the means, i.e., $\hat{\theta}(\mathbf{x}) = ||\bar{I}^{[1]}(\mathbf{x}) - \bar{I}^{[2]}(\mathbf{x})||^2$. Note that more sophisticated statistics (e.g. Hotelling's T^2-statistic) can be applied here to improve performance. For the standard permutation test, the mean is computed simply by averaging across images in the same group. For BBS, the mean is computed instead using weighted averaging using the weighted samples, i.e.,

$$\bar{I}^{[g]}(\mathbf{x}) \equiv \frac{\sum_{(w_{i,m},\mathbf{p}_{i,m})\in\mathbf{Z}^{[g]}(\mathbf{x})} \left[w_{i,m}\right]^{M_g^\gamma} \mathbf{p}_{i,m}}{\sum_{(w_{i,m},\mathbf{p}_{i,m})\in\mathbf{Z}^{[g]}(\mathbf{x})} \left[w_{i,m}\right]^{M_g^\gamma}}. \tag{2}$$

The exponent M_g^γ, $\gamma > 0$, is for adjusting the weights according to the number of images. This is to reduce estimation bias when a greater number of images are available. According to [8], we set $\gamma = 2/5$. Note that if we restrict the search range to $1 \times 1 \times 1$ and override the weights with 1, BBS is equivalent to

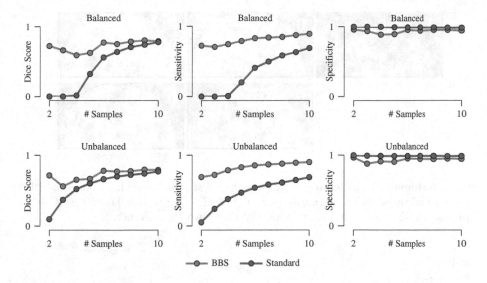

Fig. 3. Performance Statistics. Detection accuracy, sensitivity, and specificity of BBS compared with the standard permutation test. The mean values of 10 repetitions are shown. The standard deviations are negligible and are not displayed. For the case of balanced sample size, both groups have the same number of samples. For the case of unbalanced sample size, only the size of the patient dataset was varied; the size of the normal control dataset was fixed at 10.

the standard permutation test. For all experiments, we set the search range to $5 \times 5 \times 5$ and the block size to $3 \times 3 \times 3$. A search diameter of 5 is sufficient for correcting the registration errors because the images have already been non-linearly aligned.

3.1 Synthetic Data

BBS was first evaluated using synthetic data. Based on a reference vector-valued diffusion-weighted image (each element corresponding to a diffusion gradient direction, see Fig. 2(a)), 10 replicates were generated by varying the locations, sizes, and principal diffusion directions of the 'normal' structures (squares) to form the 'normal control' dataset. Based on a 'pathological' reference image (see Fig. 2(b)), created by introducing lesions ('circles') to the reference image, a corresponding 'patient' dataset was generated by varying the locations, sizes, and severity of lesions, in addition to perturbing the normal structures as before. Lesions were simulated by swelling tensors in the non-principal directions. Group comparison was repeated using 10 Rician noise realizations of the datasets.

To demonstrate the power of BBS, we performed group comparison by progressively increasing the number of samples. Voxels with ASL < 0.01 were considered to be significantly different between the two groups. Detection accuracy was evaluated using Dice score with the lesions defined on the reference image as the baseline. Both cases of balanced and unbalanced sample sizes were

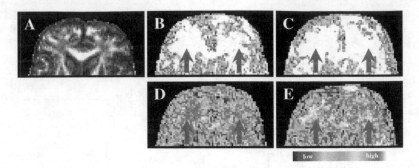

Fig. 4. Achieved Significance Level. Inverted ASL, i.e., $1 - \text{ASL}$, obtained by BBS (B & C) and the standard permutation test (D & E) using 5 (B & D) and 10 (C & E) samples. The fractional anisotropy image (A) is shown for reference.

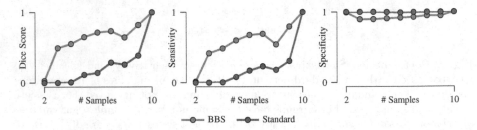

Fig. 5. Performance Statistics for Real Data. Detection accuracy, sensitivity, and specificity of BBS compared with the standard permutation test. The mean values of 10 repetitions are shown. The standard deviations are negligible and are not displayed.

considered. For the latter, only the size of the patient dataset was varied; the size of the normal control dataset was fixed at 10. The results, shown in Fig. 3, indicates that BBS yields markedly improved accuracy even when the sample size is small. Detection sensitivity is greatly increased by BBS. The specificity of both methods is comparable. The improvements given by BBS can be partly attributed to the fact that BBS explicitly corrects for alignment errors and yields sharper mean images than simple averaging, as can be observed from Fig. 2(c) and (d).

3.2   Real Data

Diffusion MR imaging was performed on a clinical routine whole body Siemens 3T Tim Trio MR scanner. We used a standard sequence: 30 diffusion directions isotropically distributed on a sphere at $b = 1,000 \, \text{s/mm}^2$, one image with no diffusion weighting, 128×128 matrix, $2 \times 2 \times 2 \, \text{mm}^3$ voxel size, TE $= 81 \, \text{ms}$, TR $= 7,618 \, \text{ms}$, 1 average. Scans for 10 healthy subjects and 10 mild cognitive impairment (MCI) subjects were used for comparison. Before group comparison was performed, the scans were all non-linearly registered to a common space using a large deformation diffeomorphic registration algorithm [9, 10].

Representative qualitative comparison results are shown in Fig. 4. The color maps present the inverted ASL values, i.e., $1-\text{ASL}$, obtained by the two methods using 5 and 10 images in each group. Warmer and brighter colors indicate differences with greater significance. When a limited number of samples are available, BBS gives results that are more consistent with results obtained with a larger sample size. In the figure, the arrows mark the regions where the standard permutation test gives inconsistent results when different sample sizes are used.

For quantitative evaluation, we used the detection results obtained using the full 10 samples as the reference and evaluated whether hypothesis testing using a smaller number of samples gives consistent results. The evaluation results shown in Fig. 5 indicate that BBS yields results that converge faster to the results given by a larger sample size. An implication of this observation is that BBS improves group comparison accuracy in small datasets.

4   Conclusion

We have presented a new method for detecting group differences with greater robustness. The method, called block-based statistics (BBS), explicitly corrects for alignment errors and shows greater detection accuracy and sensitivity compared with the standard permutation test, even when the number of samples is very low. The key benefits of BBS have been validated by the experimental results. In the future, we will improve the algorithm by using more sophisticated statistics and by incorporating resampling-based correction for multiple testing. BBS will also be applied to detect differences in quantities will greater complexity, such as orientation distribution functions and tractography streamlines.

References

1. Ashburner, J., Friston, K.J.: Voxel-based morphometry - the methods. NeuroImage **11**(6), 805–821 (2000)
2. Efron, B., Tibshirani, R.J.: An Introduction to the Bootstrap. Monographs on Statistics and Applied Probablilty. Chapman and Hall, Boca Raton (1994)
3. Buades, A., Coll, B., Morel, J.M.: A review of image denoising algorithms, with a new one. Multiscale Model. Simul. **4**(2), 490–530 (2005)
4. Härdle, W., Müller, M.: Multivariate and semiparametric kernel regression. In: Schimek, M.G. (ed.) Smoothing and Regression: Approaches, Computation, and Application. Wiley, Hoboken (2000)
5. Yap, P.T., An, H., Chen, Y., Shen, D.: Uncertainty estimation in diffusion MRI using the non-local bootstrap. IEEE Trans. Med. Imaging **33**(8), 1627–1640 (2014)
6. Härdle, W.: Applied Nonparametric Regression. Cambridge University Press, Cambridge (1992)
7. Manjón, J., Carbonell-Caballero, J., Lull, J., García-Martí, G., Martí-Bonmatí, L., Robles, M.: MRI denoising using non-local means. Med. Image Anal. **12**(4), 514–523 (2008)
8. Silverman, B.: Density Estimation for Statistics and Data Analysis. Monographs on Statistics and Applied Probablilty. Chapman and Hall, London (1998)

9. Zhang, P., Niethammer, M., Shen, D., Yap, P.T.: Large deformation diffeomorphic registration of diffusion-weighted imaging data. Med. Image Anal. **18**(8), 1290–1298 (2014)
10. Yap, P.T., Shen, D.: Spatial transformation of DWI data using non-negative sparse representation. IEEE Trans. Med. Imaging **31**(11), 2035–2049 (2012)

Automatic Collimation Detection in Digital Radiographs with the Directed Hough Transform and Learning-Based Edge Detection

Liang Zhao[2], Zhigang Peng[1(✉)], Klaus Finkler[4], Anna Jerebko[4],
Jason J. Corso[3], and Xiang (Sean) Zhou[1]

[1] Siemens Medical Solutions USA, Inc., Malvern, USA
zhigang.peng@siemens.com
[2] Computer Science and Engineering, University at Buffalo SUNY, Buffalo, USA
[3] Electrical Engineering and Computer Science, University of Michigan,
Ann Arbor, USA
[4] Siemens Healthcare, Erlangen, Germany

Abstract. Collimation is widely used for X-ray examinations to reduce the overall radiation exposure to the patient and improve the contrast resolution in the region of interest (ROI), that has been exposed directly to X-rays. It is desirable to detect the region of interest and exclude the unexposed area to optimize the image display. Although we only focus on the X-ray images generated with a rectangular collimator, it remains a challenging task because of the large variability of collimated images. In this study, we detect the region of interest as an optimal quadrilateral, which is the intersection of the optimal group of four half-planes. Each half-plane is defined as the positive side of a directed straight line. We develop an extended Hough transform for directed straight lines on a model-aware gray level edge-map, which is estimated with random forests [1] on features of pairs of superpixels. Experiments show that our algorithm can extract the region of interest quickly and accurately, despite variations in size, shape and orientation, and incompleteness of boundaries.

1 Introduction

In medical X-ray examinations, radiographers often adopt collimation to avoid unnecessary exposure to patients and improve the image quality. It is important to detect the non-collimated region for improving the visual quality in the diagnosis environment and for the processing of the image, e.g. image compression. Nevertheless, collimation detection remains a challenging problem due to the large variability in shape and appearance across collimated images. In this study, the region of interest (ROI) is the non-collimated region in the X-ray image, which is a quadrilateral caused by rectangle collimators.

There have been many works using 2D boundary detection technique for collimation detection [2,3]. However, all these methods used an unsupervised model for edge detection. Because of the large variability of the collimated images

© Springer International Publishing Switzerland 2015
G. Wu et al. (Eds.): Patch-MI 2015, LNCS 9467, pp. 71–78, 2015.
DOI: 10.1007/978-3-319-28194-0_9

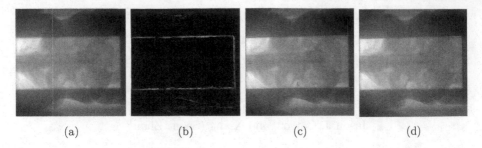

Fig. 1. An example of our algorithm: (a) Input image; (b) Edge map; (c) The optimal group of four directed straight lines; (d) Detected ROI.

and the overlap of the pixel-level feature distribution between the ROI and the collimation field, these method are not reliable. In Kawashita et al. [4], the authors detect the ROI with a plane detection Hough transform. But this method works only when the ROI is a rectangle and is not as large as the whole image. In Mao et al. [5], the authors proposed a multi-view learning-based method combining region and corner detection. The accuracy of this method highly depends on the region detection with a pixel-level two-class classification. As this method makes a classification on each pixel, the accuracy is also limited and compromises efficiency. In this paper, we develop our method based on two simple observations. First, if two pixels are near to each other, one is in the ROI and one is not, the difference of their intensity is often relatively large. Second, along a piece of boundary between the ROI and the collimation field, the directions of gradient vectors are often from the collimation field to the ROI.

The first observation indicates that, if we over-segment the image with both location and appearance information, e.g. SLIC [6], most pixels of the boundary of the ROI would be on the boundaries of superpixels. The second observation indicates that, compared with undirected straight lines, straight lines with positive normal directions specified can make stricter shape constraints for the ROI detection in X-ray images.

Hence, we proposed a novel algorithm based on superpixel-level learning-based edge estimation and a directed Hough transform. We estimate the edge strength for pixels with a random forests approach on pairs of neighbouring superpixels (Fig. 1b). As the edge map is estimated with the training data, it is robust and accurate. By computing the edge map on the superpixel level, we decrease the number of samples for learning-based classification, take advantage of superpixel-level features and decrease the number of pixels visited in the Hough transform. In Andrews and Hamarneh's work [7], the authors also used learning-based method for boundary detection. However, their method makes classifications for each boundary candidates on the pixel-level and our method only makes classifications on pairs of neighboring superpixels, which should be more efficient.

We define directed straight lines by specifying their normal vector, and extend the classical Hough transform to detect directed straight lines with the gradient vector field and the learning-based edge map. We define positive and negative half-planes for directed straight lines. And we regard the quadrilateral ROI as the intersection of four positive half-planes of the optimal group of four directed lines, as shown in Fig. 1c and d. By setting special values in the edge map and the vector field for the pixels on the four sides of the image, our method works even if the ROI is the whole image.

2   Learning-Based Edge Estimation

Given an X-ray image I, we compute its edge map I_e with the following four steps (Fig. 2).

1. We make an over-segmentation on the image with SLIC [6], resulting in a set of superpixels, S.
2. For each pair of neighbouring superpixels, we compute its probability of belonging to each of the three given classes with random forests (See Sect. 2.1 for details).
3. For each superpixel, we compute its probability of being in the ROI.
4. For each pixel $p \in I$, we compute its edge strength $I_e(p)$ based the computed superpixel-level probabilities.

As our algorithm is based on the assumption that most pixels on the boundary of the ROI are on the boundaries of some superpixels in S, we use the algorithm SLIC (Simple Linear Iterative Clustering) [6] to make the over-segmentation with pixel-level features, including intensity and texture information, which efficiently produces smooth regular-sized superpixels. We select this algorithm to guarantee our assumption above and make the features of different superpixels comparable.

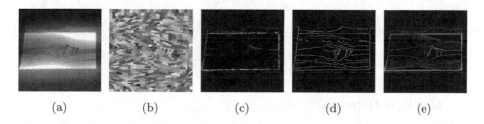

| (a) | (b) | (c) | (d) | (e) |

Fig. 2. An example of our edge estimation algorithm: (a) Input image; (b) superpixels; (c) Edge map with our method; (d) Canny edge map [8]; (e) gradient magnitude

2.1   Superpixel-Level Probability

We use a three-class random forests classifier to estimate the probability of each pair of neighbouring superpixels. The set of classes is $\{L_0, L_1, L_2\}$, which represents that 0, 1 or 2 superpixels of this pair are in the ROI, respectively. Let $Pr_{(P,Q)}(L)$ be the probability of the pair of superpixels, (P, Q), belonging to the class Ł. The features used in the classifier include the averages and the standard deviation of pixel-level features, such as intensity and gradients, of the pixels contained by either of the two superpixel, and properties of shape. By comparing the average of the intensity of P and Q, and rearranging their features, we guarantee that (P, Q) and (Q, P) have the same feature value for the random forests classifier and $Pr_{(P,Q)}(\text{Ł}) = Pr_{(Q,P)}(\text{Ł})$, $\text{Ł} = \text{Ł}_0$, Ł_1, Ł_2.

Let $Pr(P)$ be the probability for the superpixel P of being in the ROI, which is defined as: $Pr(P) = \frac{\sum_{Q \in \mathbf{N}(P)} Pr_{(P,Q)}(\text{Ł}_2)}{|\mathbf{N}(P)|}$, where $\mathbf{N}(\cdot)$ is the neighbourhood of a superpixel, $|\cdot|$ is the size of a set.

2.2   Pixel-Level Probability

Let $B(P, Q)$ be the common boundary of a pair to superpixels (P, Q), l_{four} be the set of pixels on the four sides of the image, such that $l_{four} = \{p \| p_x = 1 | p_x = M | p_y = 1 | p_y = N\}$, where $M \times N$ is the size of I.

Note that, given a perfect over-segmentation S of I, such that each superpixel P is either exactly in the ROI or exactly not, a pixel p is on the boundary of the ROI if and only if it is in one of the following two situations:

- $p \in B(P, Q)$, one of P and Q is in the ROI, the other is not.
- $p \in l_{four}$, $p \in P$, P is in the ROI

Hence we estimate the strength of edge $I_e(p)$ with the probability of pixel p being on the boundary:

$$I_e(p) = \begin{cases} \alpha Pr(P) & \text{if } p \in P \text{ and } p \in l_{four} \\ Pr_{(P,Q)}(\text{Ł}_1) & \text{if } p \in B(P, Q) \text{ and } p \notin l_{four} \\ 0 & \text{otherwise} \end{cases} \qquad (1)$$

where, α is positive constant parameter.

3   Directed Hough Transform

3.1   Classical Hough Transform

Applying the classical Hough transform (HT) to the non-negative edge map I'_e of an image I results in an 2D accumulator array $C(\rho_k, \theta_l)$, that represents the sum of edge strength (I'_e) of points satisfying the linear equation $\rho_k = p_x \cos \theta_l + p_y \sin \theta_l$, where p is a pixel in the image and (p_x, p_y) is its coordinate. Local maxima of C can be used to detect straight lines in the image. $C(\cdot)$ is defined as: $C(\rho_k, \theta_l) = \sum_{p:\ p_x \cos \theta_l + p_y \sin \theta_l - \rho_k = 0} I'_e(p)$. Where, I'_e can be binary, e.g. Canny edges, or grey-level, e.g. gradient magnitude. To compute $C(\cdot)$, for each pixel p, such that $I'_e(p) > 0$, the Hough transform algorithm calculates the parameters (ρ, θ) of lines at p, and increments the value of the corresponding bins in $C(\cdot)$ by $I'_e(p)$ [9].

3.2   Directed Straight Line

Given the coordinate (p_{0x}, p_{0y}) of a pixel p_0 and a normal vector n_0, a straight line passing through p_0 is defined with a linear equation:

$$p_x \cos \theta_0 + p_y \sin \theta_0 - \rho_0 = 0 \qquad (2)$$

where θ_0 is the angle between n_0 and the positive X-axis, ρ_0 is defined as $p_{0x} \cos \theta_0 + p_{0y} \sin \theta_0$. In this definition, $\theta_0 \in [0, \pi)$.

In this paper, we use the same equation (Eq. 2) to define a directed straight line l_{p_0, n_0} by measuring the angle θ_0 counter-clockwise from the positive X-axis to n_0. In this way, a point with two opposite normal vectors define two different directed lines passing through the same points. $\theta_0 \in [0, 2\pi)$, and θ_0 is in one-to-one correspondence to normal vectors n_0, $n_0 = (\cos \theta_0, \sin \theta_0)$.

We define the positive and negative half-plane of l_{p_0, n_0} with two linear inequalities, respectively:

$$H^+(l_{p_0, n_0}) : \quad p_x \cos \theta_0 + p_y \sin \theta_0 - \rho_0 > 0 \qquad (3)$$

$$H^-(l_{p_0, n_0}) : \quad p_x \cos \theta_0 + p_y \sin \theta_0 - \rho_0 < 0 \qquad (4)$$

Given a vector field $W = (U, V)$ for the image I, a pixel q is a supporting pixel of the directed line l_{p_0, n_0}, if and only if (q_x, q_y) satisfies Eq. 2 and $|\angle(W(q), n_0)| < \pi/2$. It is easy to see, the directions of the vectors of supporting pixels are from the negative half-plane to the positive half-plane. We define W as the supporting vector field of the image I and estimate the strength of directed straight lines with its supporting pixels in Sect. 3.3.

3.3   Directed Hough Transform with Gradient Vectors

Given the image I, its edge map I_e and its supporting vector field W, we define an 2D accumulator array $C_d(\cdot)$ for the directed Hough transform as:

$$C_d(\rho_k, \theta_l) = \sum_{\substack{p: \; |\angle(W(p), n_l)| < \pi/2 \\ p_x \cos \theta_l + p_y \sin \theta_l - \rho_k = 0}} I_e(p) \qquad (5)$$

where $n_l = (\cos \theta_l, \sin \theta_l)$.

Our goal is to guarantee that each directed line l passing through pixels on the boundary of the ROI, such that the ROI is in its positive half-plane $H^+(l)$, has a correspondent local maxima in C_d. Hence we need to define a proper supporting vector field and a good edge map.

With the observation that, along the boundary of the ROI in a X-ray image, the directions of intensity gradient vectors are often from the shadow region (non-ROI) to the ROI, we define the supporting vector field (U, V) with the estimated gradient vector $\nabla I = (I_x, I_y)$. Special values are set in the four sides of the image. As in some cases, parts of the boundary of the ROI are on the sides of the image and there is no shadow region near it.

$$W(p) = \begin{cases} (1,0) & \text{if } p_x = 1 \\ (-1,0) & \text{if } p_x = M \\ (0,1) & \text{if } p_y = 1,\ 1 < p_x < M \\ (0,-1) & \text{if } p_y = N,\ 1 < p_x < M \\ (I_x(p), I_y(p)) & \text{otherwise} \end{cases} \tag{6}$$

where, $M \times N$ is the size of the image I. And we estimate the edge map I_e with a learning-based method to take advantage of the training data (see Sect. 2 for details). The complete directed Hough transform algorithm for the ROI boundary is shown in Algorithm 1.

Algorithm 1. Directed Hough Transform

Input: Image I
 1: Compute the supporting vector field $\boldsymbol{W}$. (Eq. 6)
 2: Compute the edge map I_e. (Sect. 2)
 3: **for** each pixel $p \in I$ **do**
 4:    **if** $I_e(p) > 0$ **then**
 5:       **for** $\theta \in [0, 2\pi)$ **do**
 6:          set $n = (\cos\theta, \sin\theta)$.
 7:          set $\rho = p_x \cos\theta + p_y \sin\theta$.
 8:          **if** $|\angle(n, \boldsymbol{W}(p))| < \pi/2$ **then**
 9:             $C_d(\rho, \theta) = C_d(\rho, \theta) + I_e(p)$
10:          **end if**
11:       **end for**
12:    **end if**
13: **end for**

---

4   Optimal Quadrilateral Detection

To detect the optimal quadrilateral, we need to find the optimal group of four directed straight lines cropping the ROI.

Firstly, we detect a list of directed lines l_i, denoted as $L_{list} = \{l_i,\ i = 1 \ldots k\}$, using the directed Hough transform. l_i is in correspondence with local maxima (ρ_i, θ_i) in $C_d(\cdot)$, and $C_d(\rho_i, \theta_i) > \tau_1$, where τ_1 is a positive threshold. $\theta_i \leq \theta_j$, if $i < j$. As the optimal quadrilateral can also be regarded as the intersection of the positive half-plane of the four lines cropping it, l_i should also guarantee that its positive half-plane $H^+(l)$ contains the ROI. Let $R_{\tau_2} = \cup_{Pr(P) > \tau_2}(P)$ be a region that pixels in it have high probability in the ROI, where τ_2 is set to 0.96 in this study. Hence, each directed line l_i in L_{list} satisfies: $\dfrac{|R_{tau_2} \cap H^+(l_1)|}{|R_{tau_2}|} > \tau_3$, where $0 < \tau_3 < 1$.

Secondly, we detect a group of four directed lines $\boldsymbol{l_i} = (l_{i_1}, l_{i_2}, l_{i_3}, l_{i_4})$ in L_{list}, such that $i_1 < i_2 < i_3 < i_4$, satisfying that $\left|\theta_{i_{j+1}} - \theta_{i_j} - \pi/2\right| < \tau_\theta$, $j = 1, 2, 3$,

$|\theta_{i_1} - \theta_{i_4} + 3\pi/2| < \tau_\theta$, $|\theta_{i_{j+2}} - \theta_{i_j} - \pi| < \tau_\theta$, $j = 1, 2$, $\rho_{i_{j+2}} + \rho_{i_j} < -\tau_\rho$, $j = 1, 2$, to maximize the function f:

$$f_{l_i} = \beta \sum_{j=1}^{4} C_d(\rho_{i_j}, \theta_{i_j}) - \sum_{j=1}^{3} (\theta_{i_{j+1}} - \theta_{i_j} - \pi/2)^2 - (\theta_{i_1} - \theta_{i_4} + 3\pi/2)^2 \qquad (7)$$

where, τ_θ, τ_ρ and β are positive constant parameters.

We optimize Eq. 7 with a constrained exhaustive search. For $l_i \in L_{list}$, let $s(i) = \min\{j|\theta_j > \theta_i + \pi/2 - \tau_\theta\}$, $e(i) = \max\{j|\theta_j < \theta_i + \pi/2 + \tau_\theta\}$, it is easy to see that, in the optimal group of $(l_{i_1}, l_{i_2}, l_{i_3}, l_{i_4})$, $s(i_j) \leq i_{j+1} \leq e(i_j)$, for $j = 1, 2, 3$. We compute $s(\cdot)$ and $e(\cdot)$ beforehand to speed up the exhaustive search.

With the optimal group of $(l_{i_1}, l_{i_2}, l_{i_3}, l_{i_4})$, we can generate the optimal quadrilateral as the detected region of the interest (ROI), as in Fig. 1c.

Table 1. Comparative success rate: our method (s^*), proposed directed Hough transform with gradient magnitude map (s^1), undirected Hough transform with proposed learning-based edge map (s^2), and the method in Mao et al. [5] (s^A). D_1' and D_2' are the sets of testing images in D_1 and D_2, respectively. The success rate is computed with expert identification. The running time of the method in [5] is about 15 s per case in average, and ours is about 1.8 s.

Success rate	s^*	s^1	s^2	s^A	Number of images
D_1'	**95 %**	90 %	82 %	80 %	1598
D_2'	**99 %**	96 %	94 %	85 %	705

5   Experiments

To show the robustness of our proposed method and the impact of the two components, we evaluate our algorithm on two data sets, D_1 and D_2, acquired by X-ray machines. We randomly select 100 images from the union of the two data sets for training, and evaluate our method on the remaining images. We also evaluate another learning based method [5] with the same training and testing images for comparison, in Table 1. D_1 and D_2 are from different sites and the difference of the success rate between D_1' and D_2' is due to larger variability of orientation and size of images in D_1.

For each image, our algorithm takes 1.807 s in average to detect the ROI, on an Intel Core i5-3470, 3.2 GHz processor and 4 GB memory system. The average size of input images is 350×350. The training of the selected images takes about 2 h, in which the training data are labeled as ROI or not in pixel-level. In Fig. 3, we show some results of our method, including a failure case Fig. 3e, in which, almost all the right side of the ROI is very weak.

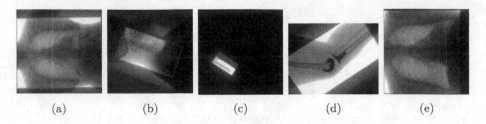

(a)   (b)   (c)   (d)   (e)

Fig. 3. Some results of our methods, (e) is a failure case

6   Discussion

In this paper, we propose a novel automatic algorithm to detect the region of interest in a X-ray image quickly and accurately. Learning-based edge maps are much more accurate than unsupervised methods, and the directed Hough transform add strict shape constraints for the quadrilateral detection. However, although we use a learning-based edge estimation, our method still cannot work if parts of the boundary are too weak, which makes the basic assumption of our method no longer hold.

References

1. Breiman, L.: Random forests. Mach. Learn. **45**(1), 5–32 (2001)
2. Luo, J., Senn, R.A.: Collimation detection for digital radiography. In: SPIE (1997)
3. Sheth, R., et al.: Region of interest identification in collimated x-ray images utilizing nonlinear preprocessing and the radon transform. J. Electron. Imaging **14**(3), 033011 (2005)
4. Kawashita, I., et al.: Collimation detection in digital radiographs using plane detection hough transform. In: Palade, V., Howlett, R.J., Jain, L. (eds.) KES 2003. LNCS, vol. 2774. Springer, Heidelberg (2003)
5. Mao, H., et al.: Multi-view learning based robust collimation detection in digital radiographs. In: SPIE Medical Imaging (2014)
6. Achanta, R., et al.: SLIC superpixels compared to state-of-the-art superpixel methods. IEEE TPAMI **34**(11), 2274–2282 (2012)
7. Andrews, S., Hamarneh, G.: The generalized log-ratio transformation: learning shape and adjacency priors for simultaneous thigh muscle segmentation. IEEE TMI **34**(9), 1773–1787 (2015)
8. Canny, F.J.: A computational approach to edge detection. IEEE PAMI **8**(6), 679–698 (1986)
9. Duda, R.O., Hart, P.E.: Use of the hough transformation to detect lines and curves in pictures. Commun. ACM **15**(1), 11–15 (1972)

Efficient Lung Cancer Cell Detection with Deep Convolution Neural Network

Zheng Xu and Junzhou Huang[(✉)]

Department of Computer Science and Engineering, University of Texas at Arlington,
Arlington, TX 76019, USA
jzhuang@uta.edu

Abstract. Lung cancer cell detection serves as an important step in the automation of cell-based lung cancer diagnosis. In this paper, we propose a robust and efficient lung cancer cell detection method based on the accelerated Deep Convolution Neural Network framework(DCNN). The efficiency of the proposed method is demonstrated in two aspects: (1) We adopt a training strategy, learning the DCNN model parameters from only weakly annotated cell information (one click near the nuclei location). This technique significantly reduces the manual annotation cost and the training time. (2) We introduce a novel DCNN forward acceleration technique into our method, which speeds up the cell detection process several hundred times than the conventional sliding-window based DCNN. In the reported experiments, state-of-the-art accuracy and the impressive efficiency are demonstrated in the lung cancer histopathological image dataset.

1 Introduction

Automatic lung cancer cell detection is the basis of many computer-assisted methods for cell-based experiments and diagnosis. However, at present, very few work has been focused on lung cancer cell detection. The difficulty in lung cancer cell detection problem is basically three-fold. First, the density of lung tumor cells is generally very high in the histopathological images. Second, the cell size might vary and cell clumping is usual. Third, the time cost of cell detection method, especially in high-resolution histopathological images, is very high in cell-based diagnosis. With these challenges mentioned above, it is still in great demand for researchers to develop efficient and robust lung cancer cell detection methods. To alleviate these problems, we propose an efficient and robust lung cancer cell detection method based on the Deep Convolution Neural Network(DCNN) [1]. Other than computationally-intensive frameworks [2,3], or ROI(region of interest)-based detection method [4,5], it exploits the deep architecture to learn the hierarchical discriminative features, which has recently achieved significant success in biomedical image analysis [6,7].

This work was partially supported by U.S. NSF IIS-1423056, CMMI-1434401, CNS-1405985.

G. Wu et al. (Eds.): Patch-MI 2015, LNCS 9467, pp. 79–86, 2015.
DOI: 10.1007/978-3-319-28194-0_10

In the proposed method, the training process is only performed on the local patches centered at the weakly annotated dot in each cell area with the non-cell area patches of the same amount as the cell areas. This means only weak annotation of cell area (a single dot near the center of cell area) are required during labeling process, significantly relieving the manual annotation burden. Another benefit for this technique is to reduce the over-fitting effect and make the proposed method general enough to detect the rough cell shape information in the training image, providing the benefit for further applications, e.g. cell counting, segmentation and tracking.

During testing stage, the conventional sliding window manner for all local pixel patches is inefficient due to the considerable redundant convolution computation. To accelerate the testing process for each testing image, we present a fast forwarding technique in DCNN framework. Instead of preforming DCNN forwarding in each pixel patch, the proposed method performs convolution computation in the entire testing image, with a modified sparse convolution kernel. This technique almost eliminates all redundant convolution computation compared to the conventional pixel-wise classification, which significantly accelerates the DCNN forwarding procedure. Experimental result reports the proposed method only requires around 0.1 s to detect lung cancer cells in a 512×512 image, while the state-of-the-art DCNN requires around 40 s.

To sum up, we propose a novel DCNN based model for lung cancer cell detection in this paper. Our contributions are summarized as three parts: (1) We built up a deep learning-based framework in lung cancer cell detection with modified sliding window manner in both training and testing stage. (2) We modify the training strategy by only acquiring weak annotations in the samples, which decreases both labeling and training cost. (3) We present a novel accelerated DCNN forwarding technology by reducing the redundant convolution computation, accelerating the testing process several hundred times than the traditional DCNN-based sliding window method. To the best of our knowledge, this is the first study to report the application of accelerated DCNN framework for lung cancer cell detection.

2   Methodology

Given an input lung cancer histopathological image I, the problem is to find a set $D = \{d_1, d_2, \ldots, d_N\}$ of detections, each reporting the centroid coordinates for a single cell area. The problem is solved by training a detector on training images with given weakly annotated ground truth information $G = \{g_1, g_2, \ldots, g_M\}$, each representing the manually annotated coordinate near the center of each cell area. In the testing stage, each pixel is assigned one of two possible classes, *cell* or *non-cell*, the former to pixels in cell areas, the latter to all other pixels. Our detector is a DCNN-based pixel-wise classifier. For each given pixel p, the DCNN predicts its class using raw RGB values in its local square image patch centered on p.

2.1   Training the Detector

Using the weakly annotated ground truth data G, we label each patch centered on the given ground truth g_m as positive(*cell*) sample. Moreover, we randomly sample the negative(*non-cell*) samples from the local pixel patches whose center are outside of the boundary of positive patches. The amount of negative sample patches is the same as the positive ones. If a patch window lies partly outside of the image boundary, the missing pixels are fetched in the mirror padded image.

For these images, we only feed very few patches into the proposed model for training, therefore extremely accelerating the training stage. Besides, this technique also partly eliminates the effect of over-fitting due to the under-sampling usage of sample images (Fig. 1).

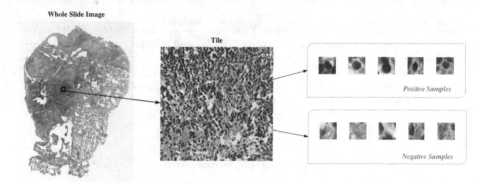

Fig. 1. The illustration of generation of training samples: (1) Tiles are randomly sampled from the whole slide images. (2) The sampled tiles are manually annotated by well-trained pathologists, which construct the weakly annotated information. (3) We only feed the local pixels patches center on the annotated pixels and the randomly sampled non-cell patches of the same amount as the cell ones.

2.2   Deep Convolution Neural Network Architecture

Our DCNN model contains two pairs of convolution and max-pooling layers, followed by a fully connected layer, rectified linear unit layer and another fully connected layer as output. Figure 2 illustrates the network architecture for training stage. Each **convolution layer** performs a 2D-convolution operation with a square filter. If the activation from previous layer contains more than one map, they are summed up first and then convoluted. In the training process, the stride of **max-pooling layer** is set the same as its kernel size to avoid overlap, provide more non-linearity and reduce dimensionality of previous activation map. The **fully connected layer** mixes the output from previous map into the feature vector. A **rectified linear unit layer** is followed because of its superior non-linearity. The output layer is simply another fully connected layer with just two neurons(one for cell class, the other for non-cell class), activated by a softmax function to provide the final possibility map for the two classes. We detail the

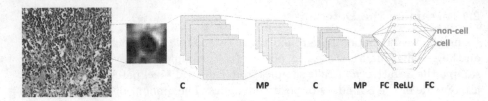

Fig. 2. The DCNN architecture used in the training process of the proposed framework. C, MP, FC, ReLU represents the convolution layer, max pooling layer, fully connected layer and rectified linear unit layer, respectively.

Table 1. Backward (left) and accelerated forward (right) network architecture. M: the number of patch samples, N: the number of testing images. Layer type: I - Input, C - Convolution, MP - Max Pooling, ReLU - Rectified Linear Unit, FC - Fully Connected

Type	Maps and neurons	Filter size	Filter num	Stride	Type	Maps and neurons	Filter size	Filter number	Stride
I	$3 \times 20 \times 20M$	-	-	-	I	$3 \times 531 \times 531N$	-	-	-
C	$20 \times 16 \times 16M$	5	20	1	C	$20 \times 527 \times 527N$	5	20	1
MP	$20 \times 8 \times 8M$	2	-	2	MP	$20 \times 526 \times 526N$	2	-	1
C	$50 \times 4 \times 4M$	5	50	1	C	$50 \times 518 \times 518N$	9	50	1
MP	$50 \times 2 \times 2M$	2	-	2	MP	$50 \times 516 \times 516N$	3	-	1
FC	$500M$	1	-	-	FC(C)	$500 \times 512 \times 512N$	5	-	1
ReLU	$500M$	1	-	-	ReLU	$500 \times 512 \times 512N$	1	-	-
FC	$2M$	1	-	-	FC(C)	$2 \times 512 \times 512N$	1	-	-

layer type, neuron size, filter size and filter number parameters of the proposed DCNN framework in the left of Table 1.

2.3   Acceleration of Forward Detection

The traditional sliding window manner requires the patch-by-patch scanning for all the pixels in the same image. It sequentially and independently feeds patches to DCNN and the forward propagation is repeated for all the local pixel patches. However, this strategy is time consuming due to the fact that there exists a lot of redundant convolution operations among adjacent patches when computing the sliding-windows.

To reduce the redundant convolution operations, we utilize the relations between adjacent local image patches. In the proposed acceleration model, at the testing stage, the proposed model takes the whole input image as input and can predict the whole label map with just one pass of the accelerated forward propagation. If a DCNN takes $n \times n$ image patches as inputs, a testing image of size $h \times w$ should be padded to size $(h + n - 1) \times (w + n - 1)$ to keep the size consistency of the patches centered at the boundary of images. The proposed method, in the testing stage, uses the exact weights solved in the training stage to generate the exactly same result as the traditional sliding window method does. To achieve this goal, we involve the k-sparse kernel technique [8] for convolution and max-pooling layers into our approach. The k-sparse kernels are created by inserting all-zero rows and columns into the original kernels to make every two original neighboring entries k-pixel away. To accelerate the forward process of fully connect layer, we treat fully connected layer as a special convolution layer. Then the fully connect layer could be accelerated by the modified convolution layer. The proposed fast forwarding network is detailed in Table 1(right). Experimental results show that around 400 times speedup is achieved on 512×512 testing images for forward propagation (Fig. 3).

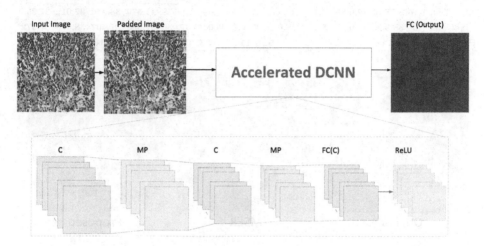

Fig. 3. The illustration of acceleration forward net: (1) The proposed method takes the whole image as input in testing stage. (2) The input image is mirror padded as the sampling process in the training stage. (3) The padded image is then put into the accelerated forward network which generates the whole label map in the rightmost. Note that the fully connected layer is implemented via a modified convolution layer to achieve acceleration.

3   Materials, Experiments and Results

3.1   Materials and Experiment Setup

Data Set. The proposed method is evaluated on part of the National Lung Screening Trial (NLST) data set [9]. Totally 215 tile images of size 512×512 are selected from the original high-resolution histopathological images. The nuclei in these tiles are manually annotated by the well-trained pathologist. The selected dataset contains a total of 83245 nuclei objects.

Experiments Setup. We partition the 215 images into three subsets: training set (143 images), validation set (62 images) and evaluation set (10 images). The evaluation result is reported on evaluation subset containing 10 images. We compare the proposed method with the state-of-the-art method in cell detection [4] and the traditional DCNN-based sliding window method [1].

Table 2. F_1 scores on the evaluation set

	1	2	3	4	5	6	7	8	9	10	Mean
MSER [4]	0.714	0.633	0.566	0.676	**0.751**	0.564	0.019	0.453	0.694	0.518	0.559
Proposed	**0.790**	**0.852**	**0.727**	**0.807**	0.732	**0.804**	**0.860**	**0.810**	**0.770**	**0.712**	**0.786**

Table 3. Mean time cost comparison on the evaluation set

	1	2	3	4	5	6	7	8	9	10	Mean
MSER [4]	37.897	29.000	37.172	43.332	42.806	37.843	28.548	41.570	38.346	37.012	37.353
Pixel-wise [10]	38.936	38.923	38.306	38.080	37.126	38.038	37.030	37.398	37.407	38.470	37.972
Proposed	**0.128**	**0.124**	**0.116**	**0.115**	**0.114**	**0.125**	**0.115**	**0.127**	**0.116**	**0.126**	**0.121**

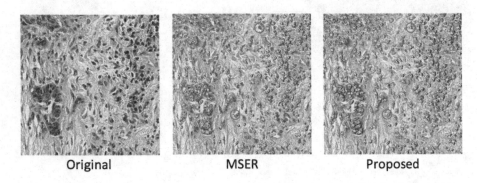

Original   MSER   Proposed

Fig. 4. Visual Comparison between the proposed method and MSER-based method [4]. The green area denotes the detected cell area by the corresponding method. Blue dots denote the ground-truth annotation. The proposed method is able to detect the cell area missed by the MSER-based method as denoted in red circle. Better viewed in ×4 pdf (Color figure online).

3.2   Results

Training Time Cost. The mean training time for the proposed method is 229 s for the training set described below. The unaccelerated version with the same training strategy costs the same time as the proposed method. Besides, the state-of-the-art MSER-based method [4] costs more than 400000 s, roughly 5 days for training 143 images of size 512×512. The proposed method is able to impressively reduce several thousand times time cost of training stage than the state-of-the-art MSER-based method due to the proposed training strategy.

Accuracy of Testing. Table 2 reports the F_1 score metric comparison between the proposed method and MSER-based method. The proposed method outperforms the state-of-the-art method in almost all of the evaluation images in terms of F_1 scores. We also visually compares our results with the MSER-based method in Fig. 4. The proposed method detects almost all of the cell regions even in images with intensive cells.

Testing Time Cost. As shown in Table 3, the proposed method only costs around 0.1 s for a single 512×512 tile image, which is the fastest among the three methods. The proposed method accelerates the forwarding procedure around 400 times compared with the traditional pixel-wise sliding-window method, which is due to the accelerated forwarding technique.

4   Conclusion

In this paper, we propose an efficient and robust lung cancer cell detection method. The proposed method is designed based on the Deep Convolution Neural Network framework [10], which is able to provide state-of-the-art accuracy with only weakly annotated ground truth. For each cell area, only one local patch containing the cell area is fed into the detector for training. The training strategy significantly reduces the time cost of training procedure due to the fact that only around one percent of all pixel labels are used. In the testing stage, by utilizing the relation of adjacent patches, the proposed method provides the exact same results within a few hundredths time. Experimental results clearly demonstrate the efficiency and effectiveness of the proposed method for large-scale lung cancer cell detection. In the future, we shall attempt to combine the structured techniques [11–13] to further improve the accuracy.

Acknowledgments. The authors would like to thank NVIDIA for GPU donation and the National Cancer Institute for access to NCI's data collected by the National Lung Screening Trial. The statements contained herein are solely those of the authors and do not represent or imply concurrence or endorsement by NCI.

References

1. LeCun, Y., Bottou, L., Bengio, Y., Haffner, P.: Gradient-based learning applied to document recognition. Proc. IEEE **86**(11), 2278–2324 (1998)
2. Bernardis, E., Stella, X.Y.: Pop out many small structures from a very large microscopic image. Med. Image Anal. **15**(5), 690–707 (2011)
3. Nath, S.K., Palaniappan, K., Bunyak, F.: Cell segmentation using coupled level sets and graph-vertex coloring. In: Larsen, R., Nielsen, M., Sporring, J. (eds.) MICCAI 2006. LNCS, vol. 4190, pp. 101–108. Springer, Heidelberg (2006)
4. Arteta, C., Lempitsky, V., Noble, J.A., Zisserman, A.: Learning to detect cells using non-overlapping extremal regions. In: Ayache, N., Delingette, H., Golland, P., Mori, K. (eds.) MICCAI 2012, Part I. LNCS, vol. 7510, pp. 348–356. Springer, Heidelberg (2012)
5. Girshick, R., Donahue, J., Darrell, T., Malik, J.: Rich feature hierarchies for accurate object detection and semantic segmentation. In: Computer Vision and Pattern Recognition (2014)
6. Hinton, G.E., Osindero, S., Teh, Y.W.: A fast learning algorithm for deep belief nets. Neural Comput. **18**(7), 1527–1554 (2006)

7. Li, R., Zhang, W., Suk, H.-I., Wang, L., Li, J., Shen, D., Ji, S.: Deep learning based imaging data completion for improved brain disease diagnosis. In: Golland, P., Hata, N., Barillot, C., Hornegger, J., Howe, R. (eds.) MICCAI 2014, Part III. LNCS, vol. 8675, pp. 305–312. Springer, Heidelberg (2014)
8. Li, H., Zhao, R., Wang, X.: Highly efficient forward and backward propagation of convolutional neural networks for pixelwise classification (2014). arXiv preprint arXiv:1412.4526
9. Team, N.L.S.T.R., et al.: The national lung screening trial: overview and study design. Radiology **258**, 243–253 (2011)
10. Jia, Y., Shelhamer, E., Donahue, J., Karayev, S., Long, J., Girshick, R., Guadarrama, S., Darrell, T.: Caffe: Convolutional architecture for fast feature embedding (2014). arXiv preprint arXiv:1408.5093
11. Huang, J., Huang, X., Metaxas, D.: Simultaneous image transformation and sparse representation recovery. In: 2008 IEEE Conference on Computer Vision and Pattern Recognition, CVPR 2008, pp. 1–8. IEEE (2008)
12. Huang, J., Huang, X., Metaxas, D.: Learning with dynamic group sparsity. In: 2009 IEEE 12th International Conference on Computer Vision, pp. 64–71. IEEE (2009)
13. Huang, J., Zhang, S., Li, H., Metaxas, D.: Composite splitting algorithms for convex optimization. Comput. Vision Image Underst. **115**(12), 1610–1622 (2011)

An Effective Approach for Robust Lung Cancer Cell Detection

Hao Pan[1,2], Zheng Xu[1], and Junzhou Huang[1]($\boxtimes$)

[1] Department of Computer Science and Engineering, University of Texas
at Arlington, Arlington, USA
jzhuang@uta.edu
[2] Department of Information Systems,
Beijing Institute of Petro-chemical Technology, Beijing, China

Abstract. As lung cancer is one of the most frequent and serious disease
causing death for both men and women, early diagnosis and differenti-
ation of lung cancers is clinically important. Lung cancer cell detection
is the most basic step among the Computer-aided histopathology lung
image analysis applications. We proposed an automatic lung cancer cell
detection method based on deep convolutional neural network. In this
method, we need only the weakly annotated images to achieve the image
patches as the training set. The detection problem is formulated into a
deep learning framework using these patches efficiently. Then, the feature extraction is made through the training of the deep convolutional
neural networks. A challenging clinical use case including hundreds of
patients' lung cancer histopathological images is used in our experiment.
Our method has achieved promising performance on the lung cancer cell
detection in terms of accuracy and efficiency.

1 Introduction

Lung cancer is the leading cause of cancer death for men and women worldwide. In
United States alone, it is estimated that 115,610 for men and 105,590 for women
new cases of lung bronchus cancer will be diagnosed, and with 86,380 for men
and 71,660 for women of lung bronchus cancer death in 2015[1]. Early detection
and diagnosis of lung cancers is clinically important to improve the survival rates
[1]. The five-year survival rate increases to 54 percent if detected early. Otherwise, it drops to 4 percent if detected when the cancer has spread out of the lungs.
Histopathology images provide detailed view of the disease, and is a golden standard to the diagnosis of lung cancer. It is a very time-consuming and tedious job to
pathologists, since a whole slide histopathological image may have billions of pixels, and even a region-of-interest (ROI) contains thousands of cells. An automatic
lung cancer analysis and diagnosis method is promising to reduce the burden of
manual examination and avoid the subjectivity of the doctors.

Z. Huang—This work was partially supported by U.S. NSF IIS-1423056, CMMI-
1434401, CNS-1405985.

[1] http://www.cancer.org/acs/groups/content/@editorial/documents/.

© Springer International Publishing Switzerland 2015
G. Wu et al. (Eds.): Patch-MI 2015, LNCS 9467, pp. 87–94, 2015.
DOI: 10.1007/978-3-319-28194-0_11

Computer-aided histopathology image analysis and diagnosis has attracted more and more attention in the enhancement of the accuracy and efficiency of diagnosis. Automatic lung cancer cell detection technique is the critical prerequisite for the other image analysis tasks. It is challenging in handling the difficulties of the histopathological images of lung tumor, such as large variations in the shape and the size of lung tumor cells, high density of lung tumor cells, and cell clumping. Some works have been made at lung cancer analysis method, they are based on conventional machine learning methods which is heavily dependent on a robust region detector and priori knowledge [1,2]. However, to the best of our knowledge, few works have been done on the lung cancer cell detection problems using Deep Convolutional Neural Network(DCNN) [3]. Currently, deep neural networks have been shown to excel at learning the hierarchical discriminative features and achieved great performance in biomedical image analysis [4].

In this paper, we propose a fully automatic lung cancer cell detection method using DCNN. Our contributions in this work are two-fold: firstly, in the training process, we need only the weakly annotated images to achieve the cell image patches as the training set. The pathologists just annotate the center of the lung cancer cell in the histopathological images, which means no need to annotate every pixel of the images so as to significantly ease the burden of manually annotated works. The proposed method also improves the training efficiency through providing less than one percent of the number of pixel patches for the training model. Secondly, No priori knowledge has been provided during the training stage, automatic feature extraction and classification is made through the training and testing of our proposed DCNN, which has the advantages of automatically learning the feature descriptors in spite of the variations in the shape and size of the training image patches. Experiments is made on a challenging clinical use case including histopathological images from hundreds of lung cancer patients. Our method has achieved promising performance on the lung cancer cell detection in terms of accuracy and efficiency.

2   Related Work

Automatic cell detection and analysis of biomedical images has attracted a number of interests for decades. Machine learning methods has been used in this area and made great progress. Automatic cell detection and analysis methods can be roughly divided into two categories. In one category, domain specific priori information of cellular features has been used to build the analysis model. The accurate cell segmentation and diagnosis depends on the quality of complex cell level feature patterns, like the shape, texture and morphology of the tissue [1]. Since the shape and size features of lung cancer cells are highly heterogeneous, these patterns tend to significantly differ in the diseased tissue which is related to different morphology tissue architecture. It is very difficult to define a generic model representative of a realistic distribution of lung cell nucleus features. Another problem of this method is about efficiency. It is time consuming to analyze a histopathological image with billions of pixels. Some methods analyze the image as a whole by representing the statistics of cell level information [5]. Other category for biomedical image analysis considers little prior knowledge, and depends on the low level image features where different strategies for image representation can be tried. Therefore, classical machine learning techniques, likely Support Vector Machine (SVM) can be used for the classification [6].

In the last few years, deep learning methods have gained great success in the field of histopathology image analysis [7]. The preprocessing of the biometric images has been preprocessed to unmix the RGB image into different biologically meaningful color channels. Then automatic immune cell detection has been realized using convolutional neural networks (CNN) [4]. To the best of our knowledge, CNNs have not been utilized efficiently for the lung cancer cell detection problems. Lung cancer can be classified as small cell lung cancer (SCLC) and non-small cell lung cancer (NSCLC). NSCLC has two major types of adenocarcinoma and squamous cell carcinoma. The diverse characteristics of different types of lung cancer have enhanced the complexity of the cell detection problems. In this paper, CNN is used to handle the general lung cancer cell detection problems. We explore the preprocessed method and CNN architecture for the lung cancer cell detection considering the complexity of the lung cancer histopathology image. Experiments have validated the effectiveness and efficiency of the proposed method.

3   Methodology

3.1   Overview

An overview of our method is presented in Fig. 1. The proposed framework is based on pixel-wise lung cancer cell detection over CNN. Slides of hematoxylin and eosin stained lung biopsy tissue are scanned at 40x magnification. Since the extreme high resolution of the original slide, smaller image patches are randomly extracted as the datasets. There are two parts, training part and cell detection testing part. In the training part, the provided training images are preprocessed into image patches first. There are two types of image patches, positive image patches(lung cancer cell) and negative image patches(non-lung cancer cell), which are produced according to the human annotation of the training images. Then the convolutional neural network is trained using the manually annotated image patches of the training data. In the cell detection testing part, the testing image is input into the trained CNN to get the output possibility map, and then the image moment analysis method is applied to get the lung cancer cell centroids.

3.2   Deep Convolutional Neural Network

Deep Convolutional Neural Network (DCNN) have been developed to be a powerful framework in the domains of computer vision, DCNN is a type of feed forward artificial neural network, which is very effective in the extraction of the

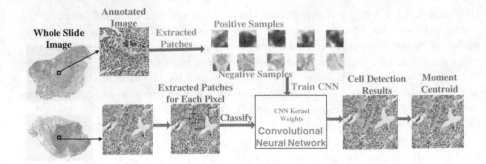

Fig. 1. Overview of the proposed framework.

hierarchical feature expressions for the image classification and recognition tasks without any prior knowledge of domain specific image features. Convolution layer and pooling layer are DCNN typical layers

Our DCNN model is a 7-layer network(excluding input) with 2 convolutional layers(C), 2 max-pooling layers(MP), 1 fully connected layer(FC), 1 rectified linear unit layer(ReLU) followed by the output layer, which is the special case of fully connected layer with the softmax function as the activation function with 2 output classes(lung cancer cell or non-lung cancer cell), as shown in Fig. 2. The architecture and mapped proximity patches of our proposed DCNN model are illustrated in Fig. 2. The detailed configuration of our DCNN is: Input($20 \times 20 \times 3$) - C($16 \times 16 \times 20$) - MP($8 \times 8 \times 20$) - C($4 \times 4 \times 50$) - MP($2 \times 2 \times 50$) - FC(500) - ReLu(500) - FC(2). The sizes of the layers are defined as $width \times height \times depth$, where the depth represents the number of feature maps and $width \times height$ represents the dimensionality of the feature map. The filter size of the convolution layer is 5×5, the max pooling layer is 2×2 with the stride of 2. For the output layer, the activation function is softmax function, $softmax(x) = exp(x)/Z$, where Z is a normalization constant. This function converts the computation result x into positive values(the summation to the values is one), so as to be interpreted as a probability distribution.

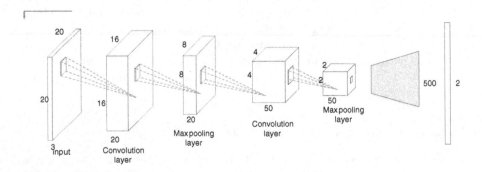

Fig. 2. DCNN architecture used for the experiments.

3.3   Implementation

The training set is composed of the image patches extracted from the weakly annotated images. All of the true lung cancer cell centers are manually annotated in the training images. The task of training data preparation is to generate image patches according to the annotated lung cancer cell centers. We extract the square image patches from the training images within the distance d_1 from the lung cancer cell center as positive training samples. The square image patches from the training images that locate far from the lung cancer cell centers (d_2) are considered as negative training samples. As the number of pixel marked as the negative samples is far more than the number as positive, we randomly selected the same number of negative image patches avoiding the ones in-balance problems.

In the testing stage, we first extract the image patches centered at each pixel of the testing image, then apply the trained DCNN classifier to these patches for producing the output probability labels.

The last step of our method is to approximate the location of cell nuclei based on the rough shape information provided by the proposed patch-by-patch manner. For each cell area, we estimate the centroid of the lung cancer cell area as the nuclei location via the *image raw moments*:

$$M_{p,q,i} = \sum_x \sum_y x^p y^q I_i(x,y), \tag{1}$$

where x, y indicate the pixel location coordinate, i denotes the i-th cell area. $I_i(x,y)$ is the image intensity function for the binary image at i-th cell area. $I_i(x,y) = 1$ if pixel located at (x,y) is in the i-th cell area, otherwise $I_i(x,y) = 0$. With the calculated image raw moments, we are able to approximate the centroid of i-th cell area by:

$$(x_i, y_i) = (\frac{M_{1,0,i}}{M_{0,0,i}}, \frac{M_{0,1,i}}{M_{0,0,i}}). \tag{2}$$

4   Experiments

4.1   Dataset Description and Experiment Setup

We evaluate the proposed method on part of the National Lung Screening Trial (NLST) data set (Fig. 3) [9]. 215 tiles of size 512×512 are selected from the original high-resolution histopathological images. The nuclei in these tiles are manually weakly annotated by the well-trained pathologist. The selected dataset contains a total of 83245 nuclei objects. The 215 images are divided into three subsets: T_1 (143 images), T_2 (62 images), E (10 images). T_1 is used for training procedure, T_2 is used for testing procedure. The evaluation result is reported on subset E containing 10 images. We compare the proposed method with the state-of-the-art method in cell detection [10]. Its code is downloaded from their website.

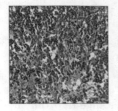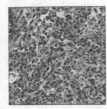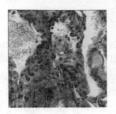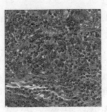

Fig. 3. Sample data from the data set: The red dots in the slide images are the manual weak annotation of nuclei location (Color figure online).

4.2 Method Evaluation

Table 1 shows the F_1 score metric of the proposed method and Arteta's method. We can see almost every F1 score of our proposed method is higher than the other method that means our method achieves high accuracy and low detection loss on the lung cancer cell detection. It is obvious that our proposed method achieved better performance than Arteta's method due to the superior performance of the DCNN.

Table 1. F_1 scores for the evaluation set

	1	2	3	4	5	6	7	8	9	10	Mean
Arteta et al. [10]	0.714	0.633	0.566	0.676	**0.751**	0.564	0.019	0.453	0.694	0.518	0.559
Proposed	**0.790**	**0.852**	**0.727**	**0.807**	0.732	**0.804**	**0.860**	**0.810**	**0.770**	**0.712**	**0.786**

From the visual comparison of these two methods, shown in Fig. 4, we can observe that our proposed method detects almost every lung cancer cell. However, it is obvious that only a few lung cancer cells have been detected in Arteta's method, while lot of lung cancer cells have not yet been detected. In one of the evaluating histopathology images shown in Fig. 4, two lung cancer cells marked with the black circle in the same location have been detected in our proposed method but not in Arteta's method. Overall, our proposed method achieves higher precision and recall than Arteta's method.

The mean training time of the proposed method is 229 seconds for the training set described. The Arteta's method [10] costs more than 5 days for training 143 images. The proposed method greatly reduces time cost of training stage than Arteta's method. The mean testing time of the proposed method is 37.972 seconds and 37.353 of Arteta's method for the image with size 512×512. The time cost of the two methods is almost the same. However, the standard deviation of the testing time is 0.668 of our proposed method and 4.819 of Arteta's method. The reason is that the testing time of our proposed method is only related to the number of pixels, while Arteta's method is also related with the number of the objects. Therefore the time cost of our proposed method is robust to the number of the object in the image, which is a favorable feature in large scale lung cancer cell detection.

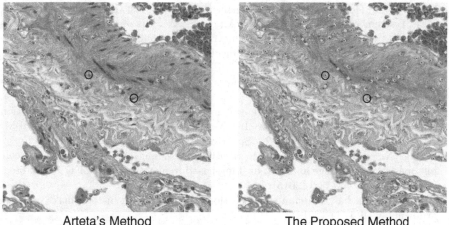

Arteta's Method   The Proposed Method

Fig. 4. Visual Comparison between the proposed method and Arteta's method [10]. The green area denotes the detected cell area by the corresponding method. Blue dots denote the ground-truth annotation. The proposed method is able to detect the cell area missed by the Arteta's method (Color figure online).

5   Conclusion

In this paper, we introduce an automatic lung cancer cell detection method on the histopathological image. DCNN is used to improve the training speed and lung cancer cell detection accuracy. No preprocessing or feature extraction is required during the training and testing procedure in our DCNN framework. Our image patch extraction method on weakly annotated lung cancer histopathological images greatly reduces the cost of the training data and improves the efficiency of the training process. The experiments on clinical image data demonstrate the promising results in terms of the training speed and lung cancer cell detection accuracy compared with the state-of-the-art method. Also, inspired by recent structure sparse learning techniques [11–13], we will use feature selection methods based on structured sparsity to select important features and further improve the accuracy.

Acknowledgments. The authors would like to thank NVIDIA for GPU donation and the National Cancer Institute for access to NCI's data collected by the National Lung Screening Trial. The statements contained herein are solely those of the authors and do not represent or imply concurrence or endorsement by NCI.

References

1. Edwards, S., Roberts, C., McKean, M., Cockburn, J., Jeffrey, R., Kerr, K.: Preoperative histological classification of primary lung cancer: accuracy of diagnosis and use of the non-small cell category. J. Clin. Pathol. **53**(7), 537–540 (2000)

2. Krebs, M.G., Hou, J.M., Sloane, R., Lancashire, L., Priest, L., Nonaka, D., Ward, T.H., Backen, A., Clack, G., Hughes, A., et al.: Analysis of circulating tumor cells in patients with non-small cell lung cancer using epithelial marker-dependent and-independent approaches. J. Thorac. Oncol. **7**(2), 306–315 (2012)

3. Krizhevsky, A., Sutskever, I., Hinton, G.E.: Imagenet classification with deep convolutional neural networks. In: Advances in Neural Information Processing Systems, pp. 1097–1105 (2012)

4. Chen, T., Chefd'hotel, C.: Deep learning based automatic immune cell detection for immunohistochemistry images. In: Wu, G., Zhang, D., Zhou, L. (eds.) MLMI 2014. LNCS, vol. 8679, pp. 17–24. Springer, Heidelberg (2014)

5. Zhang, X., Liu, W., Dundar, M., Badve, S., Zhang, S.: Towards large-scale histopathological image analysis: hashing-based image retrieval. IEEE Trans. Med. Imaging **34**(2), 496–506 (2015)

6. Barbu, T.: Svm-based human cell detection technique using histograms of oriented gradients. Cell **4**, 11 (2012)

7. Cireşan, D.C., Giusti, A., Gambardella, L.M., Schmidhuber, J.: Mitosis detection in breast cancer histology images with deep neural networks. In: Mori, K., Sakuma, I., Sato, Y., Barillot, C., Navab, N. (eds.) MICCAI 2013, Part II. LNCS, vol. 8150, pp. 411–418. Springer, Heidelberg (2013)

8. Jia, Y., Shelhamer, E., Donahue, J., Karayev, S., Long, J., Girshick, R., Guadarrama, S., Darrell, T.: Caffe: convolutional architecture for fast feature embedding. In: Proceedings of the ACM International Conference on Multimedia, pp. 675–678. ACM (2014)

9. Team, N.L.S.T.R., et al.: The national lung screening trial: overview and study design1. Radiology (2011)

10. Arteta, C., Lempitsky, V., Noble, J.A., Zisserman, A.: Learning to detect cells using non-overlapping extremal regions. In: Ayache, N., Delingette, H., Golland, P., Mori, K. (eds.) MICCAI 2012, Part I. LNCS, vol. 7510, pp. 348–356. Springer, Heidelberg (2012)

11. Huang, J., Huang, X., Metaxas, D.: Simultaneous image transformation and sparse representation recovery. In: 2008 IEEE Conference on Computer Vision and Pattern Recognition. CVPR 2008, pp. 1–8. IEEE (2008)

12. Huang, J., Huang, X., Metaxas, D.: Learning with dynamic group sparsity. In: 2009 IEEE 12th International Conference on Computer Vision, pp. 64–71. IEEE (2009)

13. Huang, J., Zhang, S., Li, H., Metaxas, D.: Composite splitting algorithms for convex optimization. Comput. Vis. Image Underst. **115**(12), 1610–1622 (2011)

Laplacian Shape Editing with Local Patch Based Force Field for Interactive Segmentation

Chaowei Tan[1], Zhennan Yan[1], Kang Li[2], Dimitris Metaxas[1],
and Shaoting Zhang[3]($\boxtimes$)

[1] CBIM, Department of Computer Science, Rutgers University, Piscataway, NJ, USA
[2] Department of Industrial and Systems Engineering, Rutgers University,
Piscataway, NJ, USA
[3] Department of Computer Science, UNC Charlotte, Charlotte, NC, USA
szhang16@uncc.edu

Abstract. Segmenting structure-of-interest is a fundamental problem in medical image analysis. Numerous automatic segmentation algorithms have been extensively studied for the task. However, misleading image information and the complex organ structures with high curvature boundaries may cause under- or over-segmentation for the deformable models. Learning based approaches can alleviate this issue, while they usually require a large number of representative training samples for each use case, which may not be available in practice. On the other hand, manually correcting segmentation errors produces good results and doctors would like such tools to improve accuracy in local areas. Therefore, we propose a 3D editing framework to interactively and efficiently refine the segmentation results, by editing the mesh directly. Specifically, the shape editing framework is modeled by integrating the Laplacian coordinates, image context information and user specified control points. We employ a local patch based optimization to enhance the supplement force field near the control points to improve correction accuracy. Our method requires few (and intuitive) user inputs, and the experimental results show competitive performance of our interactive refinement compared to other state-of-the-art methods.

1 Introduction

Medical image segmentation is one of the most important and fundamental problems in medical image analysis. In recent decades, numerous automatic segmentation algorithms have been studied, e.g., deformable model families and learning based segmentation approaches, aiming to generate accurate and robust results for clinical use. Despite the deformable models [3,4,12] have good popularity, but they are sensitive to initialization and not stable for low-contrast or ambiguous images. Learning based methods [6,11,13,15] usually require a large number of representative training samples for each specific use case. On the other hand, in many clinical applications, doctors or researchers may prefer to edit the segmentation result for better accuracy considering the limitation of automated

© Springer International Publishing Switzerland 2015
G. Wu et al. (Eds.): Patch-MI 2015, LNCS 9467, pp. 95–103, 2015.
DOI: 10.1007/978-3-319-28194-0_12

methods in dealing with high variability of medical images. Motivated by this, interactive segmentation methods [1, 2, 9] have been investigated recently. Such approaches have the potential to be widely applied in practice because they combine the efficiency of the automated methods with the reliability of manual guidance and domain knowledge from the experts.

Interactive segmentation strategies usually take different types of user input to initialize the editing process, and then generate the intermediate results based on the specialized evaluation criteria. Users can provide or update inputs to refine the segmentation result iteratively. For example, interactive graph cut [1] utilizes a user's input of foreground and background seeds to segment the foreground objects, based on the intensity statistics and spatial connectivity. Active learning based interactive segmentation [9] allows a user to delineate a set of 2D contours of the 3D object in an active learning framework and reconstruct a 3D surface based on the labeled 2D contours. In general, these existing interactive approaches apply user inputs implicitly to the segmentation results. Specifically, graph cut requires users to provide seeds to constrain the weak or misleading appearance cues and correct the mislabeled regions. However, the additional user inputs affect the global statistics and may bring some additional mislabeled regions. In addition, graph cut consumes large amounts of memories due to the graph construction and requires a complete computation for the whole ROI in each iteration. The active learning approach generates surface mesh model as the segmentation result, but the users can only edit the surfaces by editing 2D contours due to the uncertainty of the effect introduced by the additional contours.

Different from the previous approaches, we propose an effective framework to edit the 3D object boundary directly. Specifically, the framework is modeled through the Laplacian coordinates [7], which is a classical mesh model in computer graphics and is able to edit shapes without loosing detail information. However, this model only relies on the geometric information. For medical image segmentation, image context is also needed to incorporate into the interactive mesh editing. Therefore, in this paper, we propose a novel interactive framework to edit the segmentation results by adapting and integrating the Laplacian detail-preserving mesh editing, image context information and user labeled control points. The control points specify the expected segmentation targets and then drive the deformable mesh to the correct locations. These specified information also provide reliable landmarks whose local image information is emphasized. We employ a local patch based vector field convolution (VFC) [5] to optimize the supplement force field and improve the boundary extraction. With the aid of geometric optimization and image guidance, the proposed framework allows the doctors or researchers to explicitly edit the segmented shapes in an intuitive fashion. The refined results can be utilized to do clinical analysis with more confidence. We evaluate this framework extensively on two different applications, e.g., segmentation of CT lungs, MRI livers. Our proposed method is compared favorably with other state-of-the-art methods such as interactive graph cut [1] and active learning-based [9] approaches.

2   Methods

In this section, we start by defining our notation and introducing the overview of our framework in the energy formulation. Then we analyze each energy term and the integration of the influence from the user-defined control points.

Let $S : \Lambda \subset R^2 \to R^3$ denotes a surface representing object boundary, $\mathcal{I} \in R^3$ denotes a 3D image. The surface model S can be discretized as a simplex triangle mesh represented by a graph $G = (V, E)$ with vertices V connected by edges E. $V = [v_1, v_2, \ldots, v_n]^T$, $v_i = [v_{ix}, v_{iy}, v_{iy}]^T \in R^3$. Let $G_0 = (V_0, E_0)$, $G_t = (V_t, E_t)$ denote the initial and target shape, respectively. We aim to edit G_0 to $G_d = (V_d, E_d)$ which can best approximate G_t. Inspired by the framework of the Metamorphs model [3], the process of mesh editing can be formulated as an energy minimization problem:

$$E_{total} = E_{model}(G_0, G_d) + E_{shape}(G_0, G_d) + E_{target}(G_d, G_t). \tag{1}$$

Here, model energy E_{model} measures the similarity between G_0 and G_d. It preserves the initial geometric characteristics during the deformation of G_d. Shape energy E_{shape} is designed for shape optimization. It constrains the shape's tension and rigidity to ensure the global smoothness, while preserving the local details as much as possible. Target energy E_{target} reflects the distance between G_d and G_t. It introduces an external force driving the shape model evolving towards the target shape G_t. In image segmentation, the G_t represents the boundary of the object-of-interest. By minimizing these three energies, the model will deform to the target boundary while preserving its geometric properties. At the meantime, it avoids the mesh degeneration during the deformation and produces an optimized result.

To optimize the above energy function, we use iterative gradient descent method according to the forces derived using variational calculus and the Euler-Lagrange theory. E_{model} and E_{shape} derive the internal forces to preserve and optimize the shape properties. E_{target} derive the external forces to attract the model towards the target object boundary. The minimization is computed in small time step. In our study, we keep the same topology of the model and only change the coordinates of V during the deformation. Given a deformable mesh either from an initialization or a segmentation result by any algorithm, we can do interactive mesh editing and segmentation refinement by setting control points in the ROI. The control points constrain the internal force and provide a supplement external force to ensure the correct estimate of target model.

2.1   Internal Forces with Detail-Preserved Smoothing

Let C be the set of control points (landmarks) from user. c_j, $j \in C$, denotes the coordinates of a control point. v_k, $k \in V$, is the coordinates of a selected point responding to the control of c_j. The model energy E_{model} and shape energy E_{shape} are defined as:

$$E_{model} = \gamma \|V^{(t)} - V^{(t-1)}\|^2 \tag{2}$$

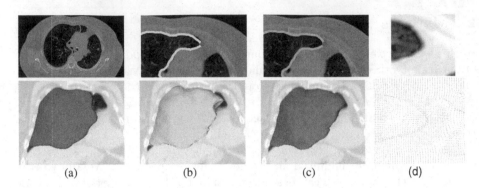

(a)   (b)   (c)   (d)

Fig. 1. Example of interactive CT lung segmentation. (a) The initial segmentation (red) and user specified control point (blue); (b) The editing result with only internal constraints introduced by control point (yellow); (c) The editing result with both geometric and image information (green); (d) An axial local image patch and the supplement force field F_{Ctrl} (Color figure online).

$$E_{shape} = \alpha \| L_u V_p^{(t)} - W L_c V_p^{(t-1)} \|^2 + \beta \| L_u^2 V_p^{(t)} \|^2 + \sum_{j,k} \omega_{kj}^2 |v_{kp}^{(t)} - c_{jp}|^2 \quad (3)$$

where $V^{(t)}$ is the model's vertices at the t-th iteration. γ, α and β are the weights. $V_p = [v_{1p}, v_{2p}, \ldots, v_{np}]^T$, $p \in \{x, y, z\}$ are coordinates along p direction. $L_u V_p$ and $L_c V_p$ are uniform and cotangent Laplacian used to approximate the discretization of Laplace operator to V [7,8]. Minimizing the two Laplacians makes the model smooth while keeping some details of the original shape. The diagonal weight matrix W for the cotangent Laplacian can be assigned as in [8]. The second term of E_{shape} controls the rigidity which simulates the surface as a thin plate to segment objects with complex shapes or high curvature regions. $\omega_{kj} = \frac{1 - \hat{dist}_{kj}}{\sum_k 1 - \hat{dist}_{kj}}$ encodes the strength of the attraction from c_j to v_k, where $\hat{dist}_{kj} \in [0, 1]$ is the normalized ℓ_2 distance to the control point c_j.

2.2 External Forces via Control Points and Local Patch Based Optimization

A resulting surface minimizing E_{target} corresponds to a smooth object boundary. The external force F_{Ext} derived by E_{target} can be defined as the similar fashions in traditional approaches (e.g., the Snakes [4], the GVF (gradient vector field) [12], the Metamorphs [3], or other variations). For these deformable models, inaccurate segmentation result is usually caused by ambiguous edges or low contrast around some parts of object boundaries. The intuitive goal of interactive aids is to emphasize the desired edges to overcome misleading appearance cues in local areas. Internal constraints can pull vertices towards the desired position, but limited number of control points may cause sharp spines (Fig. 1(b)). To overcome such limitation and improve the efficiency of user inputs, we utilize the local image information indicated by control points to form a new external force field $\tilde{F}_{Ext}$ as a supplement to the ambiguous image information and abrupt internal constraints:

$$\tilde{F}_{Ext} = F_{Ext} + \lambda F_{Ctrl} \tag{4}$$

In Eq. 4, F_{Ext} is the traditional field. λ is a weight balancing the control points field F_{Ctrl}, which is defined as:

$$F_{Ctrl} = K(x, y, z) * |\nabla[G_\sigma * \mathcal{I}_s]|^2 \tag{5}$$

Here, $\mathcal{I}_s$ is a local image patch with control point as the center and window size s. G_σ is a 3D Gaussian function with standard deviation σ. $K(x, y, z)$ is a 3D VFC kernel [5] in which all the vectors point to the kernel origin. The F_{Ctrl} optimizes the supplement force field by the VFC method, thus the field has larger capture ranges, and is more robust and computationally efficient. The radius of the kernel K is set to $s/4$. Figure 1(d) shows the optimized supplement force field by the local image patch based method.

2.3   Optimization

Combining all the energy terms via the shape optimization, image context and control points, the overall minimization problem is formed as a sparse and over-determined linear system:

$$\begin{bmatrix} A \\ diag(\sum_j \omega_{kj}) I_k \end{bmatrix} V_p^{(t)} = \begin{bmatrix} \hat{f}_p^{\,(t-1)} \\ \Omega C_p \end{bmatrix} \tag{6}$$

$$A = \gamma I - \alpha L_u + \beta L_u^2 \tag{7}$$

$$\hat{f}_p^{\,(t-1)} = \gamma V_p^{(t-1)} + \kappa \tilde{F}_{Ext}(V_p^{(t-1)}) - \alpha W L_c V_p^{(t-1)} \tag{8}$$

where Ω is a matrix formed by putting weight ω_{kj} at position (k, j) and each row in I_k is the indicator vector e_k^T. $\tilde{F}_{Ext}(V_d^{(t-1)})$ is the column vector representing p-axis force values at vertices $V^{(t-1)}$ by trilinear interpolations. κ is also a balancing weight. This linear system can be solved efficiently in a least squares fashion.

3   Experiments

In this section, we evaluate our method and compare it with other two state-of-the-art interactive methods for image segmentation. One is interactive graph cut method (GC [1]), the other one is active learning based method (AL [9]).

Data Sets. We validate our proposed method thoroughly on two data sets. The first data set includes 10 3D CT chest scans from which we segment the right lungs. The second data set includes 13 3D MRI abdominal scans from which we segment the livers. The CT chest images have 0.98 mm in-plane resolution and 3 mm between-slice resolution. The in-plance sizes are 512 × 512, the number of

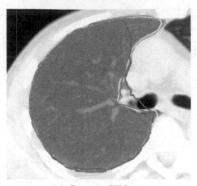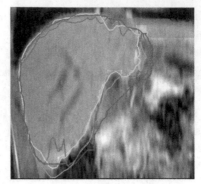

(a) Case 1: CT lung   (b) Case 2: MRI liver

Fig. 2. 2D visual comparison of refined results by different methods. The objects of interest are masked. Red lines are for initial models; yellow, green and blue lines are for our model, AL and GC refinement, respectively (Color figure online).

slices range from 97 to 148. The MRI abdomen scans are T1-weighted MRI. In this data set, images have $0.78 - 1.87$ mm in-plane resolution with $3.5 - 7$ mm between-slice resolution. The in-plane sizes range from 256×192 to 512×512. The number of slices is from 30 to 104.

Experimental Settings. We first use the TurtleSeg software [9,10] to obtain all the initial segmentations with no more than 7 labeled contours per subject. The initial segmented objects are exported as surface meshes and binary mask images for different interactive methods to refine. Since it is hard to measure the interaction efforts during the refinement, we limit different methods to only edit or correct labels at roughly same location in the same amount of slices. Then we compare the refined segmentation results. The graph cut is conducted with 26-neighborhood connectivity in down-sampled input images due to the large memory consumptions. Our model is initialized by decimated surface meshes. For each data set (CT and MRI), the parameters are firstly tuned for one data and applied to all other data in the set. We first analyze the improvements generated by control points in our framework. Then we qualitatively and quantitatively compare the refinements using different interactive methods. Dice Similarity Coefficient ($DSC = \frac{2TP}{2TP+FP+FN}$) between ground truth labels and segmentation results and the surface distance error between the surfaces of segmentation results and those of the ground truth are reported.

Experimental Results. Since our interactive framework is integrated in a parametric deformable model approach, the traditional matrix A and the internal constraints by control points are assembled once before the iteration. In each iteration, only $\hat{f}^{(t-1)}$ is updated and new $V^{(t)}$ is solved efficiently. In our cases, the surface meshes have about 2000 vertices, and the online computation is fast, about 5 frames per second, which allows real-time feedbacks of the interactive controls.

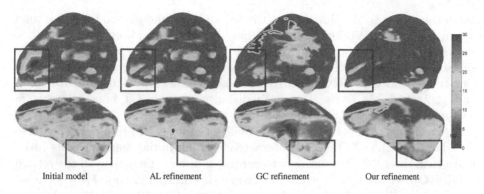

Fig. 3. 3D visual comparison of surface distance errors to the ground truth for two cases. The black boxes indicate rough locations where we did interactive refinement using different methods. The top row is for a CT lung case, the bottom row for a MRI liver case. The left to right are the surface error maps of the initial model, AL, GC and the proposed method, respectively (Color figure online).

Table 1. Quantitative comparison of segmentations in overlapping measurement and Hausdorff distance. Initial means the initial models. CG and AL stand for Graph Cut and Active Learning-based refinement, respectively.

Method	CT Lung						MRI Liver					
	Global DSC		Local DSC		Local hausdorff		Global DSC		Local DSC		Local hausdorff	
	$\mu(\%)$	σ	$\mu(\%)$	σ	$\mu(mm)$	σ	$\mu(\%)$	σ	$\mu(\%)$	σ	$\mu(mm)$	σ
Initial	90.08	0.03	24.63	0.27	10.50	7.2	84.61	0.07	44.35	0.19	8.41	4.29
GC [1]	87.28	0.05	74.05	0.28	4.14	4.13	81.89	0.09	65.87	0.10	7.84	4.20
AL [9]	90.89	0.03	71.48	0.14	4.51	2.49	86.31	0.06	67.14	0.05	7.91	4.71
Ours1	92.21	0.02	83.20	0.03	4.08	2.28	86.69	0.06	65.84	0.16	5.45	3.50
Ours2	**92.43**	**0.02**	**85.00**	**0.03**	**3.96**	**2.26**	**87.27**	**0.06**	**71.79**	0.12	**5.12**	**2.24**

Before comparing different approaches, we first show the difference between our method with or without image context information. As shown in Fig. 1, (a) shows the initial model to be edited, and the blue point in 2D slice indicates the control point we set; (b) shows the refined model by editing with only geometry constraints; (c) shows the result by editing with both geometry and image information introduced by the control point. In this case, only one control point easily correct the segmentation error in the initial model. And we can observe that only geometric editing may not produce nice boundaries for the object-of-interest. By combining both geometric and image forces, it achieves better improvement.

After showing the effectiveness of our proposed interactive framework, we compare the qualitative and quantitative performances of different approaches. Figure 2 shows two cases by 2D visual comparisons. In Fig. 3, it shows the visual comparisons in 3D view of two cases. The surface distance errors are plotted for one lung and one liver. The red color represents large surface errors, while blue color indicates small errors. We only did interactive refinement in areas indicated by the black boxes. We observe that the GC and AL produce good result around interactive sites, but other places may have little or bad side-effects. This figure shows that our proposed method has the best performance with regard to the surface error. The mean errors for initial model, Active Learning result, Graph Cut result, and Ours result in MRI liver data set are 8.30, 7.65 mm, 10.28 mm and 7.42 mm, respectively. The mean distance errors in CT lung data set are 5.61 mm, 5.13 mm, 6.24 mm and 4.21 mm, respectively.

Quantitative comparisons of overlapping accuracies and Hausdorff distances are shown in Table 1. Here we interactively refine initial segmentations in no more than three 2D slices using different methods and summarize all the refined results. **Ours1** are results with only geometric editing (without F_{Ctrl}). **Ours2** are results with all information via control points. Since the overall overlapping measurement may not reflect the local refinement clearly, we measure local performances in a small ROI containing the interaction site. It shows that all the methods except GC improve the global dice scores, because graph cut may need much more background labels to avoid mislabeling. In both global and local measurements, Ours2 produces the best performance, demonstrating the efficacy of our method.

4   Conclusions and Future Work

In this work, we proposed a novel framework for interactive mesh editing in 3D medical image segmentation. Our method seamlessly integrates the Laplacian coordinates, image context information and user specified control points to refine the segmentation results. The internal force constraints and the local patch based supplement external force introduced by control points are embedded to form a unified segmentation correction framework. We show the matrix representation of the formulated energy function, which is convenient in computation. The proposed method is evaluated on one CT dataset and one MRI dataset. We observe accuracy improvement in global and local accuracy measurement compared to two state-of-the-art interactive methods. Since our framework requires fewer user interaction and provides real-time results, it can help the doctors or researchers to interactively and intuitively refine the segmentation results in many clinical applications. In the future, we will incorporate shape prior [14] during the editing process, to further constrain the deformation and improves the reliability of the final segmentation results.

References

1. Boykov, Y.Y., Jolly, M.P.: Interactive graph cuts for optimal boundary & region segmentation of objects in N-D images. In: ICCV 2001, vol. 1, pp. 105–112. IEEE (2001)
2. Grady, L.: Random walks for image segmentation. IEEE Trans. Pattern Anal. Machine Intell. **28**(11), 1768–1783 (2006)
3. Huang, X., Metaxas, D.N.: Metamorphs: deformable shape and appearance models. IEEE Trans. Pattern Anal. Mach. Intell. **30**(8), 1444–1459 (2008)

4. Kass, M., Witkin, A., Terzopoulos, D.: Snakes: active contour models. IJCV **1**(4), 321–331 (1988)
5. Li, B., Acton, S.T.: Active contour external force using vector field convolution for image segmentation. IEEE Trans. Image Process. **16**(8), 2096–2106 (2007)
6. Ling, H., Zhou, S., Zheng, Y., Georgescu, B., Suehling, M., Comaniciu, D.: Hierarchical, learning-based automatic liver segmentation. In: CVPR, pp. 1–8. IEEE (2008)
7. Nealen, A., Igarashi, T., Sorkine, O., Alexa, M.: Laplacian mesh optimization. In: Proceedings of the 4th International Conference on Computer Graphics and Interactive Techniques in Australasia and Southeast Asia, pp. 381–389. ACM (2006)
8. Shen, T., Huang, X., Li, H., Kim, E., Zhang, S., Huang, J.: A 3D laplacian-driven parametric deformable model. In: ICCV 2011, pp. 279–286. IEEE (2011)
9. Top, A., Hamarneh, G., Abugharbieh, R.: Active learning for interactive 3D image segmentation. In: Fichtinger, G., Martel, A., Peters, T. (eds.) MICCAI 2011, Part III. LNCS, vol. 6893, pp. 603–610. Springer, Heidelberg (2011)
10. Top, A., Hamarneh, G., Abugharbieh, R.: Spotlight: automated confidence-based user guidance for increasing efficiency in interactive 3D image segmentation. In: Menze, B., Langs, G., Tu, Z., Criminisi, A. (eds.) MICCAI 2010. LNCS, vol. 6533, pp. 204–213. Springer, Heidelberg (2011)
11. Wu, G., Wang, Q., Zhang, D., Nie, F., Huang, H., Shen, D.: A generative probability model of joint label fusion for multi-atlas based brain segmentation. Med. Image Anal. **18**(6), 881–890 (2014)
12. Xu, C., Prince, J.L.: Snakes, shapes, and gradient vector flow. IEEE Trans. Image Process. **7**(3), 359–369 (1998)
13. Zhan, Y., Dewan, M., Zhou, X.S.: Cross modality deformable segmentation using hierarchical clustering and learning. In: Yang, G.-Z., Hawkes, D., Rueckert, D., Noble, A., Taylor, C. (eds.) MICCAI 2009, Part II. LNCS, vol. 5762, pp. 1033–1041. Springer, Heidelberg (2009)
14. Zhang, S., Zhan, Y., Dewan, M., Huang, J., Metaxas, D.N., Zhou, X.S.: Towards robust and effective shape modeling: sparse shape composition. Med. Image Anal. **16**(1), 265–277 (2012)
15. Zheng, Y., Barbu, A., Georgescu, B., Scheuering, M., Comaniciu, D.: Four-chamber heart modeling and automatic segmentation for 3-d cardiac ct volumes using marginal space learning and steerable features. IEEE Trans. Med. Imag. **27**(11), 1668–1681 (2008)

Hippocampus Segmentation Through Distance Field Fusion

Shumao Pang, Zhentai Lu, Wei Yang, Yao Wu, Zixiao Lu,
Liming Zhong, and Qianjin Feng[✉]

School of Biomedical Engineering, Southern Medical University,
Guangdong, China
qianjinfeng08@gmail.com

Abstract. In this paper, we propose a novel automatic hippocampus segmentation framework called distance field fusion (DFF). We perform a distance transformation for each label image of training subjects and obtain a distance field (DF), which contains the shape prior information of hippocampus. Magnetic resonance (MR) and DF dictionaries are constructed for each voxel in the testing MR image. We combine the MR dictionary through local linear representation to present the testing sample and the DF dictionary by using the corresponding coefficients derived from local linear representation to predict the DF of the testing sample. We predict the label of testing images through threshold processing for DF. The proposed method was evaluated on brain images derived from the MICCAI 2013 challenge dataset of 35 subjects. The proposed method is proven effective and yields mean Dice similarity coefficients of 0.8822 and 0.8710 for the right and left hippocampi, respectively.

Keywords: Hippocampus segmentation · Distance field

1 Introduction

Hippocampus, a brain structure situated in the temporal lobe, is associated with learning and memory. Comprehensive atrophy of brain, particularly in hippocampus and medial temporal lobe, is the pathological characteristic of Alzheimer's disease [1]. For accurate disease diagnosis and prognosis, the size and shape of hippocampus should be compared between healthy and diseased subjects. Magnetic resonance imaging (MRI) is a method used to observe brain structures and delineate hippocampus to calculate its volume. Therefore, accurate and reliable segmentation of hippocampus in MR images is important for clinical applications; this technique has attracted significant attention with the widespread use of MRI.

Various methods have been proposed for hippocampus segmentation. Atlas-based methods exhibit superior performance over other state-of-the-art techniques [2]. In atlas-based methods, an anatomical image from an atlas is registered to the target image to be segmented; the target image is then segmented by warping the manual label of the atlas to the target image space via the deformation field derived from the registration procedure [3]. Biased segmentation is likely to occur when using only one atlas but can be reduced using multiple atlases. In multi-atlas segmentation methods, we register the

G. Wu et al. (Eds.): Patch-MI 2015, LNCS 9467, pp. 104–111, 2015.
DOI: 10.1007/978-3-319-28194-0_13

anatomical image intensity of each atlas to the target image to be segmented; the manual label of each atlas is then warped to the target image space via the corresponding deformation field derived from the registration procedure. A fused label is generated by combining the warped labels from all atlases and regarded as the segmentation of the target image [3].

Atlas-based methods present two limitations. On one hand, segmentation accuracy in these methods is dependent on the registration procedure. On the other hand, segmentation accuracy can be improved with development of accurate and reliable label-fusion techniques, which exhibit an inherent constraint in segmentation accuracy because they do not utilize the shape prior information of hippocampus. To overcome these limitations, we propose a method in the present study.

In this study, a patch-based method is developed for hippocampus segmentation in MR brain images. Considering that the distance field (DF) of the training dataset contains sufficient shape prior information, we combine DFs, rather than the labels of the dataset. The proposed method was evaluated on 35 subjects, including 20 training subjects and 15 testing subjects. Results show that the proposed distance field fusion (DFF) is a promising technique for hippocampus segmentation.

2   Methods

2.1   Basic Idea of DFF

A segmentation problem can be described as follows. Given a training dataset, $T = \left\{ x_i^{MR}, x_i^{DF} \right\}_{i=1}^{N}$, which consists of N MR/DF image patch pairs, we calculate the patch x^{DF} of a testing MR image patch x^{MR}, which is sampled from the MR image centered at point x. The proposed method is based on two assumptions:

Assumption I: Image patches from MR image and DF are located on different nonlinear manifolds, and a patch can be approximately represented as a linear combination of several nearest neighbors from its manifolds.

Assumption II: Under a local constraint, the mapping from MR manifold to DF manifold f: $M^{MR} \rightarrow M^{DF}$ approximates a diffeomorphism.

Assumption I has been verified in several studies [4, 5]. In this paper, the manifolds of MR and DF patches are denoted as M^{MR} and M^{DF}, respectively, and M^{MR} and M^{DF} are assumed to be spanned by the patches in the training dataset T. To simplify the calculation, we transform the patch x^{MR} to a column vector, $\overrightarrow{x^{MR}}$. The column vector $\overrightarrow{x^{MR}}$ can be linearly represented as follows:

$$\overrightarrow{x^{MR}} = D^{MR}\overrightarrow{w} + \varepsilon = \sum_{i=1}^{n} \overrightarrow{x_i^{MR}} w_i + \varepsilon$$

$$s.t. \ \|\varepsilon\| < \tau \tag{1}$$

$$\forall \overrightarrow{x_i^{MR}} \notin N_k\left(\overrightarrow{x^{MR}}\right), \ w_i = 0$$

where $D^{MR} = \left[\overrightarrow{x_1^{MR}}, \overrightarrow{x_2^{MR}}, \ldots \overrightarrow{x_n^{MR}} \right]$ is a matrix called MR dictionary. The column

vectors of D^{MR} are derived from the training dataset T. $\overrightarrow{w} = [w_1, w_2, \ldots, w_n]^T$ is a column vector, whose elements are the coefficients of linear combination. ε is the reconstruction error of the sample x^{MR} and is lower than a small non-negative number τ. $N_k \left(\overrightarrow{x^{MR}} \right)$ is a set that consists of k-nearest neighbors (i.e., red circles filled with

yellow in Fig. 2) of the sample $\overrightarrow{x^{MR}}$ in the dictionary D^{MR}.

We use f to denote the mapping between M^{MR} and M^{DF}. According to assumption II, f is locally linear; thus, the DF patch x^{DF} of the testing MR patch x^{MR} can be calculated as follows:

$$\overrightarrow{x^{DF}} = f\left(\overrightarrow{x^{MR}} \right) \approx f\left(\sum_{i=1}^{n} \overrightarrow{x_i^{MR}} w_i \right) = \sum_{i=1}^{n} f\left(\overrightarrow{x_i^{MR}} \right) w_i$$

$$= \sum_{i=1}^{n} \overrightarrow{x_i^{DF}} w_i = D^{DF} \overrightarrow{w} \tag{2}$$

where $\overrightarrow{x^{DF}}$ is the DF corresponding to the testing sample $\overrightarrow{x^{MR}}$, $D^{DF} = \left[\overrightarrow{x_1^{DF}}, \overrightarrow{x_2^{DF}}, \ldots, \overrightarrow{x_n^{DF}} \right]$ is a matrix called DF dictionary, and $\overrightarrow{x_i^{DF}}$ is the DF of $\overrightarrow{x_i^{MR}}$; thus, the DF of point x is defined as:

$$M(x) = \begin{cases} -dist(x, B), & x \ outside \ C \\ dist(x, B), & otherwise \end{cases} \tag{3}$$

where C is the boundary of the hippocampus, B is the nearest point from x, and $B \in C$. $dist(x, B)$ denotes the distance between x and B.

The proposed method contains three main parts: pre-processing (including registration, distance transformation, etc.), fusion (including local dictionary construction, local linear representation, and DF prediction), and threshold segmentation. The framework of the proposed method and detailed procedures of fusion in DFF are shown in Figs. 1 and 2, respectively.

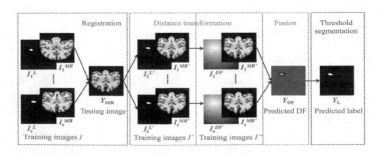

Fig. 1. The framework of the proposed DFF

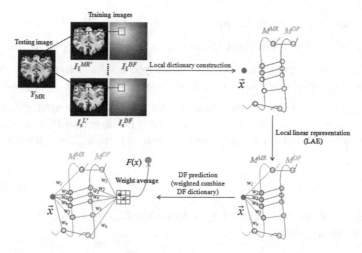

Fig. 2. The detailed procedures of fusion in DFF (Color figure online)

Local Dictionary Construction. We use $I'' = \left\{ \left(I_j^{MR'}, I_j^{DF} \right) \mid j = 1, 2, \ldots, s \right\}$ to denote the pre-processed training dataset, which is registered to the testing image and undergoes distance transformation procedure; in the formula, s denotes the number of training subjects and I_j^{DF} is the DF corresponding to the MR image $I_j^{MR'}$. For a testing image Y_{MR}, we aim to construct local dictionaries for each point x.

For a point x on the testing subject, we extract patch pairs x_i^{MR}/x_i^{DF} on the training dataset I'' in the search window centered at point x. We vectorize patches x_i^{MR} and x_i^{DF} to column vectors $\overrightarrow{x_i^{MR}} \in R^m$ and $\overrightarrow{x_i^{DF}} \in R^m$, respectively. We collect vectors $\overrightarrow{x_i^{MR}}$ and $\overrightarrow{x_i^{DF}}$ and to build dictionaries $D^{MR} = \left[\overrightarrow{x_1^{MR}}, \overrightarrow{x_2^{MR}}, \ldots, \overrightarrow{x_n^{MR}} \right] \in R^{m \times n}$ and $D^{DF} = \left[\overrightarrow{x_1^{DF}}, \overrightarrow{x_2^{DF}}, \ldots, \overrightarrow{x_n^{DF}} \right] \in R^{m \times n}$, respectively.

Local Linear Representation. Several methods have been proposed to linearly represent a testing sample by combining training samples. Sparse coding with L1 (least absolute shrinkage and selection operator) [6] emphasizes the sparsity of coefficients. This coding represents a testing sample with the least training samples and minimum construction error. By contrast, local linear classification (LCC) [7] accentuates locality, rather than sparsity. LCC represents a testing sample by using several training samples located in a local region, where the training samples are similar to the testing sample. Compared with LLC, local anchor embedding (LAE) [8] combines a non-negative constraint to coefficients. Therefore, in the current paper, we solve the linear representation problem using LAE because the testing sample in the proposed method is represented by convex combination of its closest neighbors.

DF Prediction. For a testing sample $\overrightarrow{x^{MR}}$, we predict the DF $\overrightarrow{x^{DF}}$ via Eq. (2). Each testing sample $\overrightarrow{x^{MR}}$ has a predicted DF $\overrightarrow{x^{DF}}$, and several overlapping points exist for different testing samples. Hence, the DF of the point x for a testing sample $\overrightarrow{x^{MR}}$ is determined using several predicted DFs near the point x. As such, a weighted-average strategy is introduced. First, we reshape the vector $\overrightarrow{x^{DF}} \in R^m$ to a patch $x^{DF} \in R^{a \times b \times c}$, where $m = a \times b \times c$. The weight for a point u in the region $P(x)$, which denotes the area centered at point x, with size similar to that of patch x^{DF}, is defined as follows:

$$w_u^x = \frac{1}{m} \tag{4}$$

Second, we obtain the average DF in the region $P(x)$ to predict DF for point x by using the following formula:

$$F(x) = \frac{\sum_{u \in P(x)} w_u^x I_u^x}{\sum_{u \in P(x)} w_u^x} \tag{5}$$

where I_u^x denotes the DF of x predicted by patch x^{MR} centered at the point u using Eq. (2).

2.2   Threshold Segmentation

Basing on the definition of DF in Eq. (3), we can predict the label for a point x by using a threshold:

$$L(x) = \begin{cases} 1, & F(x) > 0 \\ 0, & F(x) \leq 0 \end{cases} \tag{6}$$

where $F(x)$ is the predicted DF of the point x in Eq. (5). After predicting the label of each voxel, we obtain a binary image and the point with the value of one belongs to hippocampus.

3   Experiment Results

A dataset was obtained from MICCAI Challenge Workshop on Segmentation: Algorithms, Theory and Applications ("SATA")[1]. We applied the proposed method to the subdataset with 35 subjects, including 20 subjects as the training dataset and 15 subjects as the testing dataset. The BET approach [9] was used to remove the skull in the MR images, and the N4 algorithm [10] was utilized to remove bias field artifacts from the images. All training MR images were non-rigidly registered to a testing MR image

---

[1] https://masi.vuse.vanderbilt.edu/workshop2013/.

via different deformation fields, which were applied to all corresponding label training images. The images were registered through DRAMMS [11], and the registered label training images were transformed to DFs via Eq. (3). The parameters were set as follows: a patch size of $5 \times 5 \times 5$, a search window size of $7 \times 7 \times 7$ for constructing dictionaries, and 30 nearest neighbors in LAE.

We used dice similarity coefficient (DSC), a common evaluation measure, to quantify the effectiveness of the proposed method for hippocampus segmentation and compare with other state-of-the-art segmentation algorithms. All experiments were conducted with MATLAB.

3.1 Influence of Distance Field Fusion Compared with Label Fusion

Two sets of experiments were performed to verify the effectiveness of DFF. First, we used the proposed DFF method. Second, after obtaining the coefficient vector $\vec{w}$ of the local linear representation via Eq. (1), we combined the label corresponding to the center point of the element of the dictionary D^{MR}. Table 1 shows the mean DSC values of 15 testing subjects by using DFFs; these values were improved by 1.21 % and 1.11 % for the right and left hippocampi, respectively. The results show that DFF can improve the accuracy of hippocampus segmentation.

Table 1. Mean and standard deviation of Dice similar coefficient obtained using LF and DFF.

Subject\Method	Label fusion(LF)	Distance field fusion(DFF)
Right hippocampus	0.8701 ± 0.0160	0.8822 ± 0.0154
Left hippocampus	0.8599 ± 0.0207	0.8710 ± 0.0185

3.2 Comparison with the Relevant Methods

To investigate the contribution of DFF, we compared the proposed method with several state-of-the-art fusion algorithms, such as major voting [12], weight voting [13], SIMPLE [14], STAPLE [15], and spatial STAPLE [16]. Comparison was performed using MASI Label Fusion toolbox[2] with default parameters. Table 2 shows the mean

Table 2. Mean and standard deviation of Dice similar coefficient for 15 testing subjects using the proposed method and five relevant methods.

Method\Subject	Right hippocampus	Left hippocampus
Major voting	0.8521 ± 0.0373	0.8387 ± 0.0502
Weight voting	0.8531 ± 0.0369	0.8384 ± 0.0523
SIMPLE	0.8525 ± 0.0373	0.8394 ± 0.0479
STAPLE	0.8481 ± 0.0434	0.8351 ± 0.0610
Spatial STAPLE	0.8526 ± 0.0374	0.8384 ± 0.0538
Our	0.8822 ± 0.0154	0.8710 ± 0.0185

---

[2] http://www.nitrc.org/projects/masi-fusion.

and standard deviation of DSC for 15 testing subjects by using the proposed method and the five relevant methods. The mean and standard deviations of DSC obtained by the proposed method are 0.8822 ± 0.0154 for the right hippocampus and 0.8710 ± 0.0185 for the left hippocampus. The results show that the proposed method is more accurate than the five relevant fusion algorithms.

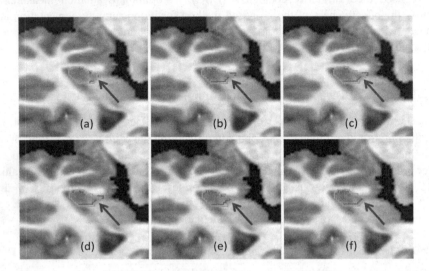

Fig. 3. Coronal view of the right hippocampus segmentation results for the testing subject by our method (Fig. 3. (a)), and five other methods (Fig. 3. (b)–(f)): Major Voting, Weight Voting, SIMPLE, STAPLE and Spatial STAPLE, along with the manual segmentation. Red contour and green contour denote the automatic segmentation results and manual segmentation results, respectively (Color figure online).

For visual comparison, we present the coronal view of the segmentation of the right hippocampus of the testing subject by using the proposed method (Fig. 3. (a)) and the five other methods (Fig. 3. (b)–(f)). The hippocampus segmented by the proposed method is similar to the ground truth than any of the five methods. In particular, in the blue arrow region, the proposed method can delineate the boundary of hippocampus, whereas the five other methods lead to large estimation errors.

4   Conclusion

In this study, we propose a novel DFF-based method to segment hippocampus in MR images. The method was established using the following procedures: (1) we used a distance transformation for label training images to obtain DF and utilize the shape information of hippocampus in training subjects; and (2) the local diffeomorphic mapping from the MR manifold was introduced to the DF manifold to predict the DF for a testing subject. The proposed method was evaluated for MR brain images on a dataset including 35 subjects. The proposed method exhibits superior performance over other fusion algorithms.

References

1. Wurtman, R.: Biomarkers in the diagnosis and management of Alzheimer's disease. Metabolism **64**, S47–S50 (2015)
2. Babalola, K.O., Patenaude, B., Aljabar, P., Schnabel, J., Kennedy, D., Crum, W., Smith, S., Cootes, T., Jenkinson, M., Rueckert, D.: An evaluation of four automatic methods of segmenting the subcortical structures in the brain. Neuroimage **47**, 1435–1447 (2009)
3. Pipitone, J., Park, M.T., Winterburn, J., Lett, T.A., Lerch, J.P., Pruessner, J.C., Lepage, M., Voineskos, A.N., Chakravarty, M.M., Alzheimer's Disease Neuroimaging Initiative: Multi-atlas segmentation of the whole hippocampus and subfields using multiple automatically generated templates. Neuroimage **101**, 494–512 (2014)
4. Huang, M., Yang, W., Jiang, J., Wu, Y., Zhang, Y., Chen, W., Feng, Q., Alzheimer's Disease Neuroimaging Initiative: Brain extraction based on locally linear representation-based classification. Neuroimage **92**, 322–339 (2014)
5. Zhang, P., Wee, C.-Y., Niethammer, M., Shen, D., Yap, P.-T.: Large deformation image classification using generalized locality-constrained linear coding. In: Mori, K., Sakuma, I., Sato, Y., Barillot, C., Navab, N. (eds.) MICCAI 2013, Part I. LNCS, vol. 8149, pp. 292–299. Springer, Heidelberg (2013)
6. Tibshrani, R.: Regression shrinkage and selection via the LASSO. J. Roy. Stat. Soc. **58**, 267–288 (1996)
7. Wang, J., Yang, J., Yu, K., Lv, F., Huang, T., Gong, Y.: Locality-constrained Linear Coding for image classification. In: IEEE Conference on Computer Vision and Pattern Recognition, pp. 3360–3367 (2013)
8. Liu, W., He, J., Chang, S.F.: Large graph construction for scalable semi-supervised learning. In: International Conference on Machine Learning, pp. 679–686 (2010)
9. Smith, S.M.: Fast robust automated brain extraction. Hum. Brain Mapp. **17**, 143–155 (2002)
10. Tustison, N.J., Avants, B.B., Cook, P.A., Zheng, Y., Egan, A., Yushkevich, P.A., Gee, J.C.: N4ITK: improved N3 bias correction. IEEE Trans. Med. Imaging **29**, 1310–1320 (2010)
11. Ou, Y., Sotiras, A., Paragios, N., Davatzikos, C.: DRAMMS: deformable registration via attribute matching and mutual-saliency weighting. Med. Image Anal. **15**, 622–639 (2011)
12. Cabezas, M., Oliver, A., Llado, X., Freixenet, J., Cuadra, M.B.: A review of atlas-based segmentation for magnetic resonance brain images. Comput. Meth. Programs Biomed. **104**, e158–e177 (2011)
13. Wu, G., Wang, Q., Zhang, D., Nie, F., Huang, H., Shen, D.: A generative probability model of joint label fusion for multi-atlas based brain segmentation. Med. Image Anal. **18**, 881–890 (2014)
14. Langerak, T.R., van der Heide, U.A., Kotte, A.N., Viergever, M.A., van Vulpen, M., Pluim, J.P.: Label fusion in atlas-based segmentation using a selective and iterative method for performance level estimation (SIMPLE). IEEE Trans. Med. Imaging **29**, 2000–2008 (2010)
15. Warfield, S.K., Zou, K.H., Wells, W.M.: Simultaneous truth and performance level estimation (STAPLE): an algorithm for the validation of image segmentation. IEEE Trans. Med. Imaging **23**, 903–921 (2004)
16. Asman, A.J., Landman, B.A.: Formulating spatially varying performance in the statistical fusion framework. IEEE Trans. Med. Imaging **31**, 1326–1336 (2012)

Learning a Spatiotemporal Dictionary for Magnetic Resonance Fingerprinting with Compressed Sensing

Pedro A. Gómez[1,2,3]($\boxtimes$), Cagdas Ulas[1], Jonathan I. Sperl[3], Tim Sprenger[1,2,3], Miguel Molina-Romero[1,2,3], Marion I. Menzel[3], and Bjoern H. Menze[1]

[1] Computer Science, Technische Universität München, Munich, Germany
`pedro.gomez@tum.de`
[2] Biomedical Engineering, Technische Universität München, Munich, Germany
[3] GE Global Research, Munich, Germany

Abstract. Magnetic resonance fingerprinting (MRF) is a novel technique that allows for the fast and simultaneous quantification of multiple tissue properties, progressing from qualitative images, such as T1- or T2-weighted images commonly used in clinical routines, to quantitative parametric maps. MRF consists of two main elements: accelerated pseudorandom acquisitions that create unique signal evolutions over time and the voxel-wise matching of these signals to a dictionary simulated using the Bloch equations. In this study, we propose to increase the performance of MRF by not only considering the simulated temporal signal, but a full spatiotemporal neighborhood for parameter reconstruction. We achieve this goal by first training a dictionary from a set of spatiotemporal image patches and subsequently coupling the trained dictionary with an iterative projection algorithm consistent with the theory of compressed sensing (CS). Using data from BrainWeb, we show that the proposed patch-based reconstruction can accurately recover T1 and T2 maps from highly undersampled k-space measurements, demonstrating the added benefit of using spatiotemporal dictionaries in MRF.

1 Introduction

Quantitative magnetic resonance imaging (qMRI) techniques measure relevant biological parameters, providing a profound characterization of the underlying tissue. In contrast to conventional weighted MRI, where the image signal is represented by intensity values and different tissues are described relative to each other, qMRI generates parametric maps of absolute measures that have a physical interpretation, leading to reduced bias and reproducible diagnostic information. On the other hand, obtaining quantitative maps is a time consuming task. It requires the repeated variation of typical MR acquisition parameters, such as flip angle (FA) or repetition time (TR), and the fitting of the measured signal to a model in order to estimate the parameters of interest, including the MR specific longitudinal (T1) and transversal (T2) relaxation times. Long acquisition times, together with high sensitivity to the imaging device

© Springer International Publishing Switzerland 2015
G. Wu et al. (Eds.): Patch-MI 2015, LNCS 9467, pp. 112–119, 2015.
DOI: 10.1007/978-3-319-28194-0_14

and system setup, are the main restrictions to clinical applications of qMRI techniques.

A recently proposed qMRI method, magnetic resonance fingerprinting (MRF), aims to overcome these limitations through accelerated pseudorandom acquisitions [6]. It is based on the idea that pseudorandom variations on acquisition parameters cause the signal response for different tissue types to be unique. This unique signal evolution can be matched to a precomputed dictionary created from known combinations of the parameters of interest (e.g. T1 and T2). Therefore, by matching the measured signal to one atom in the dictionary, all of the parameters used to simulate the corresponding atom can be simultaneously extracted. Furthermore, since the form of the signal evolution used for pattern matching is known *a priori*, MRF is less sensitive to measurement errors, facilitating accelerated acquisitions through the undersampling of the measurement space (k-space). It should be noted that, so far, all matching is done for one-dimensional temporal signals only.

The notion of reconstructing signals from undersampled measurements comes from the theory of compressed sensing (CS) [5]. CS has been successfully applied to accelerate parameter mapping [4] and recently Davies et al. [3] demonstrated a CS strategy for MRF that does not rely on pattern matching for error suppression and has exact recovery guarantees, resulting in increased performance for shorter pulse sequences. The authors further extend their CS model to exploit global spatial structure by enforcing sparsity in the wavelet domain of the estimated density maps, slightly improving the performance of their approach.

Spatial information can also be incorporated locally by using image patches. Patch-based dictionaries have the advantage of being able to efficiently represent complex local structure in a variety of image processing tasks. Furthermore, the use of overlapping patches allows for averaging, resulting in the removal of both noise and incoherent artefacts caused by undersampling. Patch-based dictionaries have been previously used for the task of MR image reconstruction [7], where the sparsifying dictionary was learnt directly from the measured data, resulting in accurate reconstructions for up to six fold undersampling.

In this work, we propose to use a dictionary with both temporal and local spatial information for parametric map estimation. We create a training set by using the Bloch equations to simulate the temporal signal response over a predefined spatial distribution obtained from anatomical images and train a spatiotemporal dictionary by clustering similar patches. The trained dictionary is incorporated into a patch-based iterative projection algorithm to estimate T1 and T2 parametric maps. We see two main benefits of our approach:

1. Incorporating spatial data increases the atom length, i.e. the amount of descriptive information available per voxel, requiring less temporal points for an accurate reconstruction.
2. Training improves the conditioning of the dictionary by creating atoms distinct to each other, leading to a better signal matching.

The rest of this paper is structured as follows. In Sect. 2 we describe the method, in particular the proposed patch-based algorithm for MRF. Section 3 depicts the experiments and demonstrates the application of recovering parametric maps from undersampled data, and in Sect. 4 we offer conclusions.

2 Methods

The goal of MRF is to obtain parametric maps $\boldsymbol{\theta} \in \mathbb{R}^{N \times Q}$ from a sequence of undersampled measurements $\mathbf{Y} \in \mathbb{C}^{M \times T}$, where Q is the number of tissue relaxation parameters (T1 and T2), T is the sequence length, every map $\boldsymbol{\theta}_q \in \mathbb{R}^N$ has a total of N voxels, every measurement $\mathbf{y}_t \in \mathbb{C}^M$ is sampled M times, and $M \ll N$. This is achieved in three steps: image reconstruction, template matching, and parameter extraction.

Image reconstruction is the task of obtaining the image sequence $\mathbf{X} \in \mathbb{C}^{N \times T}$ from the measurements $\mathbf{Y}$. This is generally formulated as a inverse problem: $\mathbf{Y} = \mathbf{EX}$, where $\mathbf{E} \in \mathbb{C}^{M \times N}$ is the encoding operator. The reconstructed image is then matched to a precomputed dictionary $\mathbf{D} \in \mathbb{C}^{T \times L}$ of L atoms, to find the dictionary atom $\mathbf{d}_l \in \mathbb{C}^T$ that best describes it. This is done at every voxel location $\mathbf{x}_n \in \mathbb{C}^T$ by selecting the entry l_n that maximizes the modulus of the atom and the conjugate transpose of the signal:

$$\hat{l}_n = \arg \max_{\substack{l \\ l=1,\ldots,L}} |\mathbf{x}_n^* \mathbf{d}_l| \tag{1}$$

where both, $\mathbf{d}_l$ and $\mathbf{x}_n$, were previously normalized to have unitary length. Finally, the T1 and T2 parameters used to construct the matching entry are assigned to the voxel n, creating $\boldsymbol{\theta}_n = \{T1_n, T2_n\}$. Thus, by repeating the matching over all voxels of the image, the parametric T1 and T2 maps are found.

Davies et al. [3] interpret the template matching as a projection of $\mathbf{x}_n$ onto the cone of the Bloch response manifold, and propose an iterative projection algorithm to accurately extract parametric maps. The algorithm, termed Bloch response recovery via iterated projection (BLIP), iteratively alternates between a gradient step, a projection step, and a shrinkage step to reconstruct the image sequence $\mathbf{X}$ and estimate the corresponding parameter maps $\boldsymbol{\theta}$.

2.1 Spatiotemporal Dictionary Design

Given a set of fully sampled 2D spatial parametric maps $\boldsymbol{\theta} \in \mathbb{R}^{N \times Q}$, where $N = N_i \times N_j$ and $Q = 2$, an image sequence $\mathbf{X} \in \mathbb{C}^{N \times T}$ of T temporal points can be created at each voxel using the Bloch equations to simulate the magnetization response of an inversion-recovery balanced steady state free-precession (IR-bSSFP) sequence with pseudorandomized acquisition parameters (see Fig. 1) [6]. $\mathbf{X}$ can be processed to create a spatiotemporal dictionary as follows.

Let $\mathbf{R}_n \in \mathbb{C}^{P \times N}$ be the operator that extracts 2D image patches of size $P = P_i \times P_j$, so that the spatiotemporal image patch $\tilde{\mathbf{x}}_n \in \mathbb{C}^{P \times T}$ at a given spatial location n is given by

$$\tilde{\mathbf{x}}_n = \mathbf{R}_n \mathbf{X}. \tag{2}$$

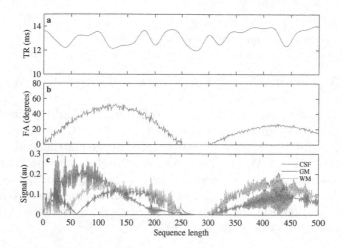

Fig. 1. Pseudorandom acquisition sequence and the corresponding signal response. **a,** TR values following a Perlin noise pattern. **b,** Flip angle series of repeating sinusoidal curves and added random values. **c,** Signal evolution for different tissue classes: white matter (WM), grey matter (GM), and cerebrospinal fluid (CSF).

It is then possible to create the patch-based image matrix $\tilde{\mathbf{X}} \in \mathbb{C}^{PT \times N}$ by concatenating the vector representation of every spatiotemporal patch of dimension $P_i \times P_j \times T$ for each spatial location in $\mathbf{X}$. Repeating the operation on θ creates the patch-based multiparametric matrix $\tilde{\theta} \in \mathbb{R}^{PQ \times N}$. The spatiotemporal dictionary $\tilde{\mathbf{D}} \in \mathbb{C}^{PT \times K}$ is then constructed by using k-means to cluster atoms in $\tilde{\mathbf{X}}$ with similar signal values into K clusters, averaging the corresponding T1 and T2 values in $\tilde{\theta}$ to create the clustered patch-based matrix $\boldsymbol{\Theta} \in \mathbb{C}^{PQ \times K}$, and simulating the signal evolution for each cluster. A new simulation of the signal evolution ensures that the atoms in $\tilde{\mathbf{D}}$ correspond exactly to the entries in $\boldsymbol{\Theta}$.

2.2   Patch-Based BLIP Reconstruction (P-BLIP)

The BLIP algorithm [3] reconstructs the image sequence $\mathbf{X}$ in an iterative fashion. Given an image sequence $\mathbf{X}^{(i)}$ at iteration i, the reconstructed sequence $\mathbf{X}^{(i+1)}$ in the next iteration is determined by

$$\mathbf{X}^{(i+1)} = \mathcal{P}_{\mathcal{A}}(\mathbf{X}^{(i)} + \mu \mathbf{E}^H (\mathbf{Y} - \mathbf{E}\mathbf{X}^{(i)})), \tag{3}$$

where $\mathcal{P}_{\mathcal{A}}$ represents the projection onto the signal model $\mathcal{A}$, $\mathbf{E}^H$ is the Hermitian adjoint of the encoding operator, and μ equals the step size. P-BLIP builds on this algorithm, incorporating the patch extraction operator in (2) and an update step to make (3) applicable to a spatiotemporal signal model.

At every iteration the updated sequence $\mathbf{X}$ is transformed into the patch-based matrix $\tilde{\mathbf{X}}$ by (2). $\tilde{\mathbf{X}}$ is related to the trained dictionary $\tilde{\mathbf{D}}$ by

$$\tilde{\mathbf{X}} = \tilde{\mathbf{D}}\mathbf{W}, \tag{4}$$

where $\mathbf{W} \in \mathbb{R}^{K \times N}$ represents the weights. Equation 4 can be readily solved using greedy algorithms that find sparse solutions to linear systems of equations by adding a sparsity constraint to the ℓ_0-norm of each column vector $\mathbf{w}_n$:

$$\hat{\mathbf{W}} = \arg\min_{\mathbf{W}} \|\tilde{\mathbf{X}} - \tilde{\mathbf{D}}\mathbf{W}\|_2^2, \text{ s.t. } \|\mathbf{w}_n\|_0 \leq \gamma, \ n = 1, ..., N. \tag{5}$$

We set the sparsity constraint to $\gamma = 1$, equivalent to finding one dictionary atom, as done in the template matching used in [3,6].

After estimating the weights, the patch-based image matrix is projected onto the dictionary by $\hat{\mathbf{X}} = \tilde{\mathbf{D}}\hat{\mathbf{W}}$. At this point, each voxel is overrepresented a total of P times, requiring an update step to return to the original image sequence $\mathbf{X}$. This update is achieved by averaging the P temporal signals that contribute to a given voxel location. Finally, the parametric maps $\boldsymbol{\theta}$ are estimated by applying the weights and patch-wise updates on $\boldsymbol{\Theta}$.

3   Experiments and Results

Image Data. Experiments were performed using twenty digital brain phantoms from BrainWeb [2]. Of these, ten were used to train the spatiotemporal dictionary and ten to test the performance of three different reconstruction algorithms: the original MRF reconstruction [6], BLIP [3], and the proposed P-BLIP. Experiments were designed to evaluate the performance of each algorithm as a function of sequence length and acceleration factors, and, for the case of P-BLIP, also as a function of spatial patch size. Ground truth datasets were generated by selecting a slice of crisp datasets labeled with different tissue classes, and resampling them to a matrix size of 256×256 to accelerate computations. Quantitative maps were then obtained by replacing the tissue labels with their corresponding T1 and T2 values. The values for the three main tissue types grey matter (GM), white matter (WM), and cerebrospinal fluid (CSF) were equaled to those reported in [6], while the values for the rest of the classes (fat, bone, muscle, vessels, dura matter, and connective tissue) were obtained directly from [1].

Modeling the Signal Evolution. At every voxel, the ground truth quantitative maps served as a basis to simulate the temporal evolution of the signal based on the IR-bSSFP pulse sequence with acquisition parameters displayed in Fig. 1, where the TRs follow a Perlin noise pattern, FAs are a series of repeating sinusoidal curves with added random values, and the radio frequency phase alternates between 0° and 180° on consecutive pulses. Off-resonance frequencies were not taken into account. This pulse sequence was combined with all possible combinations of a given range of T1 and T2 values to create a temporal dictionary used in both MRF and BLIP. The selected range was reported in [3], where T1 spans from 100 ms to 6000 ms and T2 from 20 ms to 1000 ms, both sampled at varying step sizes. Additionally, the dictionary included the exact T1 and T2 combinations corresponding to the different tissue classes.

Spatiotemporal Dictionary. To train the spatiotemporal dictionary used in P-BLIP, a region of interest that accounted for the entire head area was defined.

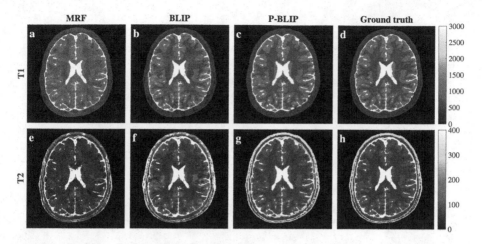

Fig. 2. Exemplary reconstruction results of one dataset with $T = 200$, $R = 10$, and $P = 3 \times 3$. The upper row shows T1 maps for all algorithms and the ground truth; and the bottom row the corresponding T2 maps. Most visible in T2 maps, subsampling artefacts can be effectively removed with P-BLIP.

The space covered by this region of interest was randomly and equally subsampled and each of the subsampled sets was assigned to a training subject. The selected parametric maps of each subject were then used as an input to train the dictionary as described in Sect. 2.1 with a total of $K = 200$ clusters.

Subsampling Strategy. We use a random EPI subsampling strategy for all experiments: the k-space is fully sampled in the read direction (k_x) and uniformly undersampled in the phase encoding direction (k_y) by an acceleration factor R. The sampling pattern is shifted by a random a number of k_y lines at every shot of the sequence.

Experimental Setup. An initial experiment was performed with spatiotemporal patches of size $3 \times 3 \times 200$ and an acceleration factor $R = 10$ to visually evaluate the reconstructed maps (see Fig. 2). Subsequently, three experiments assessed the reconstruction performance with respect to sequence length, acceleration factor and spatial patch size. The first experiment varied sequence lengths from 100 to 500 in step sizes of 100, the second experiment used acceleration factors of $R = \{2, 5, 10, 15, 20\}$, and the final experiment used spatial patches of sizes $P = \{1 \times 1, 3 \times 3, 5 \times 5, 7 \times 7\}$. The reconstruction error of the first two experiments was calculated using the signal-to-error ratio (SER) in decibels (dB), defined as $20 \log_{10} \frac{\|x\|_2}{\|x - \hat{x}\|_2}$; and the third experiment with the SSIM values [8].

Results. Figure 2 displays the reconstructed parametric maps of an exemplary dataset. The MRF estimates show the characteristic ghosting artefacts caused by sub-Nyquist sampling. BLIP removes most of these artefacts from the T1 estimation, though they are still visible in the T2 maps. P-BLIP effectively removes these artefacts from both maps, resulting in reconstructions very close to the ground truth. These visual observations can be confirmed with quantitative

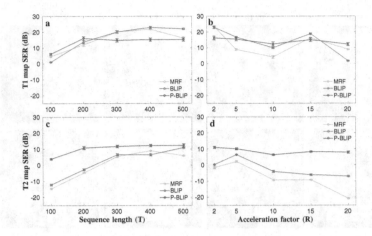

Fig. 3. a,c, Performance as a function of sequence length with $R = 10$, $P = 3 \times 3$; and b,d, as a function of acceleration factor with $T = 200$, $P = 3 \times 3$. P-BLIP is best in estimating T2 maps and shows better results for shorter sequences and higher acceleration for T1 maps.

Table 1. Average SSIM values for T1 and T2 map estimation with respect to different spatial patch sizes, $T = 200$ and $R = 10$.

Method	Baseline		Proposed: P-BLIP			
	MRF	BLIP	1×1	3×3	5×5	7×7
T1	0.761	0.814	0.848	**0.852**	0.691	0.625
T2	0.616	0.591	0.769	**0.857**	0.667	0.601

results. Figure 3c and d show how P-BLIP achieves better T2 estimates independently of the sequence length or acceleration factor. On the other hand, T1 maps for P-BLIP remain relatively constant for sequence lengths larger than 100 (Fig. 3a) and all acceleration factors (Fig. 3b), whilst the performance of MRF and BLIP increases with the sequence length and lower acceleration factors. The reason for these results is twofold. First, the IR-bSSFP sequence is mostly T1-weighted, favoring a better T1 matching over T2 matching for all methods. Second, a trained dictionary containing a longer sequence, but fixed K, is less flexible, and if the trained dictionary does not exactly contain the ground truth values, the quantitative error will be higher.

Table 1 indicates the performance of P-BLIP for different patch sizes in comparison to the performance of MRF and BLIP. A spatial patch size of $P = 1 \times 1$ implies that the training dataset was created from voxel-wise temporal evolutions and that the trained dictionary is a clustered version of the temporal dictionary. It can be seen that clustering a temporal dictionary alone improves the reconstruction with respect to MRF and BLIP, and that the spatiotemporal dictionary further improves these results for $P = 3 \times 3$. At larger spatial patch sizes the results begin to decline, indicating that the cluster size of $K = 200$ is not enough to capture the entire spatial variability of the parametric maps.

4   Conclusions

This work presents a novel patch-based reconstruction scheme for MRF consistent with the theory of CS. It is based on a spatiotemporal signal model and relies on the training of the corresponding dictionary from a set of examples. This patch-based scheme shows improved performance for shorter pulse sequences and at higher acceleration factors, leading to an increased efficiency of parameter mapping with MRF.

An important discussion point of our approach is the size of the dictionary in terms of space, time, and atoms. Larger spatial patches allow, in theory, for the acquisition of less temporal points, but the amount of atoms in the dictionary should in turn be large enough to account for large spatial variability. We have seen from our results that a dictionary size of $K = 200$ is not enough for spatial patch sizes larger than 3×3 for structures in the brain. A potencial solution to this shortcoming might be to make K dependant on the atom length or arbitrarily large at the cost of computational complexity. This point is currently under investigation and future work will focus on extending the method to incorporate 3D spatial patches and applying it to real datasets.

References

1. Aubert-Broche, B., Evans, A.C., Collins, L.: A new improved version of the realistic digital brain phantom. NeuroImage **32**, 138–145 (2006)
2. Aubert-Broche, B., Griffin, M., Pike, G.B., Evans, A.C., Collins, D.L.: Twenty new digital brain phantoms for creation of validation image data bases. IEEE Trans. Med. Imaging **25**(11), 1410–1416 (2006)
3. Davies, M., Puy, G., Vandergheynst, P., Wiaux, Y.: A compressed sensing framework for magnetic resonance fingerprinting. SIAM J. Imaging Sci. **7**(4), 2623–2656 (2014)
4. Doneva, M., Börnert, P., Eggers, H., Stehning, C., Sénégas, J., Mertins, A.: Compressed sensing reconstruction for magnetic resonance parameter mapping. Magn. Reson. Med. **64**, 1114–1120 (2010)
5. Donoho, D.L.: Compressed sensing. IEEE Trans. Inf. Theor. **52**, 1289–1306 (2006)
6. Ma, D., Gulani, V., Seiberlich, N., Liu, K., Sunshine, J.L., Duerk, J.L., Griswold, M.A.: Magnetic resonance fingerprinting. Nature **495**, 187–192 (2013)
7. Ravishankar, S., Bresler, Y.: MR image reconstruction from highly undersampled k-space data by dictionary learning. IEEE Trans. Med. Imaging **30**(5), 1028–1041 (2011)
8. Wang, Z., Bovik, A.C., Sheikh, H.R., Simoncelli, E.P.: Image quality assessment: from error visibility to structural similarity. IEEE Trans. Image Proc. **13**, 600–612 (2004)

Fast Regions-of-Interest Detection in Whole Slide Histopathology Images

Ruoyu Li and Junzhou Huang[✉]

Department of Computer Science and Engineering, University of Texas at Arlington,
Arlington, TX 76019, USA
jzhuang@uta.edu

Abstract. In this paper, we present a novel superpixel based Region of Interest (ROI) search and segmentation algorithm. The proposed superpixel generation method differs from pioneer works due to its combination of boundary update and coarse-to-fine refinement for superpixel clustering. The former maintains the accuracy of segmentation, meanwhile, avoids much of unnecessary revisit to the 'non-boundary' pixels. The latter reduces the complexity by faster localizing those boundary blocks. The paper introduces the novel superpixel algorithm [10] to the problem of ROI detection and segmentation along with a coarse-to-fine refinement scheme over a set of image of different magnification. Extensive experiments indicates that the proposed method gives better accuracy and efficiency than other superpixel-based methods for lung cancer cell images. Moreover, the block-wise coarse-to-fine scheme enables a quick search and segmentation of ROIs in whole slide images, while, other methods still cannot.

1 Introduction

The detection and segmentation of region of interest (ROI) is a crucial intermediate step between histopathology images acquisition [4] and computer-aided automated diagnosis [11,12] for those hazardous diseases, such as infectious diseases and cancers, which are still big threats to both personal health and public sanitation.

Thinking about the scenarios of clinic application and the pathophysiology requirements, we have some challenging but natural technical requirements, e.g. the low time and energy cost of the ROI search process as well as the high fidelity and the trustworthiness of segmented ROIs. The whole slide images (WSI) are here the digitized histopathology images of highest resolution (e.g. $10^6 \times 10^6$). The size of typical WSI in original data of lung cancer slide is roughly as large as 1.5 GByte. We need a novel efficient solution to handle such big volume of data without losing too much accuracy. Our main task is to accelerate the search for specific patches or patch clusters, e.g. ROI, and then to increase the accuracy of classification for ROI and background pixels via a much improved segmentations.

Z. Huang—This work was partially supported by U.S. NSF IIS-1423056, CMMI-1434401, CNS-1405985.

© Springer International Publishing Switzerland 2015
G. Wu et al. (Eds.): Patch-MI 2015, LNCS 9467, pp. 120–127, 2015.
DOI: 10.1007/978-3-319-28194-0_15

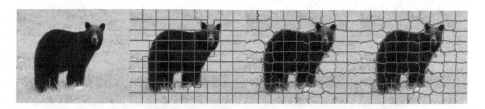

Fig. 1. An example of the brand new coarse-to-fine/boundary-only update based superpixel segmentation algorithm first presented in [10]. The basic manipulation unit is the rectangular block instead of pixels during each stage. We start from a coarse segmentation and end with pixel-level refinement on superpixel boundary. The block size is respectively 10×10, 2×2, 1×1 (single pixel) from left to right.

Fortunately, we are not alone in solving the problem by harnessing the latest machine learning and computer vision techniques. In [2], a multi-scale superpixel classification approach has been proposed for efficient detection of ROIs in WSI. However, the method does not correctly notice the effect of wrong labeling in early classification stage may not be compensated by later more accurate classification. The classifier worked on different scales of magnification, and so it has to be trained multiple times with samples extracted from superpixels of different magnification. The [7] reduced the workload of labeling and grading by two ways: by excluding the areas of definitely normal tissues within a single specimen or by excluding entire specimens which do not contain any tumor cells. Besides, [7] presented a multi-resolution cancer detection algorithm to boost the latter. Another superpixel automated segmentation method is [8], which trains a classifier to predict where mitochondrial boundaries occur using diverse cues from superpixel graph. However, because of the old superpixel algorithm [1], the slow speed and the low accuracy of superpixel encumber the overall performance. The superpixel generation algorithm used in the paper is totally different from [1] where the superpixels were clustered pixel-wise. Combining the coarse-to-fine scheme [3] and boundary-only update policy [9], our method manipulates the rectangular blocks of pixel to construct a coarse segmentation of superpixel before the more accurate refinement using boundary-only update (See Fig. 1).

The proposed approach is able to generate better superpixels of perfect snapping to the actual boundaries between the foreground and the background. The improvement brought by the algorithm on patch classification and image annotation accuracy has been proved and verified in [10], we, for the first time, apply the method and quantitatively verify the improvement of the accuracy of ROI detection in histopathology images, e.g. lung cancer H&E-stained WSI. The paper is organized as followings: we first introduce the new superpixel generation algorithm and coarse-to-fine strategy for reducing dimensionality for optimization in Sect. 1. Then we introduce the details of the algorithm as well as the mathematical and optimization background in Sect. 2. Finally, we will present experimental results and analysis in Sects. 3 and 4.

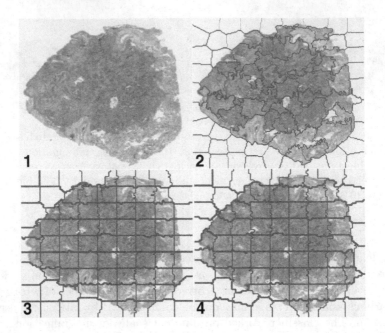

Fig. 2. The comparison of superpixel generated over lung cancer histopathology images: (1) the origin (with ROI groundtruth), (2) SLIC [1], (3) SPSS [9], (4) the new method [10]. The true ROI is contoured as green (Color figure online).

2   Methodology

Our method for detection and segmentation of ROIs has two components. We first obtain a initial identification of ROIs by clustering the superpixels at low magnification. Then the superpixels were mapped to image of higher magnification by labeling corresponding pixels. The process was repeated several times until segmentations are stable. The last, the classifier labels superpixels repretented by selected features. Different from previous classic superpixel based segmentation methods [1,9], the proposed algorithm gives topologically preserving segmentation of the image. The better segmentation the superpixels define, the more accurate the classification of ROIs will be attained.

2.1   ROIs in Lung Cancer Histopathology Images

The main idea of superpixel based segmentation methods is to cluster those pixels of similar spacial, color and topological properties and to construct a group of superpixels of all similar pixels within. As to build a fast and efficient search technique for regions of interest in lung cancer histopathology WSI, which are usually at least of trillions of pixels, previous methods may not be suitable. Because they neglected some important features in cancer cell histopathology images. The tumor cells of lung cancer patients (not only for lung cancer, but also generally appear in other subtypes of cancer) infest as cell mass. If we treat the regions where tumor cell mass appears as ROIs, it is easy to have direct observations from the H&E stained histopathology images that those tumor cells are more deeply colored due to the massive reproduction of genetic materials inside tumor nuclei (See Fig. 2).

2.2 Superpixel Clustering

As the metric of superpixel generation, we indicate the following objective functions as the one which to be minimized at each round updating the classification of pixels (or blocks):

$$E(s, \mu, c) = \sum_p E_{col}(s_p, c_{s_p}) + \lambda_{pos} \sum_p E_{pos}(s_p, \mu_{s_p}) +$$

$$\lambda_b \sum_p \sum_{q \in N_8} E_b(s_p, s_q) + E_{topo}(s) + E_{size}(s). \tag{1}$$

with $c = (c_1, c_2, \ldots, c_M)$, $\mu = (\mu_1, \mu_2, \ldots, \mu_M)$ the group of centers and mean position of each superpixels. And, the N_8 means the 8 neighbors surrounding the pixel p in a 3×3 block. $E_{col}(s_p, c_{s_p}) = (I(p) - c_{s_p})^2$ is the color intensity of pixel inside the superpixel to the average intensity value of this suerpixel, in other word, it is the variance of the color intensity distribution over $[0, 255]$, also known as appearance coherence. The shape regularization is described as the energy term averaging the distance between each contained pixel to the mean position of the superpixel, $E_{pos}(s_p, \mu_{s_p}) = \|p - \mu_{s_p}\|_2^2$, where μ_{s_p} is the center of each superpixel. On the other hand, the regularization on the size of superpixels and the connectivity of superpixels will give penalty on those superpixels of too small size and those disconnected superpixels by making the objective function positive infinity. It needs to be noted that we only consider the 4 neighbors (up, down, left and right) of the pixel (block) when we maximize $\hat{s}_{b_i^l} = arg \min_{s_i^l \in N_4} E(s, \mu, c)$.

2.3 Boundary-Only Update

The proposed superpixel generation method should be more costly efficient due to its strategy of boundary-only update at each round of pixel clustering. The boundary-only update scheme is to only update those blocks closely nearby the boundary of superpixels.

$$E_b(s_p, s_q) = \begin{cases} 1, & s_p \neq s_q, \\ 0, & otherwise. \end{cases} \tag{2}$$

$E(s_p) = \sum_{q \in N_4} E_b(s_p, s_q)$. Only if $E(s_p) = 0$, then the corresponding block p is not a boundary block. Otherwise, it is a boundary block and has at least one neighbor belongs to other superpixel. When using the boundary-only update,

---

Algorithm 1. Coarse-to-Fine ROI Search and Segmentation (CROISS)

---

for M = 1 to MagMax **do**
  for l = 1 to levelMax **do**
    if l = 1 **then**
      Initialize each block on level l with a regular grid;
    end if
    Compute the mean color and position in each block; Initialize the list of boundary blocks on level l;
    while list is not empty **do**
      Pop out boundary block b_i^l from the list;
      if connectivity is valid **then**
        $\hat{s}_{b_i^l} = arg\min_{s_i^l \in N_4} E(\mathbf{s}, \mu, \mathbf{c})$;
        if $s_{b_i^l}$ is updated **then**
          update $u_{\hat{s}_{b_i^l}}$ and $c_{\hat{s}_{b_i^l}}$ for the involved two superpixels; append the 4 neighbors of b_i^l to the list if they become boundary blocks after this update;
        end if
      end if
    end while
  end for
  Mapping **s** to the image of M+1 magnification in the term of pixel to block;
end for

---

there are two keypoints: (1) if we update the label of any block, it may change the list of boundary blocks; (2) we need to append the new boundary block to the end of the list because and follow the FIFO principle when deciding the order of blocks for consideration of changing label, in order to avoid the risk of divergence given by correlated dimensions in coordinate descent optimization.

2.4 Coarse-to-Fine Refinement

In the paper, we does not only utilize the coarse-to-fine strategy in the generation of superpixels, but also in the mapping to the images of higher magnification. When generating superpixels, the fundamental unit for manipulation is not single pixel but a series of rectangular blocks of size from large to small. We start from clustering coarse superpixels using the biggest blocks. Based on the result of last round, we then manipulate smaller blocks to form boundaries with more details. Combining with the boundary-only update strategy, the coarse-to-fine refinement could more efficiently construct the superpixels of irregular boundary. Besides, we construct superpixels over multiple layers of images of different magnification. In this way, the localization of boundary blocks will be much easier and the boundary update only happens to those blocks fallen into the boundary regions constructed at higher magnification. The effect of acceleration will become more significant as the size of whole slide image increases.

2.5 Complexity Analysis

Based on similar philosophy in sparse learning [5,6], we are able to reduce the total computational complexity from $\mathcal{O}(\sum_l N_l \times nMaxIter)$, where N is the size of image, to $\mathcal{O}(\sum_l \sum_i B_l^i)$. N is usually extremely large since the WSI has trillions of pixels. For pixel-wise methods, $nMaxIter$ should be large enough to guarantee the convergence. However, for this algorithm, at each iteration, we manipulate blocks instead of pixels in image of low resolution (size is also shrinking to $10^3 \times 10^3$ level), and then conduct mapping to image of high resolution and refine the boundaries. The boundary length B_l^i in image of magnification l for iteration i is much smaller than the size of current image N_l. Due to the reduced dimensionality, the convergence comes faster than pixel-wise methods.

3 Experiments

3.1 Experimental Setup

In the experimental stage, a random forest and a SVM classifier were built which operated on the regions defined by the superpixels generated by Algorithm 1. A total of 384 features were extracted from 100 WSIs including local binary patterns and statistics derived from the histogram of the three-channel HSD color model as well as texture features, e.g. color SIFT. The proposed method was compared with superpixels generated by SLIC [1] and tetragonum (non-superpixel). The experiments used the adenocarcinoma and squamous cell carcinoma lung cancer images from the NLST (National Lung Screening Trial) Data Portal1[1]. We conduct 10-fold cross-validation before recording and perform all experiments in a workstation of Intel i7-4770 CPU.

Table 1. The table presents the comparison results of the proposed superpixels, SLIC and tetragonum (non-superpixel) in term of classification statistics including: the rate of error classification, precision and recall. Tetragonum: sliding rectangular windows.

	Ours [10]	SLIC [1]	Tetragonum	Ours [10]	SLIC [1]	Tetragonum
	Random forest			SVM		
Error rate	**0.1326**	0.1933	0.2047	**0.3011**	0.3343	0.3061
Precision	**0.7127**	0.6835	0.6740	**0.6754**	0.6672	0.6723
Recall	**0.7333**	0.6108	0.6450	**0.7450**	0.6604	0.6972

3.2 Numerical Results

Due to the overwhelming fidelity of our superpixels, the classifier operates over the regions segmented by the proposed superpixel algorithm is able to deliver better classification accuracy (See Table 1). Since the feature descriptors were built on the patches segmented by contours of superpixels, the better the superpixel fitting the natural boundaries, the better the extracted features characterize the sample patches. In Fig. 3, we show a typical process of recursive coarse-to-fine

---

[1] https://biometry.nci.nih.gov/cdas/studies/nlst/.

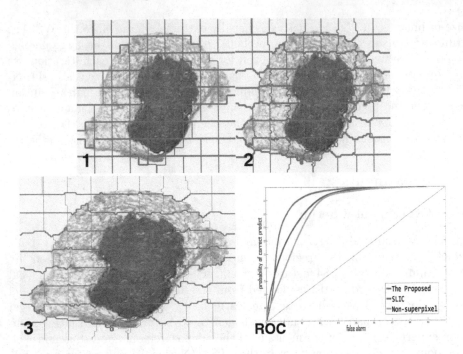

Fig. 3. A coarse-to-fine approach operates on a multi-resolution images set of a lung cancer WSI: (1) Coarse segmentation of superpixels using large blocks in images of low magnification (180×180); (2) Refine the segmentation using small blocks; (3) Mask mapping to images of higher magnification ($3 * 10^3 \times 5 * 10^3$); (4) ROC of random forest classifier trained on set of superpixel-based patches generated by our algorithm [10], SLIC [1] and rectangular patches.

refinement over the multi-resolution image set for lung cancer histopathology images. We first do a coarse-to-fine superpixel generation over low magnification image (Step 1 & 2), and then we map the superpixel mask (Fig. 3) to an image of higher magnification (Step 3) and repeat the Step 1 & 2. The recursive refinement does not stop until the image of highest resolution (WSI) with converged energy function [10]. Due to the reduced complexity of superpixel construction, we could significantly finish the patch-feature extraction in a much shorter time. Our method is possible to shrink the processing time cost to B/N, where $N \gg B$ in WSI. The ROC curves indicates the improvement on ROI detection accuracy brought by the new superpixel algorithm.

4   Conclusion

In the paper, we presented a novel solution to fast detection of ROI in whole slide lung cancer histopathology image. We integrated the novel superpixel generation algorithm with a multi-level block-wise optimization scheme. Our algorithm performed a faster and finer ROI detection and segmentation process, which ensure a more accurate classification of ROI. The effectiveness and efficiency of our algorithm has been verified on large histopathology WSI database, e.g. NLST.

References

1. Achanta, R., Shaji, A., Smith, K., Lucchi, A., Fua, P., Susstrunk, S.: Slic superpixels compared to state-of-the-art superpixel methods. IEEE Trans. Pattern Anal. Mach. Intell. **34**(11), 2274–2282 (2012)
2. Bejnordi, B.E., Litjens, G., Hermsen, M., Karssemeijer, N., van der Laak, J.A.: A multi-scale superpixel classification approach to the detection of regions of interest in whole slide histopathology images. In: SPIE Medical Imaging, pp. 94200H–94200H. International Society for Optics and Photonics (2015)
3. Van den Bergh, M., Roig, G., Boix, X., Manen, S., Van Gool, L.: Online video seeds for temporal window objectness. In: 2013 IEEE International Conference on Computer Vision (ICCV), pp. 377–384. IEEE (2013)
4. Huang, J., Huang, X., Metaxas, D.: Simultaneous image transformation and sparse representation recovery. In: IEEE Conference on Computer Vision and Pattern Recognition, CVPR 2008, pp. 1–8. IEEE (2008)
5. Huang, J., Huang, X., Metaxas, D.: Learning with dynamic group sparsity. In: 2009 IEEE 12th International Conference on Computer Vision, pp. 64–71. IEEE (2009)
6. Huang, J., Zhang, S., Li, H., Metaxas, D.: Composite splitting algorithms for convex optimization. Comput. Vis. Image Underst. **115**(12), 1610–1622 (2011)
7. Litjens, G., Bejnordi, B.E., Timofeeva, N., Swadi, G., Kovacs, I., Hulsbergen-van de Kaa, C., van der Laak, J.: Automated detection of prostate cancer in digitized whole-slide images of H and E-stained biopsy specimens. In: SPIE Medical Imaging. International Society for Optics and Photonics (2015)
8. Lucchi, A., Smith, K., Achanta, R., Lepetit, V., Fua, P.: A fully automated approach to segmentation of irregularly shaped cellular structures in EM images. In: Jiang, T., Navab, N., Pluim, J.P.W., Viergever, M.A. (eds.) MICCAI 2010, Part II. LNCS, vol. 6362, pp. 463–471. Springer, Heidelberg (2010)
9. Yamaguchi, K., McAllester, D., Urtasun, R.: Efficient joint segmentation, occlusion labeling, stereo and flow estimation. In: Fleet, D., Pajdla, T., Schiele, B., Tuytelaars, T. (eds.) ECCV 2014, Part V. LNCS, vol. 8693, pp. 756–771. Springer, Heidelberg (2014)
10. Yao, J., Boben, M., Fidler, S., Urtasun, R.: Real-time coarse-to-fine topologically preserving segmentation. Energy **2**, 2–3 (2015)
11. Zhang, X., Liu, W., Dundar, M., Badve, S., Zhang, S.: Towards large-scale histopathological image analysis: hashing-based image retrieval. IEEE Trans. Med. Imaging **34**(2), 496–506 (2015)
12. Zhang, X., Su, H., Yang, L., Zhang, S.: Fine-grained histopathological image analysis via robust segmentation and large-scale retrieval. In: The IEEE Conference on Computer Vision and Pattern Recognition (CVPR) (2015)

Reliability Guided Forward and Backward Patch-Based Method for Multi-atlas Segmentation

Liang Sun, Chen Zu, and Daoqiang Zhang[✉]

Department of Computer Science and Engineering,
Nanjing University of Aeronautics and Astronautics, Nanjing 210016, China
{sunl, chenzu, dqzhang}@nuaa.edu.cn

Abstract. Label fusion is an important step in multi-atlas based segmentation. It uses label propagation from multiple atlases to predict final label. However, most of the current label fusion methods consider each voxel equally and independently during the procedure of label fusion. In general, voxels which are misclassified are at the edge of ROIs, meanwhile the voxels labeled correctly with high reliability are far from the edge of ROIs. In light of this, we propose a novel framework for multi-atlas based image segmentation by using voxels of the target image with high reliability to guide the labeling procedure of other voxels with low reliability to afford more accurate label fusion. Specifically, we first measure the corresponding labeling reliability for each voxel based on traditional label fusion result, i.e., nonlocal mean weighted voting methods. In the second step, we use the voxels with high reliability to guide the label fusion process, at the same time we consider the location relationship of different voxels. We propagate not only labels from atlases, but also labels from the neighboring voxels with high reliability on the target. Meanwhile, an alternative method is supplied, we utilize the backward nonlocal mean patch-based method for reliability estimation. We compare our method with nonlocal mean patch-based method. In experiments, we apply all methods in the NIREP dataset to 32 regions of interest segmentation. Experimental results show our method can improve the performance of the nonlocal mean patch-based method.

1 Introduction

Magnetic resonance (MR) images can reflect anatomical structures. It is a critical step to segment different tissue types accurately for detecting pathology, clinical research, and etc. For example, hippocampus plays an important role in Alzheimer's disease. Therefore many neuroscientists seek to mark hippocampus from the MR images. A vast number of MR images are produced all the time. It costs a lot of time of medical experts to manually segment MRI. Consequently, it is meaningful to develop an accurate and robust method.

Recently, multi-atlas based segmentation achieved a great success [1–15]. There are two main steps for multi-atlas patch-based segmentation including image registration and label fusion. In the step of image registration, each atlas image is rigidly or non-rigidly warped onto the target image. Then, in the step of label fusion, labels from

G. Wu et al. (Eds.): Patch-MI 2015, LNCS 9467, pp. 128–136, 2015.
DOI: 10.1007/978-3-319-28194-0_16

different atlases will be propagated to the target image. Numerous label fusion strategies have been proposed for multi-atlas based segmentation. Among them, majority voting (MV) is the simplest one in which each atlas image is treated equally when assigned label to the target image [1]. More advanced strategy like local-weighted voting (LWV), considers the patch-wise similarity between the target and each atlas as the voting weight and it has shown that the local weighted method outperforms the global solution when segmenting the high-contrast brain structures [2]. Moreover, in order to decrease the registration errors, the nonlocal mean patch-based method (PBM) has been proposed, which propagates the labels not only from the same location, but also the neighboring patches, improving the accuracy and robustness of the labeling results [3, 4]. Recently sparse representation for multi-atlas label fusion methods are used for label fusion [5, 6]. Adding a sparse constraint, only a small number image patches with high similarity to the target image patch are selected to be used in the label fusion. This can remove the misleading candidate atlas patches, ensuring to obtain more accurate label fusion result. And more complex methods are used in multi-atlas segmentation, such as hierarchical and multi-scale feature representation [11], discriminative dictionary learning [12], and iterative method [13].

The above methods treat each voxel independently and equally and only consider the patch-wise similarity between the target and atlases. According to previous study [3], most of misclassified voxels spread at the boundary of ROIs, so the voxels far from the boundary of ROIs with high reliability are labeled correctly. Consequently the voxels in the target are useful for labeling. The voxel in the target is unlabeled. But in the target image, some voxels are easy to label and others are hard to label. Now, we assume the voxels are high reliable that soft labels are closed to 0 or 1, the soft labels will be calculated by traditional method. Therefore we use high reliable labels to guide the label fusion of the voxels with low reliable. With this assumption, in this paper, we present a novel label fusion framework for multi-atlas based segmentation. The novel label fusion framework considers not only the voxels at the atlas but also the voxels at the target with high reliability of the estimate. Thus, our method contains two steps, (1) the reliability estimation, and (2) label fusion. Our method is a general framework and can be used in the most of current state-of the-art methods. In this paper, a backward nonlocal patch-based method is supplied for reliability estimation. Our proposed method has been evaluated on NIREP dataset [16] to 32 regions of interest segmentation. Our method is able to significantly improve the labeling accuracy, comparing with the label fusion algorithm: nonlocal mean patch-based method [3].

The remainder of this paper is organized as follows. In Sect. 2, we present our novel model for label fusion. The performance of the proposed method is evaluated by comparing with PBM in Sect. 3. Finally, a brief conclusion is given in Sect. 4.

2 Methods

In Sect. 2.1, we present the nonlocal patch-based method. An alternative method for reliability estimation will be presented in Sect. 2.2. Finally, we will present the label fusion framework which consists of two step: label reliability estimation and reliability guide label fusion.

2.1   Patch-Based Method (PBM)

Here, we use T to denote the target image to be labeled. Label fusion aims to determine the label map L_T for the target image. We first register each atlas image and label maps onto the target image space. We use $A = \{A_s | s = 1, \ldots, N\}$ and $L = \{L_s | s = 1, \ldots, N\}$ to denote the N atlases and label maps and use $P_T(x)$ and $P_{A_s}(y)$ to denote the patch centered at the voxel y in the target image T and the patch centered at voxel x in the atlas A_s. We denote the neighborhood of voxel y in the target image T and atlases A as $N_T(y)$ and $N_A(y)$, respectively.

In traditional methods. For example, non-local mean patch-based method [3], we calculate the weight as follows:

$$w(y_i, x_{s,j}) = exp^{\frac{-\|I(y_i) - I(x_{s,j})\|_2^2}{\delta(y_i)}}, \tag{1}$$

with

$$\delta(y_i) = \underset{x_{s,j} \in N_A(y_i)}{\operatorname{argmin}} \|I(y_i) - I(x_{s,j})\|_2 + \varepsilon$$

where $I(y_i)$ and $I(x_{s,j})$ represent the normalized intensity of the voxels of the patches $P_T(y_i)$ and $P_{A_s}(x_{s,j})$. $\| \cdot \|_2$ is the normalized L2 norm. ε is a small constant.

For all voxels y_i of the image to be segmented, the estimation of the voxel are labeled is based on a weight label fusion $l(y_i)$ of all labeled voxels inside the neighborhood of voxel y_i:

$$l(y_i) = \frac{\sum_{s=1}^{N} \sum_{j \in N_A(y_i)} w(y_i, x_{s,j}) l_{s,j}}{\sum_{s=1}^{N} \sum_{j \in N_A(y_i)} w(y_i, x_{s,j})}, \tag{2}$$

where $l_{s,j}$ is the label given by the expert to voxel $x_{s,j}$ at the jth voxel in atlas A_s. And $w(y_i, x_{s,j})$ is a weight between voxel y_i and $x_{s,j}$, depending on the similarity of this two voxels.

2.2   Backward Patch-Based Method (B-PBM)

Compared with the nonlocal mean patch-based method, we propose the backward PBM (B-PBM), traditional method is named as forward patch-based method (F-PBM) For each voxels $x_{s,i}$ (the red patch in the Fig. 1) in the atlases, we compute the weight between $x_{s,i}$ in the atlases (the red patch in the Fig. 1) and voxels y_j (the blue patch in the Fig. 1) in the search neighborhood (the red rectangle in the Fig. 1) in the target. We denote the neighborhood of $x_{s,i}$ as $N_T(x_{s,i})$. Then, we compute the weight as:

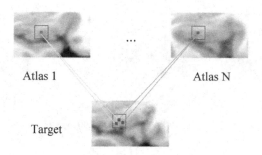

Atlas 1   Atlas N

Target

Fig. 1. Backward PBM (Color figure online)

$$w\left(x_{s,i}, y_j\right) = exp^{\frac{-\|I(x_{s,i})-I(y_j)\|_2^2}{\delta(x_{s,i})}} , \tag{3}$$

with

$$\delta\left(x_{s,i}\right) = \mathrm{argmin}_{y_j \in N_T(x_{s,i})} \|I\left(x_{s,i}\right) - I\left(y_j\right)\|_2 + \varepsilon$$

We make a soft label for each voxels in the target after the weights of all voxels $x_{s,i}$ in the atlases have been computed. We denote the set of voxels in the atlases with a nonzero weight with the voxel y_j in the target as $V(y_j)$, and we compute the soft label by:

$$l\left(y_j\right) = \frac{\sum_{s=1}^{N} \sum_{i \in V(y_j)} w(x_{s,i}, y_j) l_{s,i}}{\sum_{s=1}^{N} \sum_{i \in V(y_j)} w(x_{s,i}, y_j)} , \tag{4}$$

2.3 Reliability Guided Label Fusion

In our method, we will get a soft label by the forward or backward patch-based method. We use the soft label to get a reliability estimation, using the voxels with high reliability to guide the label fusion of voxels with low reliability. In Fig. 2, the red and blue rectangles are the search regions. In first step, the red and blue patch in the target will been given a soft label by the patch in the atlases. We assume the blue patch with high reliability and the red patch with low reliability after label fusion. In the second step, we use the blue patch to guide the labeling procedure of the red.

First, for each voxel x_i of the image to be segmented, we use the soft labels calculated by the traditional methods to estimate the voxel with right labeled reliability:

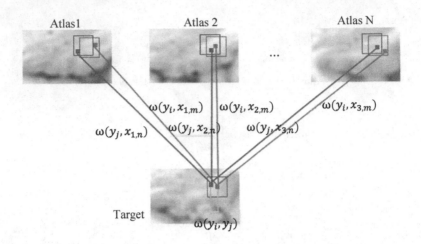

Fig. 2. Overview of the label reliability estimation and label fusion (Color figure online)

$$r(y_i) = \begin{cases} l(y_i) & l(y_i) \geq 0.5 \\ 1 - l(y_i) & l(y_i) < 0.5 \end{cases}, \tag{5}$$

If $r(y_i) > \theta$, we assume this voxel with high reliability to label right. We use this voxel with high reliability to guide the rest voxels label fusion in the next step. We use H and R to denote the set of voxels with high reliability and low reliability. We divide each voxel y_i in the target image T into two sets:

$$\begin{cases} y_i \in H & if \ r(y_i) > \theta \\ y_i \in R & otherewise \end{cases}, \tag{6}$$

At the same time, we obtain the final label of the voxel $x_i \in H$. For simplicity, we use label '1' to denote the regions of interest (ROI) on which we focus, and '0' for remaining regions. We give a label '1' when $l(y_i) \geq 0.5$ or '0' when $l(y_i) < 0.5$.

In the second step, we use the propagated soft label from atlases and the voxel with high reliability to guide the voxel y_i in R label fusion. And we consider the location relationship. We know the misclassified voxels are at the edge of the ROIs, so the voxels far from the edge will have high reliability. While we don't know the edge, for simplicity, we assume the voxels with high reliability far from the voxels with low reliability. So we want the voxels far from the center of the patch have a heavy weight. Thus for each voxel $y_i \in R$ we calculate its soft label by

$$l'(y_i) = \lambda r(y_i) + (1 - \lambda) \sum_{y_j \in (N_T(y_i) \bigcap H)} exp^{(-\frac{1}{d_{ij}\delta}\|I(y_i)-I(y_j)\|_2^2)}, \tag{7}$$

where λ is a parameter between $[0, 1]$. And d is the distance between the voxel y_i and y_j. Here we adopt the Euclidean distance. $N_T(y_i) \bigcap H$ denotes the neighborhood of voxel y_i in set of H.

Finally, the soft label is discrete into $\{0, 1\}$, the final label $L(y_i)$ is computed as:

$$L(y_i) = \begin{cases} 1 & l'(y_i) \geq 0.5 \\ 0 & l'(y_i) < 0.5 \end{cases}.$$ (8)

3   Experiments

In this section, we evaluate the performance of the proposed label fusion method on segmenting brain anatomical structure, the regions of interest (ROIs) from the MR brain image of NIREP database [16]. We compare our method with nonlocal patch-based method (F-PBM).

3.1   Dataset and Experimental Settings

The NIREP dataset [16] consist of 16 T1-weighted MR images, including 8 normal adult males and 8 females. The 16 MR images have been manually segmented into 32 ROIs. The MR images were obtained in a General Electric Signa scanner operating at 1.5 Tesla, using the following protocol: SPGR/50, TR24, TE 7, NEX 1 matrix 256 × 192, FOV 24 cm. For each of the ROIs, a Leave-One-Out cross-validation is performed to test the segmentation on each LOO fold, 15 of 16 subjects are used as atlases and aligned onto the remaining image that used as the target image.

We use the Dice ratio to assess label accuracy which measures the degree of overlap, defined as:

$$Dice(A, B) = \frac{2|A \bigcap B|}{|A| + |B|},$$ (9)

Where the $\bigcap$ denotes the overlap between automatic segmentations and ground truth, and $|\cdot|$ denotes the number of voxels of the ROI.

We use FRL-PBM denoting the new F-PBM with our framework. In order to show the advantage of utilizing location relationship, we also compare with the method without considering the location relationship, denoting as FR-PBM. We use FB-PBM and BRL-PBM denotes the backward PBM and the backward PBM with our framework. In F-PBM, FR-PBM, FRL-PBM, B-PBM and BRL-PBM, there is a common parameter, i.e., the size of $5 \times 5 \times 5$ neighborhood search region is used for our experiments. And in our experiments we fix patch size as $3 \times 3 \times 3$ voxels for all methods. We set θ in Eq. 4 as 0.8 and set λ in Eq. 6 as 0.5. And we perform a pre-selection of the patch to reduce the computational time according to the similarity of the two patch.

3.2   Experimental Results on the NIREP Dataset

We compare the segmentation results of different multi-atlas label fusion algorithms on NIREP dataset. There are 32 ROIs in the NIREP dataset, for simplicity, we treat them independently. Thus we have 32 independent binary segmentation. For each segmentation, we set the label of a voxel as 1 if it belongs to the ROI, and 0 otherwise.

Table 1 gives the average dice of the 32 ROIs. The BRL-PBM achieves the best result. Compared with F-PBM, FRL-PBM improves the average dice overlap of 32 ROIs from 75.28 % to 76.48 %. Compared with B-PBM, we can see that consider the location relationship will be improve the segmentation result. The BRL-PBM improves the overlap from 75.28 % by F-PBM to 77.06 %. Fig. 3 shows the segmentation results on the 32 ROIs using F-PBM, FR-PBM, FRL-PBM, B-PBM and BRL-PBM.

Table 1. Averaged Dice overlap of 32 ROIs using F-PBM, FR-PBM, FRL-PBM, B-PBM and BRL-PBM on NIREP dataset.

	F-PBM	FR-PBM	FRL-PBM	B-PBM	BRL-PBM
Mean	75.28 %	76.08 %	76.48 %	76.16 %	77.06 %

We can see from Fig. 3, FR-PBM outperforms F-PBM on all 32 ROIs segmentation. Using the location relationship, the FRL-PBM outperforms FR-PBM. In most cases, the BRL-PBM achieves the best result. For example, on 'L occipital lobe' the Dice overlap of F-PBM, FR-PBM, FRL-PBM, B-PBM and BRL-PBM are 77.44 %, 78.05 %, 78.45 %, 78.32 %, 78.97 %.

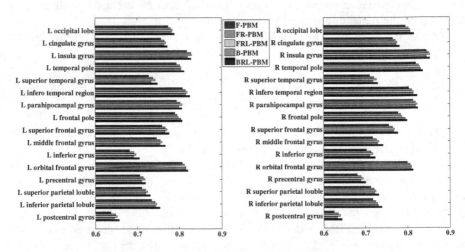

Fig. 3. Averaged Dice overlap of 32 ROIs

Finally, in Fig. 4 we visually plot the segmentation results of the F-PBM, FR-PBM FRL-PBM, B-PBM and BRL-PBM. On segmenting L insula gyrus. We also show the

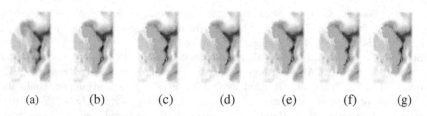

(a)   (b)   (c)   (d)   (e)   (f)   (g)

Fig. 4. Visual views on original image, ground truth and segmentation result of F-PBM (c), FRPBM (d), FRL-PBM (e), B-PBM (f) and BRL-PBM (g) algorithms on *L insula gyrus*

ground truth of the original for comparison. We can see from Fig. 4, FRL-PBM and BRL-PBM achieve a better visual quality of segmentation results.

4   Conclusion

In this paper, we proposed a novel label fusion framework for multi-atlas based segmentation. Using the voxels in the target image with high reliability to guide the labeling procedure of other voxels with low reliability, meanwhile we consider the location relationship. We estimation the label reliability by traditional method and using the voxels with high label reliability in the target image and the voxels in the atlases. Compared with the nonlocal mean weighted voting, our methods achieve high accuracies on the NIREP dataset. In the further work, we will adopt more state-of-the-art methods into our framework, and investigate the effect of the value of θ, patch size and neighborhood size to our method.

Acknowledgments. We thank the reviewers for their helpful comments. This study was supported by the National Natural Science Foundation of China (61422204; 61473149); Jiangsu Natural Science Foundation for Young Scholar (BK20130034).

References

1. Heckemann, R.A., Hajnal, J.V., Aljabar, P., et al.: Automatic anatomical brain MRI segmentation combining label propagation and decision fusion. NeuroImage **33**(1), 115–126 (2006)
2. Artaechevarria, X., Munoz-Barrutia, A., Ortiz-de-Solorzano, C.: Combination strategies in multi-atlas image segmentation: application to brain MR data. IEEE Trans. Med. Imag. **28**(8), 1266–1277 (2009)
3. Coupe, P., Manjon, J.V., Fonov, V., Pruessner, J.: Patch-based segmentation using expert priors: application to hippocampus and ventricle segmentation. Neuroimage **54**, 940–954 (2011)
4. Rousseau, F., Habas, P.A., Studholme, C.A.: Supervised patch-based approach for human brain labeling. IEEE Trans. Med. Imag. **30**(10), 1852–1862 (2011)

5. Zhang, D., Wu, G., Guo, Q., Shen, D.: Sparse patch-based label fusion for multi-atlas segmentation. In: Yap, P.-T., Liu, T., Shen, D., Westin, C.-F., Shen, L. (eds.) MBIA 2012. LNCS, vol. 7509, pp. 94–102. Springer, Heidelberg (2012)

6. Tong, T., Wolz, R., Hajnal, J.V., et al.: Segmentation of brain MR images via sparse patch representation. In: MICCAI Workshop on Sparsity Techniques in Medical Imaging (2012)

7. Lotjonen, J.M.P., Wolz, R., Koikkalainen, J.R., et al.: Fast and robust multi-atlas segmentation of brain magnetic resonance images. Neuroimage 49(3), 2352–2365 (2010)

8. Aljabar, P., Heckemann, R.A., Hammers, A., et al.: Multi-atlas based segmentation of brain images: atlas selection and its effect on accuracy. Neuroimage 46(3), 726–738 (2009)

9. Sanroma, G., Wu, G., Gao, Y., Shen, D.: Learning to rank atlases for multiple-atlas segmentation. IEEE Trans. Med. Imag. 33(11), 2210 (2014)

10. Wu, G., Wang, Q., Zhang, D., et al.: A generative probability model of joint label fusion for multi-atlas based brain segmentation. Med. Image Anal. 18(6), 881–890 (2014)

11. Wu, G., Kim, M., Sanroma, G., et al.: Hierarchical multi-atlas label fusion with multi-scale feature representation and label-specific patch partition. NeuroImage 106, 34–46 (2015)

12. Tong, T., Wolz, R., Coupe, P., et al.: Segmentation of MR images via discriminative dictionary learning and sparse coding: Application to hippocampus labeling. NeuroImage 76(1), 11–23 (2013)

13. Wang, H., Suh, J.W., Das, S.R., et al.: Multi-atlas segmentation with joint label fusion. Trans. Pattern Anal. Mach. Intell. 35(3), 611–623 (2013)

14. Langerak, T.R., van der Heide, U.A., Kotte, A.N., Viergever, M.A., van Vulpen, M., Pluim, J.P.: Label fusion in atlas-based segmentation using a selective and iterative method for performance level estimation (SIMPLE). IEEE Trans. Med. Imag. 29, 2000–2008 (2010)

15. Shen, D., Wu, G., Jia, H., Zhang, D.: Confidence-guided sequential label fusion for multi-atlas based segmentation. In: Fichtinger, G., Martel, A., Peters, T. (eds.) MICCAI 2011, Part III. LNCS, vol. 6893, pp. 643–650. Springer, Heidelberg (2011)

16. Grabowski, T.J., Bruss, J., Pirwani, I.A., Damasio, H., Vannier, M.W., Allen, J.S., Christensen, G.E., Kuhl, J.G., Geng, X.: Introduction to the non-rigid image registration evaluation project (NIREP). In: Pluim, J.P., Likar, B., Gerritsen, F.A. (eds.) WBIR 2006. LNCS, vol. 4057, pp. 128–135. Springer, Heidelberg (2006)

Correlating Tumour Histology and *ex vivo* MRI Using Dense Modality-Independent Patch-Based Descriptors

Andre Hallack[1]([⊠]), Bartłomiej W. Papież[1], James Wilson[2], Lai Mun Wang[3],
Tim Maughan[2], Mark J. Gooding[4], and Julia A. Schnabel[5]

[1] Institute of Biomedical Engineering, University of Oxford, Oxford, UK
andre.hallackmirandapureza@eng.ox.ac.uk
[2] Mirada Medical, Oxford, UK
[3] Oxford University Hospitals - NHS Trust, Oxford, UK
[4] Department of Oncology, Churchill Hospital, Oxford, UK
[5] Division of Imaging Sciences and Biomedical Engineering,
King's College London, Oxford, UK

Abstract. Histological images provide reliable information on tissue characteristics which can be used to validate and improve our understanding for developing radiological imaging analysis methods. However, due to the large amount of deformation in histology stemming from resected tissues, estimating spatial correspondence with other imaging modalities is a challenging image registration problem. In this work we develop a three-stage framework for nonlinear registration between *ex vivo* MRI and histology of rectal cancer. For this multi-modality image registration task, two similarity metrics from patch-based feature transformations were used: the dense Scale Invariant Feature Transform (dense SIFT) and the Modality Independent Neighbourhood Descriptor (MIND). The potential of our method is demonstrated on a dataset of eight rectal histology images from two patients using annotated landmarks. The mean registration error was 1.80 mm after the rigid registration steps which improved to 1.08 mm after nonlinear motion correction using dense SIFT and to 1.52 mm using MIND.

1   Introduction

[F-18] fluoromisonidazole positron emission tomography (FMISO-PET), perfusion computed tomography (pCT) and dynamic contrast-enhanced magnetic resonance imaging (DCE-MRI) are imaging techniques that can extract relevant quantitative information from tumours. Understanding the tumour micro-environment can improve its characterisation and enable more effective personalised treatment for patients. Recent research effort focused on exploring these imaging techniques to identify hypoxia in tumours. Having a reliable non-invasive method to quantify hypoxia will help to predict chemoradiotherapeutic treatment, and to develop and administer hypoxic sensitisers on patients undergoing treatment [15]. Determining whether and how these imaging modalities

© Springer International Publishing Switzerland 2015
G. Wu et al. (Eds.): Patch-MI 2015, LNCS 9467, pp. 137–145, 2015.
DOI: 10.1007/978-3-319-28194-0_17

can be used to determine hypoxia is inherently difficult. FMISO-PET uses a tracer that binds to hypoxic regions and it has been shown to be effective in some regions of the body [8]. However, for rectal cancers, the excretions present in the rectal region generate a very high background uptake. For this reason, clearly identifying hypoxic regions is difficult and studies must be performed to determine whether and at what level of enhancement these can be distinctively found. DCE-MRI and pCT do not directly measure hypoxia, but the perfusion information provided by these techniques could possibly be used as a surrogate measure of hypoxia and to segment tumour regions [7,13]. Determining ground truth is challenging and requires a more reliable imaging method. Histopathological imaging is a generally accepted choice to provide a localised ground truth for hypoxia. Hypoxia can be identified in these images with Pimonidazole staining.

Naturally, image registration is an appropriate way to obtain a mapping between these different images and to enable a localised comparison between them. The large amount of deformation and other distortions caused by the process of resecting, slicing and preparing tissues for histological acquisitions present the main difficulty in registering these images. The most common approach taken for the registration of *in vivo* radiological images to *ex vivo* histology is to have an intermediate radiological *ex vivo* acquisition of the resected tissue before slicing.

Previously, functional radiological imaging of cancer has been validated using histological findings in a pre-clinical study [3,13]. Rat prostate cancers were imaged using FMISO-PET, DCE-MRI and hypoxia-marked histological imaging. However, these images were only rigidly registered using fiduciary markers inserted in the animals before image acquisition, a method which cannot be used in human trials. Several works have explored *ex vivo* MRI/CT to histology registration, but the different tissue locations configure them as very different problems to the one addressed here. Most of the research to-date has focused on aligning brain images, where there is a relevant amount of coherence of the main types of brain tissue (white matter, grey matter and cerebrospinal fluid) which allows for segmentation-driven registration or histogram matching between the images [1]. Similarly, rigid registration of μCT to histology has been studied [2], which presents tissues with very well defined structures, similar representation across both modalities and very little nonrigid deformation. *Ex vivo* MRI to histology nonlinear registration was performed for prostate cancer, for which both segmentation-based and intensity-based approaches have been investigated [4].

In this work we present a new method to register *ex vivo* MRI to histology images of rectal cancer. It differs from previous works by showing an automated solution to register images with large amounts of nonlinear deformation on different imaging representations by applying non-specific methods which could be employed for different body parts and modalities (as opposed to segmentation-based and histogram matching approaches). Another relevant contribution is the application of two patch-based techniques to extract features which can be used as similarity metrics for image registration: dense SIFT and MIND [5,9].

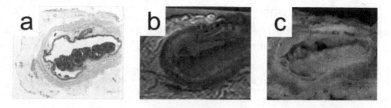

Fig. 1. Example of rectal cancer images before registration: (a) histology, (b) corresponding *ex vivo* MRI slice and (c) blockface photograph.

This paper is structured as follows. In Sect. 2 the methods developed to register *ex vivo* MRI to histology are presented. Section 3 describes the images used in this work, as well as the experiments conducted to evaluate the proposed framework and their results. Finally, Sect. 4 discusses and concludes this work.

2 Methods

The challenge addressed in this work can be described as finding a transformation T^i for each histology image I_H^i to an MRI volume I_M, where the grouping of all the histology images form a histology stack I_H. To solve this problem we have designed a three-stage solution. Firstly, a global transformation T_Z to axially (Z-direction) align I_M to I_H is estimated. Then, after applying this transformation we rigidly register each I_H^i to its corresponding MRI slice I_M^i, thus estimating T_r^i. This is followed by nonlinear registration, which ultimately computes T_{nl}^i for each of the histology slices. These steps are described in Sects. 2.1, 2.2 and 2.3.

As can be seen from Fig. 1, MRI and histology tumour images show different types of tissues, but the main feature characteristics are preserved (albeit under severe deformation). Hence, we opted to use similarity metrics with strong edge responses. Two similarity metrics with such property were explored in this work: the Scale Invariant Feature Transform, both its original form and dense variant (SIFT [10] and dense SIFT [9]), and the Modality Independent Neighbourhood Descriptor (MIND) [5]. Both of these metrics extract descriptor vectors based on the intensity relationships between voxels in regions of the images.

SIFT is a method to localise points of interest (POIs) in images and extract high dimensional discriminative descriptor vectors based on the gradient profile on the regions around these salient points [10]. Dense SIFT is a variant of this method where an image is converted to a vector-valued image by computing these descriptors at each voxel without the POI detection of classic SIFT [9].

MIND is a transform that computes a feature vector for each voxel of an image [5]. This feature vector is determined by the similarity of nonlocal patches around each voxel. Its descriptors have much smaller dimensions than SIFT and have already shown to generate good results in medical image registration tasks.

Both dense SIFT and MIND can be used as a similarity measure. Each of the images being registered (I_1, I_2) is transformed using these methods generating the vector-valued images $(\text{SIFT}(I(\mathbf{x}))$ or $\text{MIND}(I(\mathbf{x})))$ with d descriptors. Then the sum-of-squared differences (SSD) can be computed between these images resulting in a similarity measure (SIM). For the SIFT case this is expressed as:

$$\text{SIM}_{\text{SIFT}}(I_1(\mathbf{x}), I_2(\mathbf{x})) = \left\|\left|\text{SIFT}(I_1(\mathbf{x})) - \text{SIFT}(I_2(\mathbf{x}))\right|\right\|_2 \qquad (1)$$

An analogous equation can be used for SIM_{MIND}.

2.1 Histology to MRI Axial Registration

Initialisation is one of the main difficulties in registering 2D histological slices to 3D MRI. In general, the specimens are sliced axially before the histology image acquisition, hence finding corresponding axial MRI slices for each histology image is a good first step towards image registration.

SIFT is a fitting solution for this problem as it reduces the large MR volume space to a small number of POIs which can be matched to the histology slices ones. However, due to the large amount of deformations found in the histology, the POIs from the histology may not always be similar to the MRI ones. Thus, to robustly perform this step we opted to jointly register all the histology slices from a tumour to the corresponding MRI volume. This is done by first generating a histology stack by placing each of the slices on their expected relative axial positions (which can be determined with the aid of the blockface images Fig. 1(c)). This initial axial translational transformation (T_Z) is obtained with the following sequence of steps:

- SIFT is applied to the histology stack, generating a set of POIs and descriptors P_H. Where $P^n = [\mathbf{x}, \mathbf{D}]$, $\mathbf{x}$ denoting the interest point's coordinates and $\mathbf{D}$ its descriptor vector.
- SIFT is applied to the MRI volume, finding a set of POIs P_M.
- For each POI of the histology stack (P_H^n) the most similar point in the MRI volume (P_M^k) is found by minimising the SSD between descriptors:

$$[P_H^n, P_M^k] = \arg \min_{P_M^m}\left(\left|\left|P_H^n[\mathbf{D}] - P_M^m[\mathbf{D}]\right|\right|_2\right) \qquad (2)$$

- Each correspondence pair denotes an axial translation $T_Z^n = P_M^n[z] - P_H^k[z]$ between the histology and MRI stacks.
- A final axial transformation (T_Z) is obtained as the mode of all these transformations: $T_Z = \text{Mode}\{T_Z^n\}$.

Reconstruction of a 3D histology volume is not possible in our case, as the histology images are not contiguous and sometimes incomplete, but individual slices can be matched to the MR volume. For that reason, we can only perform a translation in the axial direction in this first step. Note that, a similar approach was proposed to estimate rigid transforms for histology to μCT registration of bone structures [2].

2.2   2D MRI Rigid Registration

After finding a corresponding MRI slice (I_M^i) for each histology image (I_H^i), the next step is to perform 2D to 2D rigid registration between this image pair (estimating T_r^i). We investigated both dense SIFT and MIND similarity metrics for this step (using Eq. 1), by iteratively minimising:

$$\hat{T}_r = \arg \min_{T_r} \left(\int_{\mathbf{x}=0}^{\Omega} \mathrm{SIM}(I_1, I_2)(\mathbf{x}) d\mathbf{x} \right) \qquad (3)$$

where Ω is the image domain and SIM denotes Eq. 1 using either dense SIFT or MIND. This minimisation was performed using a Levenberg-Marquandt optimizer from the *alglib* library[1].

The results for this step using dense SIFT were very unsatisfactory (and thus will not be reported in the results section). The cause for this is that regions with very low match values with dense SIFT dominate its response as a global similarity metric. Thus, its use as a global measure requires some adaptations (such as mutual saliency weighting [11]).

2.3   2D MRI Nonlinear Registration

Histological images show high levels of nonlinear deformation, especially as some regions shrink while others expand, in addition to tissue tearing and shearing. We performed nonlinear motion correction in this work using logDemons [14], which provides invertible diffeomorphic transformation fields (T_{nl}). Even though the deformation present in these images are not diffeomorphic, such approach is chosen as a one-to-one correspondence is relevant for future data analysis between functional and histology images. A multi-resolution framework was applied for this registration and we compared the use of dense SIFT, MIND (minimising Eq. 1) and local cross-correlation (LCC) [6], a standard similarity metric.

3   Experiments and Results

3.1   Data Acquisition, Preparation and Landmark Selection

T2-weighted MRI images were acquired from 2 resected rectums with adenocarcinomas while in formalin for 12 to 24 h. The images were acquired using 1.5 T scanner (TwinSpeed, GE Healthcare) with 3 mm oblique axial sections with 0.3 mm spacing. The specimens were then sectioned in 3 mm sections when possible and 6 mm at more friable sections of the tumour. Haematoxylin and eosin stains were applied and histological imaging acquisitions were performed. A total of 8 histological slices with axial resolution of 2 μm were obtained this way.

A number of steps were taken to prepare the images for the proposed method. The *ex vivo* MRI images of the resected cancer possessed a much larger field of

---

[1] *alglib*, available on http://mloss.org/software/view/231/.

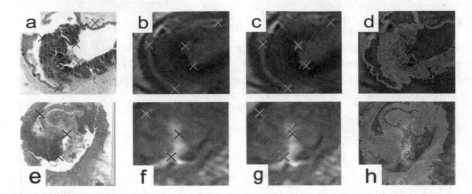

Fig. 2. Registration of two cases from different patients (row 1 and 2, respectively). (a,e) Histology and (b,f) corresponding MRI slice after rigid registration, (c,g) after nonlinear registration using dense SIFT and (d,h) after nonlinear registration with yellow overlay of the histology. Landmarks are shown by the crosses: histology (blue), MRI after rigid registration (green) and MRI after nonlinear registration (red) (Color figure online).

view than the histology, thus, to facilitate the registration algorithm a region around the tumour was cropped. For each of the histology images, an expert histologist and oncologist jointly annotated a set of two to five landmarks (25 in total) in both the histology and the *ex vivo* MRI using the software *VV* [12].

3.2   Framework Parameters and Results

The parameters for the registration framework were empirically determined. For the initial slice estimation, an off-the-shelf implementation of SIFT, $ezSIFT^2$, was used along with its standard parameters: 36 bins, threshold set to 8 and number of layers set to 3. For nonlinear registration, the logDemons framework was applied with three resolution levels with 40 iterations at each level and transformation field smoothing $\sigma_{diff} = 4$ pixels. The SIFT Flow library was used for dense SIFT with the standard parameters: cell size $= 2$ and 8 bins [9]. For MIND, the search region was $R = 2$ and the Gaussian weighting $\sigma_{MIND} = 0.5$.

The proposed method was quantitatively evaluated using the annotated landmarks. For each of the histological images, the obtained transformations were applied to the landmarks and the mean distance to the MRI landmarks were computed. The mean registration error for each of the images was evaluated after the rigid registration steps and after nonlinear registration, Table 1 presents these results. It can be observed that nonlinear registration was able to compensate some of the deformation in these images and considerably decrease the distance between the landmarks, in the best case, with dense SIFT, an average improvement of 60 % was observed which corresponds to a mean error of 1.08 mm. Figure 2 presents some registered images using this similarity metric.

---

2 *ezSIFT*, available on http://sourceforge.net/projects/ezsift/.

Table 1. Average mean squared error and standard deviation of the landmarks after rigid and nonlinear registration with different similarity metrics.

Registration	Rigid (mm)	Nonlinear (mm)		
Patient	MIND	Dense SIFT	MIND	LCC
Patient 1	1.97 ± 0.45	1.10 ± 0.58	1.61 ± 0.44	1.80 ± 0.53
Patient 2	1.51 ± 0.42	1.06 ± 0.57	1.37 ± 0.64	1.42 ± 0.33
Overall	1.80 ± 0.44	1.08 ± 0.58	1.52 ± 0.49	1.62 ± 0.57

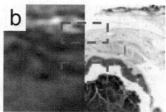

Fig. 3. Histology slice (right) and MRI image (left) after nonlinear registration using (a) MIND and (b) dense SIFT. A close inspection shows that both methods are good at matching edges, but MIND is not very discriminative and consequently registers noncorresponding edges, while dense SIFT is more accurate.

As expected, the similarity metrics with a strong edge response, dense SIFT and MIND, could better characterise and compare the images being registered, leading to better registration results. However, despite MIND being very good at identifying edges, it is not as good as dense SIFT in discriminating them, this is observed in Fig. 3, a case where MIND matches noncorresponding edges.

4   Discussion and Conclusions

We have presented a comprehensive framework that addresses the challenging tasks of aligning histological slices through a tumour with volumetric *ex vivo* MRI of the tumour. Despite it being developed for a rectal cancer application, the proposed method does not use any specific characteristic of the region of the body being analysed and thus could be employed for other similar histology registration tasks. The framework was evaluated through landmarks, and visual inspection also confirmed its validity of this solution for this problem.

For this, we have investigated the potential of dense SIFT as a patch-based similarity metric within the logDemons framework, achieving good results compared to other multi-modality and feature vector based similarity metric. Due to some limiting factors dense SIFT has not been widely used yet for medical image registration: its descriptors have very high dimensions and were originally developed for 2D images, two aspects that need to be adapted to be used with the very large 3D volumes found in medical imaging.

To-date, the validation was performed in a small dataset, which is one of the difficulties when working with histology images and we intend to increase the number of cases as part of an ongoing trial. There are several aspects that can be explored in future works. Dense SIFT was not a viable option as a global similarity metric and could be further developed for such task. Moreover, this application should be extended to also account for nonlinear deformation across MRI volume slices. This work will follow by registering *ex vivo* to *in vivo* MRI volumes and then to the functional acquisitions (DCE-MRI, pCT and FMISO-PET), obtaining a correspondence between the histology and these acquisitions.

Acknowledgements. We would like to acknowledge the funding from CRUK/EPSRC Cancer Imaging Centre at Oxford. AH also acknowledges the support of the Research Council UK Digital Economy Programme EP/G036861/1 (Oxford Centre for Doctoral Training in Healthcare Innovation) and CAPES Foundation, process BEX 0725/12-9.

References

1. Ceritoglu, C., Wang, L., Selemon, L.D., Csernansky, J.G., Miller, M.I., Ratnanather, J.T.: Large deformation diffeomorphic metric mapping registration of reconstructed 3D histological section images and in vivo MR images. Front Hum. Neurosci. **4**, 43 (2010)
2. Chicherova, N., Fundana, K., Müller, B., Cattin, P.C.: Histology to μCT data matching using landmarks and a density biased RANSAC. In: Golland, P., Hata, N., Barillot, C., Hornegger, J., Howe, R. (eds.) MICCAI 2014, Part I. LNCS, vol. 8673, pp. 243–250. Springer, Heidelberg (2014)
3. Cho, H., Ackerstaff, E., Carlin, S., Lupu, M.E., Wang, Y., Rizwan, A., O'Donoghue, J., Ling, C.C., Humm, J.L., Zanzonico, P.B., et al.: Noninvasive multimodality imaging of the tumor microenvironment: registered dynamic MRI and PET studies of a preclinical tumor model of tumor hypoxia. Neoplasia **11**(3), 247–259 (2009)
4. Feldman, M., Tomaszewski, J., Davatzikos, C.: Non-rigid registration between histological and MR images of the prostate: a joint segmentation and registration framework. In: IEEE CVPR, pp. 125–132 (2009)
5. Heinrich, M.P., Jenkinson, M., Bhushan, M., Matin, T., Gleeson, F., Brady, M., Schnabel, J.A.: MIND: modality independent neighbourhood descriptor for multi-modal deformable registration. Med. Image Anal. **16**(7), 1423–1435 (2012)
6. Hermosillo, G., Chefd'hotel, C., Faugeras, O.: Variational methods for multimodal image matching. Int. J. Comput. Vis. **50**(3), 329–343 (2002)
7. Irving, B., Cifor, A., Papież, B.W., Franklin, J., Anderson, E.M., Brady, S.M., Schnabel, J.A.: Automated colorectal tumour segmentation in DCE-MRI using supervoxel neighbourhood contrast characteristics. In: Golland, P., Hata, N., Barillot, C., Hornegger, J., Howe, R. (eds.) MICCAI 2014, Part I. LNCS, vol. 8673, pp. 609–616. Springer, Heidelberg (2014)
8. Koh, W.J., Bergman, K.S., Rasey, J.S., Peterson, L.M., Evans, M.L., Graham, M.M., Grierson, J.R., Lindsley, K.L., Lewellen, T.K., Krohn, K.A.: Evaluation of oxygenation status during fractionated radiotherapy in human nonsmall cell lung cancers using [f-18]fluoromisonidazole PET. Int. J. Radiat. Oncol. Biol. Phys. **33**(2), 391–398 (1995)
9. Liu, C., Yuen, J., Torralba, A.: SIFT flow: dense correspondence across scenes and its applications. IEEE Trans. Pattern Anal. Mach. Intell. **33**(5), 978–994 (2011)

10. Lowe, D.G.: Object recognition from local scale-invariant features. In: ICCV, vol. 2, pp. 1150–1157. IEEE (1999)
11. Ou, Y., Sotiras, A., Paragios, N., Davatzikos, C.: DRAMMS: Deformable registration via attribute matching and mutual-saliency weighting. Med. Image Anal. 15(4), 622–639 (2011)
12. Seroul, P., Sarrut, D.: VV: a viewer for the evaluation of 4D image registration. In: MICCAI-Systems and Architectures for Computer Assisted Interventions (2008)
13. Stoyanova, R., Huang, K., Sandler, K., Cho, H., Carlin, S., Zanzonico, P.B., Koutcher, J.A., Ackerstaff, E.: Mapping tumor hypoxia in vivo using pattern recognition of dceMRI data. Trans. Oncol. 5(6), 437–447 (2012)
14. Vercauteren, T., Pennec, X., Perchant, A., Ayache, N.: Symmetric log-domain diffeomorphic registration: a demons-based approach. In: Metaxas, D., Axel, L., Fichtinger, G., Székely, G. (eds.) MICCAI 2008, Part I. LNCS, vol. 5241, pp. 754–761. Springer, Heidelberg (2008)
15. Zahra, M.A., Hollingsworth, K.G., Sala, E., Lomas, D.J., Tan, L.T.: Dynamic contrast-enhanced MRI as a predictor of tumour response to radiotherapy. Lancet Oncol. 8(1), 63–74 (2007)

Multi-atlas Segmentation Using Patch-Based Joint Label Fusion with Non-Negative Least Squares Regression

Mattias P. Heinrich$^{(\boxtimes)}$, Matthias Wilms, and Heinz Handels

Institute of Medical Informatics, University of Lübeck, Lübeck, Germany
heinrich@imi.uni-luebeck.de
http://www.mpheinrich.de

Abstract. This work presents a patch-based multi-atlas segmentation approach based on non-negative least squares regression. Our approach finds a weighted linear combination of local image patches that best models the target patch, jointly for all considered atlases. The local coefficients are optimised with the constraint of being positive or zero and serve as weights, of the underlying segmentation patches, for a multi-atlas voting. The negative influence of erroneous local registration outcome is shown to be reduced by avoiding negative weights. For challenging abdominal MRI, the segmentation accuracy is significantly improved compared to standard joint least squares regression and independent similarity-based weighting. Our experiments show that restricting weights to be non-negative yields significantly better segmentation results than a sparsity promoting ℓ_1 penalty. We present an efficient numerical implementation that rapidly calculates correlation matrices for all overlapping image patches and atlases in few seconds.

Keywords: Linear regression · Generative model · Cross-correlation

1 Introduction

Automatic segmentation of anatomical structures is an essential part of medical imaging applications, including but not limited to visualisation, computer-aided diagnosis and image-guided interventions. Atlas-based segmentation, in particular when employing multiple atlases and deformable registration, has demonstrated to achieve high accuracy and very good generalisation to different modalities, application domains and anatomic sights. Several algorithms have been proposed to rate different atlases [1] based on their suitability to segment a given target image in order to optimally fuse them. Patch-based approaches have the advantage against global methods of being able to estimate locally varying weights and can therefore better deal with local registration errors or imaging artefacts [2]. Recently, generative models that jointly estimate atlas weights have become popular [3,4]. In Sect. 3, we present an elegant mathematical formulation that jointly estimates a linear combination of all atlas image patches

© Springer International Publishing Switzerland 2015
G. Wu et al. (Eds.): Patch-MI 2015, LNCS 9467, pp. 146–153, 2015.
DOI: 10.1007/978-3-319-28194-0_18

that best approximates the target patch using **only positive or zero coefficients**. By employing non-negative least squares [5], we can avoid unrealistic negative weights of atlases, which may cancel out correct label votes. Furthermore, we present a numerically efficient solution that enables rapid calculation of local correlation matrices and makes our fusion approach at least an order of magnitude faster than previous joint fusion methods [4]. Together with a fast deformable registration our method enables computation times of < 2 min per scan, which closes the performance gap to machine learning approaches. In Sect. 4, we demonstrate the suitability of our approach for the segmentation of organs in clinical abdominal magnetic resonance images (MRI) that pose different challenges than more commonly studied brain images. We show experimental comparisons with majority voting, locally weighted fusion (based on normalised correlation), sparse Lasso regression [6], least squares regression [3] and joint label fusion [4].

2   Related Work

Multi-atlas label fusion is an active field of research in medical imaging. Global performance of multiple raters or atlases can been estimated by the popular STAPLE (Simultaneous truth and performance level estimation) framework [1]. Recent work has shown that segmentation and registration errors are highly non-uniform across the image domain so that locally varying performance levels should be estimated [2] for every overlapping patch within the target scan. STAPLE estimates dependency across atlases based on their agreement of segmentation labels, however, atlas-based registration provides additional intensity information (of registered atlas images), which has been exploited e.g. in [7,8]. In these works, label fusion is formulated as a generative model, which explains the formation of the target appearance through multiple atlases. Non-local patch based approaches that directly obtain weights from distance measures of image similarity [9,10] are popular when only a rough (e.g. affine) alignment of atlases to the target scan is available. These methods, with the exception of [11], usually rate each atlas independently and may miss relations between them. Joint label fusion with least square regression was proposed in [3] and similarity-based distances between atlases and target scan and amongst atlases themselves in [4]. An additional sparsity constraint together with least squares regression was used in [6]. Yet, the task to select the right number of atlases is difficult in this context as discussed in [12]. Our work is closely related to the joint least square approaches of [3,6], but demonstrates the potential degradation of the label fusion through negative weights and proposes an elegant and effective solution by using a non-negativity constraint in the regression.

3   Methods

Our aim is to segment an unseen 3D intensity target scan $\mathbf{I}$ using n atlas scans $\mathbf{J}_1, \mathbf{J}_2, \ldots, \mathbf{J}_n$ and their corresponding manual segmentations $\mathbf{L}_1, \mathbf{L}_2, \ldots, \mathbf{L}_n$, which have already been brought into spatial alignment by deformable registration. To find the optimal label for a location x in the target scan, we consider its intensity patch $\mathbf{X}(x)$ (in $\mathbf{I}$) for a neighbourhood radius r defined by Ω_x with a size of $R = (2r + 1)^3$. From the atlas database, we have n patches $\mathbf{Y}_1(x), \mathbf{Y}_2(x), \ldots, \mathbf{Y}_n(x)$. To avoid the negative influence of local contrast variations we first subtract the mean of all patches and divide them by their standard deviations, yielding normalised patches $\mathbf{X}'(x)$, $\mathbf{Y}'_1(x)$, etc.:

$$\mathbf{X}'(x) = \frac{\mathbf{X}(x) - \overline{\mathbf{X}(x)}}{\sqrt{\frac{1}{R} \sum_{y \in \Omega_x} (\mathbf{X}(y) - \overline{\mathbf{X}(x)})^2}} \text{with } \overline{\mathbf{X}(x)} = \frac{1}{R} \sum_{y \in \Omega_x} \mathbf{X}(y) \qquad (1)$$

We now seek the coefficient vector $\mathbf{c} = c_1, c_2, \ldots, c_n$ that minimises the least squares error ρ^2 of a linear weighted combination of atlas patches:

$$\rho^2 = \sum_{y \in \Omega_x} (\mathbf{X}'(y) - \sum_i^n c_i \mathbf{Y}'_i(y))^2 \qquad (2)$$

Let $\mathbf{A}$ be a $R \times n$ matrix, where the i-th column represents the atlas patch $\mathbf{Y}'_i(x)$ and $\mathbf{b}$ a vector of length R, which stands for the target patch $\mathbf{X}'(x)$. The straightforward solution of the optimal $\mathbf{c}$ in Eq. 2 without further constraints can be obtained by least squares regression. In our method, we propose to add the constraint that all coefficients have to be non-negative, hence solving a non-negative least squares problem [5]:

$$\underset{\mathbf{c}}{\operatorname{argmin}} ||\mathbf{A}\mathbf{c} - \mathbf{b}||_2^2 \text{ subject to } c_i \geq 0 \ \forall \ i = \{1, 2, \ldots, n\} \qquad (3)$$

The estimated $\mathbf{c}$ can be used to obtain an optimal reconstruction of the target patch from a weighted combination of all atlas patches for which $c_i > 0$. Figure 1 shows an example, where the advantages of the non-negativity constraint can be clearly seen in comparison to the classical least squares solution. Patches with poor visual similarity (bottom row) are assigned zero weights in our approach. Using least squares, these weights become negative and lead to a cancellation of any votes for the kidney (shown with red labels) in the patch-based fusion.

Relations to Sparsity Promoting Minimisation. An alternative solution to finding an optimal patch combination, [6], introduces an additional ℓ_1 penalty on the coefficients: $\lambda^* |\mathbf{c}|_1$, where $\lambda^* = \lambda \max(|\mathbf{A}\mathbf{b}|)$. Adding this term for Eq. 3 instead of the non-negativity constraint transforms the minimisation into a Lasso problem [13], which promotes a sparse selection of atlases. In [6] it was shown that a sparse selection of atlases may improve label fusion. It, however, adds an additional free parameter λ, which regulates the degree of sparsity. The minimisation of Lasso is computationally more expensive than NNLS and no gain is achieved for the image registration step (since all registered atlases are required regardless). Furthermore, it has been recently shown in [14] that a non-negativity constraint may achieve a superior sparse selection without the need for balancing the ℓ_1 penalty. We will further strengthen this theoretical assumption in our experiments.

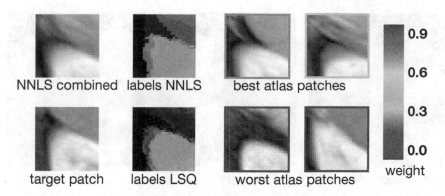

Fig. 1. Visual example of non-negative least square (NNLS) patch-based fusion for a challenging anatomical location close to spleen and kidney. After calculating the coefficients c the best and worst patches from the atlas database can be determined. The coloured borders indicate the NNLS-weights (both bottom patches have zero weight). When the NNLS weights are applied for patch-based label the probabilistic segmentation estimate (green indicates kidney, red spleen) is improved compared to least squares (LSQ) and the combined intensity patches reconstruct the target patch visually well. In the least squares approach the negative weight of e.g. the patch at the bottom right cancels out votes for the spleen (red colour) and leads to a deterioration of the fusion (Color figure online).

Efficient Implementation for Overlapping Patches. We assume $R > n$, i.e. the resulting linear system is overdetermined and the same solution is obtained for $\mathbf{A}^T\mathbf{A}c = \mathbf{A}^T\mathbf{b}$. Using matrix notation this yields the following equations (omitting x for brevity):

$$\begin{bmatrix} \sum(\mathbf{Y}_1')^2 & \sum\mathbf{Y}_1'\mathbf{Y}_2' & \cdots & \sum\mathbf{Y}_1'\mathbf{Y}_n' \\ \sum\mathbf{Y}_2'\mathbf{Y}_1' & \sum(\mathbf{Y}_2')^2 & \cdots & \sum\mathbf{Y}_2'\mathbf{Y}_n' \\ \vdots & \vdots & \ddots & \vdots \\ \sum\mathbf{Y}_n'\mathbf{Y}_1' & \sum\mathbf{Y}_n'\mathbf{Y}_2' & \cdots & \sum(\mathbf{Y}_n')^2 \end{bmatrix} \begin{bmatrix} c_1 \\ c_2 \\ \vdots \\ c_n \end{bmatrix} = \begin{bmatrix} \mathbf{Y}_1'\mathbf{X}' \\ \mathbf{Y}_2'\mathbf{X}' \\ \vdots \\ \mathbf{Y}_n'\mathbf{X}' \end{bmatrix} \quad (4)$$

This reduces the number of equations from R to n and it becomes clear that all entries are normalised cross-correlations (scaled by a factor R) between the locally considered patches. Since the elements in Eq. 4 have to be calculated for nearly all overlapping patches in an image, many calculations are repetitive. Following the work of [15] on local canonical correlation, which is based on the principle of guided filtering [16], we can replace the summations in Eq. 4 with box convolution filters. The filter operations have a computational complexity that is independent of the patch size R and thus enables fast computation for large neighbourhoods. For implementation details we refer to [15], but in contrast to that work, we consider correlation (not covariance) matrices and we have to calculate local standard deviations (numerator of Eq. 1). Note that this simplification cannot be used in *joint label fusion*, since the product of absolute differences cannot be expanded that way (c.f. Eq. 18 [4]). To stabilise the solution a small regularisation constant ϵ may be added to the diagonal of $\mathbf{A}^T\mathbf{A}$.

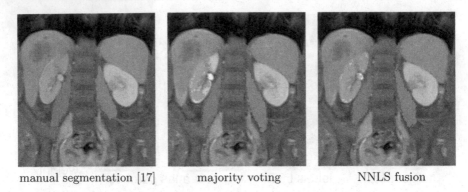

manual segmentation [17]   majority voting   NNLS fusion

Fig. 2. Visual comparison of segmentation outcome for two different multi-atlas label fusion techniques. The coronal slices show the following segmented abdominal organs: ■ liver, ■ spleen, ■ left, ■ right kidney, ■ left psoas major muscle (pmm) and ■ right pmm. Substantially improved organ delineation can be seen for the proposed non-negative least square regression compared to majority voting, especially for the right kidney and liver. Note that the bladder is not visible in this slice (Color figure online).

The choice of this parameter will be discussed later. After an atlas weighting vector c has been obtained for every voxel x, a structured label combination of the overlapping patches is considered. Each voxel votes for all voxels in its neighbourhood Ω_x based on its local label patch. This is equivalent to spatially filtering the weighting field of each label with a uniform kernel of size Ω_x and has already been used in [4,16].

4   Experiments

We evaluated our method for ten abdominal MRI scans from the VISCERAL3 training dataset [17] (see Fig. 2). The images were first resampled to uniform voxel-spacings and cropped to have same dimensions. Pair-wise deformable registrations were performed using the **deeds** framework [18], which is based on discrete optimisation together with self-similarity context [19] as matching term. For image resolutions of 2.5 mm ($\approx$3 million voxels per volume) a single registration takes only $\approx$10 s. Five multi-scale levels with control-point spacings of $[8, 7, 6, 5, 4]$ voxels, $l_{\max} = [6, 5, 4, 3, 2]$ displacement steps, and quantisations of $q = [5, 4, 3, 2, 1]$ voxels were used, which yields a capture range of 75 mm.

   We used a leave-one-out cross-validation for our experiments, i.e. for every target scan there are $n = 9$ atlases. The patch-radius was fixed to $r = 4$ voxels, as this yielded the best accuracy for all evaluated techniques on our data. In our NNLS implementation, we first calculate cross-correlations between all atlases and between all atlases and the target scan using roughly $\frac{(n+3)n}{2} = 65$ box filter operations. Each volumetric filter takes about 0.05 s (in total of 3 s). Figure 3 demonstrates the advantages compared to a naïve implementation. Only voxels without unanimous decision of all atlases (and voxels within a margin of

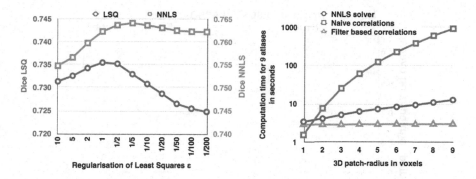

Fig. 3. Left: Influence of regularisation weight ϵ for least square regression with and without non-negative constraint on segmentation accuracy (note: the y-scales are different). Best results for NNLS are obtained for $0.5 \leq \epsilon \leq 0.1$ and $1 \leq \epsilon \leq 0.5$ for LSQ. Right: Computation times (on logarithmic scale) for calculation of all correlation matrices in Eq. 4 using naïve approach and our proposed filter-based (exact) solution, which is independent of the radius. The NNLS solution takes slightly longer for larger radii because more voxels are considered (larger spatial influence of each patch).

r around them) need to be considered for weighted NNLS fusion (so only for these, correlation matrices have to be stored). The NNLS optimisation was then performed for an average of 500×10^3 voxels per atlas in 6 s. for all atlases. This computation time compares favourably (roughly 15 times faster) with an average of 120 s for *joint label fusion* using the original implementation of [4] on the same machine. Our reference implementation will be made available at www. mpheinrich.de/software.html.

The visual results in Fig. 2 show an improved segmentation compared to majority voting especially at boundaries between organs, e.g. liver and right kidney, which are challenging for the deformable registration. Experiments have been performed using the same registration outcome for several comparable state-of-the-art approaches. The resulting segmentations S have been numerically evaluated using the manual annotations M of seven organs (see Fig. 2 for a description) provided by [17] using the Dice overlap $D = 2|S \cap M|/(|S| + |M|)$. Our approach significantly improves with an average Dice of $D = 0.764$ over majority voting ($D = 0.713$), independent local NCC-similarity weighted fusion ($D = 0.729$), joint least square regression [3] ($D = 0.735$) and ℓ_1-Lasso regression ($D = 0.734$). The results obtained for the joint distance based fusion of [4] are only slightly inferior to ours with $D = 0.756$, but incur a much larger computation time. Figure 4 compares the distribution of Dice overlaps for all methods. Our approach implicitly yields roughly 40 % of zero coefficient. When combining the non-negativity and ℓ_1 constraints, a larger sparsity can be obtained (69 %, 53 % and 43 % for $\lambda = 0.5$, 0.2 and 0.1 respectively). In accordance with [14] adding the ℓ_1 penalty deteriorates the coefficient estimation compared to only using NNLS. For $\lambda \leq 0.1$ both sparsity and accuracy of ℓ_1+NNLS come close to our results.

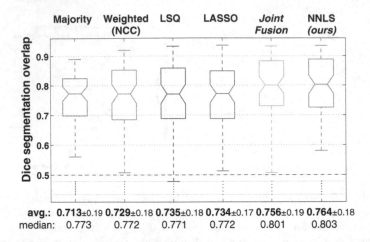

Fig. 4. Numerical results for segmentation accuracy in 10 MRI scans of [17] using multi-atlas fusion in a leave-one-out fashion. Average Dice scores over seven abdominal structures are compared for majority voting, locally weighted fusion with normalised cross-correlation (NCC), least squares regression (LSQ) analogous to [3], joint label fusion [3] and our proposed nonnegative least square (NNLS) regression. The improvements of NNLS compared to LSQ, LASSO and NCC are significant with $p = 0.049$, $p = 0.031$, and $p = 0.022$ respectively using a signed Wilcoxon rank-sum test.

5   Conclusion

We have presented a very accurate and fast multi-atlas label fusion technique that jointly models patch correlations using non-negative least squares regression. Experimental validation for abdominal scans shows significant improvements over straightforward patch-based regression or independent similarity-based weighting. On average our approach also outperforms *joint label fusion* [4], which is computationally much more involved. We have demonstrated that for this application non-negativity constraints are favourable over sparsity promoting ℓ_1 regularisation with clear advantages in computational demand and parameter choice. Future work could employ this fast and reliable fusion strategy together with approximate (pseudo-geodesic) pair-wise deformable registrations in order to further narrow the performance gap to machine learning approaches.

Acknowledgements. We are very grateful to H. Matuschek (University of Potsdam) for making available an efficient implementation for non-negative least square optimisation within the Eigen3 library (http://eigen.tuxfamily.org).

References

1. Warfield, S.K., Zou, K.H., Wells, W.M.: Simultaneous truth and performance level estimation (STAPLE): an algorithm for the validation of image segmentation. IEEE Trans. Med. Imaging **23**(7), 903–921 (2004)

2. Commowick, O., Akhondi-Asl, A., Warfield, S.K.: Estimating a reference standard segmentation with spatially varying performance parameters: local MAP STAPLE. IEEE Trans. Med. Imaging **31**(8), 1593–1606 (2012)
3. Wang, H., Suh, J.W., Das, S., Pluta, J., Altinay, M., Yushkevich, P.: Regression-based label fusion for multi-atlas segmentation. In: 2011 IEEE Conference on Computer Vision and Pattern Recognition (CVPR), pp. 1113–1120. IEEE (2011)
4. Wang, H., Suh, J.W., Das, S.R., Pluta, J.B., Craige, C., Yushkevich, P., et al.: Multi-atlas segmentation with joint label fusion. IEEE Pattern Anal. Mach. Intell. **35**(3), 611–623 (2013)
5. Lawson, C.L., Hanson, R.J.: Solving least squares problems, vol. 161. SIAM (1974)
6. Zhang, D., Guo, Q., Wu, G., Shen, D.: Sparse patch-based label fusion for multi-atlas segmentation. In: Yap, P.-T., Liu, T., Shen, D., Westin, C.-F., Shen, L. (eds.) MBIA 2012. LNCS, vol. 7509, pp. 94–102. Springer, Heidelberg (2012)
7. Wu, G., Wang, Q., Zhang, D., Nie, F., Huang, H., Shen, D.: A generative probability model of joint label fusion for multi-atlas based brain segmentation. Med. Image Anal. **18**(6), 881–890 (2014)
8. Sabuncu, M.R., Yeo, B.T., Van Leemput, K., Fischl, B., Golland, P.: A generative model for image segmentation based on label fusion. IEEE Trans. Med. Imaging **29**(10), 1714–1729 (2010)
9. Coupé, P., Manjón, J.V., Fonov, V., Pruessner, J., Robles, M., Collins, D.L.: Patch-based segmentation using expert priors: application to hippocampus and ventricle segmentation. NeuroImage **54**(2), 940–954 (2011)
10. Rousseau, F., Habas, P.A., Studholme, C.: A supervised patch-based approach for human brain labeling. IEEE Trans. Med. Imaging **30**(10), 1852–1862 (2011)
11. Asman, A.J., Landman, B.A.: Non-local statistical label fusion for multi-atlas segmentation. Med. Image Anal. **17**(2), 194–208 (2013)
12. Awate, S.P., Zhu, P., Whitaker, R.T.: How many templates does it take for a good segmentation?: error analysis in multiatlas segmentation as a function of database size. In: Yap, P.-T., Liu, T., Shen, D., Westin, C.-F., Shen, L. (eds.) MBIA 2012. LNCS, vol. 7509, pp. 103–114. Springer, Heidelberg (2012)
13. Tibshirani, R.: Regression shrinkage and selection via the lasso. J. R. Stat. Soc. Ser. B (Methodol.) **58**, 267–288 (1996)
14. Slawski, M., Hein, M.: Sparse recovery by thresholded non-negative least squares. Adv. Neural Inf. Process. Syst. **24**, 1926–1934 (2011)
15. Heinrich, M.P., Papież, B.W., Schnabel, J.A., Handels, H.: Multispectral image registration based on local canonical correlation analysis. In: Golland, P., Hata, N., Barillot, C., Hornegger, J., Howe, R. (eds.) MICCAI 2014, Part I. LNCS, vol. 8673, pp. 202–209. Springer, Heidelberg (2014)
16. He, K., Sun, J., Tang, X.: Guided image filtering. IEEE Trans. Pattern Anal. Mach. Intell. **35**(6), 1397–1409 (2013)
17. Hanbury, A., Müller, H., Langs, G., Weber, M.A., Menze, B.H., Fernandez, T.S.: Bringing the algorithms to the data: cloud–based benchmarking for medical image analysis. In: Catarci, T., Forner, P., Hiemstra, D., Peñas, A., Santucci, G. (eds.) CLEF 2012. LNCS, vol. 7488, pp. 24–29. Springer, Heidelberg (2012)
18. Heinrich, M.P., Jenkinson, M., Brady, M., Schnabel, J.A.: MRF-based deformable registration and ventilation estimation of lung CT. IEEE Trans. Med. Imaging **32**(7), 1239–1248 (2013)
19. Heinrich, M.P., Jenkinson, M., Papież, B.W., Brady, S.M., Schnabel, J.A.: Towards realtime multimodal fusion for image-guided interventions using self-similarities. In: Mori, K., Sakuma, I., Sato, Y., Barillot, C., Navab, N. (eds.) MICCAI 2013, Part I. LNCS, vol. 8149, pp. 187–194. Springer, Heidelberg (2013)

A Spatially Constrained Deep Learning Framework for Detection of Epithelial Tumor Nuclei in Cancer Histology Images

Korsuk Sirinukunwattana[1], Shan E. Ahmed Raza[1], Yee-Wah Tsang[2],
David Snead[2], Ian Cree[2], and Nasir Rajpoot[3(✉)]

[1] Department of Computer Science, University of Warwick, Coventry, UK
{k.sirinukunwattana,s.e.a.raza}@warwick.ac.uk
[2] Department of Histopathology, University Hospital of Coventry and Warwickshire,
Coventry, UK
{yeewah.tsang,david.snead,ian.cree}@uhcw.nhs.uk
[3] Department of Computer Science and Engineering, Qatar University, Doha, Qatar
nasir.rajpoot@ieee.org

Abstract. Detection of epithelial tumor nuclei in standard Hematoxylin & Eosin stained histology images is an essential step for the analysis of tissue architecture. The problem is quite challenging due to the high chromatin texture of the tumor nuclei and their irregular size and shape. In this work, we propose a spatially constrained convolutional neural network (CNN) for the detection of malignant epithelial nuclei in histology images. Given an input patch, the proposed CNN is trained to regress, for every pixel in the patch, the probability of being the center of an epithelial tumor nucleus. The estimated probability values are topologically constrained such that high probability values are concentrated in the vicinity of the center of nuclei. The location of local maxima is then used as a cue for the final detection. Experimental results show that the proposed network outperforms the conventional CNN with center-pixel-only regression for the task of epithelial tumor nuclei detection.

Keywords: Cancer nuclei detection · Spatially constrained regression · Convolutional neural networks

1 Introduction

The study of tissue architecture is as important as the molecular profile for cancer grading and prognosis [1]. Morphology and organization of epithelial cells in the tumor microenvironment are of interest to many researchers as malignant tumors arising from the epithelium (adenocarcinomas) are the most common form of cancers treated worldwide [2]. In this paper, we focus on the detection of epithelial tumor cells.

Recently published cell or nucleus detection methods rely on symmetry and stability of the cellular (nuclear) region and mainly focus on the detection of

© Springer International Publishing Switzerland 2015
G. Wu et al. (Eds.): Patch-MI 2015, LNCS 9467, pp. 154–162, 2015.
DOI: 10.1007/978-3-319-28194-0_19

regular shaped cells (nuclei) in the tissue [3–6]. These methods are likely to fail to detect epithelial tumor nuclei due to their atypical characteristics, such as irregularity in size and shape, and non-uniform chromatin texture. Ali *et al.* [7] proposed an active contour based approach to detect and segment overlapping nuclei based on shape, which is highly variable in the case of tumor nuclei. More recently, convolutional neural networks (CNNs) have become the method of choice due to their success in a number of applications in computer vision [8,9]. Ciresan *et al.* [8] trained CNNs to regress the probability of belonging to a mitotic figure for each pixel, taking a patch centered at the pixel as context. This approach has a drawback that it does not enforce the pixels close to the center of a nucleus to have a higher probability than those further away and results in poor detection results in case of epithelial tumor nuclei, as shown later in this paper, due to the challenges mentioned above.

In this paper, we introduce a new type of CNN layer, which is specifically designed for spatially constrained regression. Taking nucleus detection as the main task, we trained the spatially constrained CNN to predict the probability of a pixel being the center of an epithelial tumor nucleus, and the predicted probability values are topologically constrained such that high probability values are concentrated in the vicinity of the center of nuclei. The proposed method has been evaluated on breast and colon cancer datasets. As compared to its center-pixel-only regression counterpart [8], the proposed method shows a promising performance, despite the challenging nature of the problem.

2   Method

2.1   The Standard Convolutional Neural Network

A convolutional neural network (CNN) f is a composition of a sequence of L functions or layers $(f_1, .., f_L)$ that maps an input vector $\mathbf{x}$ to an output vector $\mathbf{y}$, i.e.,

$$\mathbf{y} = f(\mathbf{x}; \mathbf{w}_1, ..., \mathbf{w}_L)$$
$$= f_L(\,\cdot\,; \mathbf{w}_L) \circ f_{L-1}(\,\cdot\,; \mathbf{w}_{L-1}) \circ ... \circ f_2(\,\cdot\,; \mathbf{w}_2) \circ f_1(\mathbf{x}; \mathbf{w}_1), \qquad (1)$$

where $\mathbf{w}_l$ is the weight vector for the lth layer f_l. Conventionally, f_l is defined to perform one of the following operations: (a) convolution with a bank of filters; (b) spatial pooling; and (c) non-linear activation. Given a set of N training data $\{(\mathbf{x}^{(i)}, \mathbf{y}^{(i)})\}_{i=1}^{N}$, we can estimate the weight vectors $\mathbf{w}_1, .., \mathbf{w}_L$ by solving the optimization problem

$$\arg\min_{\mathbf{w}_1, ..., \mathbf{w}_L} \frac{1}{N} \sum_{i=1}^{N} \ell(f(\mathbf{x}^{(i)}; \mathbf{w}_1, ..., \mathbf{w}_L), \mathbf{y}^{(i)}), \qquad (2)$$

where ℓ is an appropriately defined loss function. Numerical optimization of (2) is often performed via backpropagation and stochastic gradient descent methods.

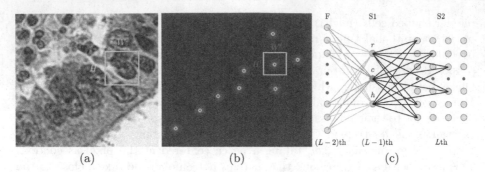

(a)   (b)   (c)

Fig. 1. An illustration of the proposed spatially constrained CNN. (a) An input patch $\mathbf{x}$ of size $H \times W$ is extracted from an image. (b) A training output patch $\mathbf{y}$ of size $H' \times W'$ is extracted from a probability map showing the probability of being the center of nuclei. (c) An illustration of the last three layers of the proposed CNN. Here, F is the fully connected layer, S1 is the new parameter estimation layer, S2 is the spatially constrained layer, and L is the total number of layers in the network.

2.2 Spatially Constrained Regression

In regression analysis, given a pair of input $\mathbf{x}$ and output $\mathbf{y}$, the task is to estimate a function g that represents the relationship between both variables. The output $\mathbf{y}$, however, may not only depend on the input $\mathbf{x}$ alone, but also on the topological domain (time, spatial domain, etc.) on which it is residing.

Let Ω be the spatial domain of $\mathbf{y}$, and suppose that the spatially constrained regression model g is known *a priori*, and is of the form

$$\mathbf{y} = g(\Omega; \boldsymbol{\theta}(\mathbf{x})), \tag{3}$$

where $\boldsymbol{\theta}(\mathbf{x})$ is an unknown parameter vector. We can employ CNN to estimate $\boldsymbol{\theta}(\mathbf{x})$ by extending the standard CNN such that the last two layers (f_{L-1}, f_L) of the network are defined as

$$\boldsymbol{\theta}(\mathbf{x}) = f_{L-1}(\mathbf{x}_{L-2}; \mathbf{w}_{L-1}), \tag{4}$$
$$\mathbf{y} = g(\Omega; \boldsymbol{\theta}(\mathbf{x})), \tag{5}$$

where $\mathbf{x}_{L-2}$ is an output of the $(L-2)$th layer of the network, (4) is the new parameter estimation layer and (5) is the layer imposing the spatial constraints.

2.3 Tumor Nucleus Detection Using a Spatially Constrained CNN

Given an image patch $\mathbf{x} \in \mathbb{R}^{H \times W \times D}$ with its height H, width W, and the number of its features D, our aim is to detect the center of a nucleus contained in $\mathbf{x}$ (Fig. 1a). To tackle this problem, we first define the training output $\mathbf{y} \in [0, 1]^{H' \times W'}$ as a probability map of size $H' \times W'$ (Fig. 1b). Let $\Omega = \{1, ..., H'\} \times \{1, ..., W'\}$ be the spatial domain of $\mathbf{y}$. The jth element of $\mathbf{y}$, $j = 1, ..., |\Omega|$, is defined as

$$y_j = \begin{cases} \frac{1}{1+(\|\mathbf{z}_j - \mathbf{z}_0\|_2^2)/2} & \text{if } \|\mathbf{z}_j - \mathbf{z}_0\|_2 \leq d, \\ 0 & \text{otherwise,} \end{cases} \tag{6}$$

where $\mathbf{z}_j$ and $\mathbf{z}_0$ denotes the coordinates of y_j and the center of the nucleus on Ω, respectively, and d is a constant radius. Pictorially, the probability map defined by (6) has a high peak in the vicinity of the center of the nucleus $\mathbf{z}_0$ and flat elsewhere.

Next, we define the predicted output $\hat{\mathbf{y}}$, generated from the spatially constrained layer (S2, the Lth layer) of the network (Fig. 1c). Following the known structure of the probability map in the training output described in (6), we define the jth element of the predicted output $\hat{\mathbf{y}}$ as

$$\hat{y}_j = g(\mathbf{z}_j; \hat{\mathbf{z}}_0, h) = \begin{cases} \left(\frac{1}{1+(\|\mathbf{z}_j - \hat{\mathbf{z}}_0\|_2^2)/2} \right) h & \text{if } \|\mathbf{z}_j - \hat{\mathbf{z}}_0\|_2 \leq d, \\ 0 & \text{otherwise,} \end{cases} \tag{7}$$

where $\hat{\mathbf{z}}_0 \in \Omega$ is an estimated center of the probability mask and $h \in [0, 1]$ is a weight that allows $\hat{\mathbf{y}}$ to become zero in case there is no nuclei present in $\mathbf{x}$. In our experiments, we set d in (6) and (7) to 4 pixels.

The parameters $\hat{\mathbf{z}}_0 = (r, c)$ and h are estimated in the parameter estimation layer (S1, the $(L-1)$th layer, as shown in Fig. 1c). Let $\mathbf{x}_{L-2}$ be the output of the $(L-2)$th layer of the network. We define r, c, h as

$$r = (H' - 1) \cdot sigm(\mathbf{W}_{L-1,r} \cdot \mathbf{x}_{L-2} + b_r) + 1, \tag{8}$$
$$c = (W' - 1) \cdot sigm(\mathbf{W}_{L-1,c} \cdot \mathbf{x}_{L-2} + b_c) + 1, \tag{9}$$
$$h = sigm(\mathbf{W}_{L-1,h} \cdot \mathbf{x}_{L-2} + b_h), \tag{10}$$

where $\mathbf{W}_{L-1,r}, \mathbf{W}_{L-1,c}, \mathbf{W}_{L-1,h}$ denote the weight vectors and b_r, b_c, b_h denote the bias variables, and $sigm(\cdot)$ denotes the sigmoid function.

To learn all the variables (i.e., weight vectors and bias values) in the network, we solve (2) using the following loss function:

$$\ell(\mathbf{y}, \hat{\mathbf{y}}) = \sum_j (y_j + \epsilon) H(y_j, \hat{y}_j), \tag{11}$$

where $H(y_j, \hat{y}_j)$ is the cross-entropy loss defined by

$$H(y_j, \hat{y}_j) = -\left[y_j \log(\hat{y}_j) - (1 - y_j) \log(1 - \hat{y}_j) \right], \tag{12}$$

and ϵ is a small constant, which is set to be the ratio of the total number of non-zero probability pixels and zero probability pixels in the training output data. The first term of the product in (11) is a weight term that penalizes the loss contributed by the output pixels with small probability. This is crucial as, in the training output data, there are a large number of pixels with zero probability as compared to the non-zero probability ones.

Finally, to detect the center of epithelial tumor nuclei from a big image, we use the sliding window strategy with overlapping windows. Since we use

Table 1. Architecture of the spatially constrained CNN. The network consists of input (I), convolution (C), max-pooling (M), fully-connected (F), parameter estimation (S1), and spatial regression (S2) layers. All convolution layers and the first fully-connected layer are followed by rectified linear unit activation.

Layer	Type	Colorectal cancer		MITOS-ATYPIA	
		Filter dimensions	Input/Output dimensions	Filter dimensions	Input/Output dimensions
0	I		27×27×4		35×35×4
1	C	4×4×4×36	24×24×36	6×6×4×36	30×30×36
2	M	2×2	12×12×36	2×2	15×15×36
3	C	3×3×36×48	10×10×48	4×4×36×48	12×12×48
4	M	2×2	5×5×48	2×2	6×6×48
5	F	5×5×48×1000	1000	6×6×48×1000	1000
6	F	1×1×1000×500	500	1×1×1000×500	500
7	S1	1×1×500×3	3	1×1×500×3	3
8	S2		11×11		11×11

full-patch regression, the predicted probability of being the center of a tumor nucleus is generated for each of the extracted patches using (7). These results are then aggregated to form a probability map. That is, for each pixel location, we average the probability values from all the patches containing that pixel. The final detection is obtained from the local maxima found in the probability map.

3   Experimental Results

The Datasets. To evaluate the proposed detection algorithm for epithelial tumor nuclei, we use the following two datasets. First, the MITOS-ATYPIA dataset[1] consists of images of H&E stained breast cancer tissues. We cropped 30 images of size 512×458 pixels from the dataset. Cancer epithelial nuclei in this dataset exhibit a high degree of nuclear atypia, often appearing hollow inside, and have a weakly stained boundary. Second, the Colorectal Cancer (CRC) dataset consists of 15 images of H&E stained colon cancer tissue of size 301×301 pixels. The cancer epithelial nuclei highly overlap each other in this dataset. The images in both datasets are at 20× optical magnification. For the MITOS-ATYPIA dataset, epithelial tumor nuclei were annotated by one of the authors and cross-validated by a trained pathologist, whereas, for the CRC datset, cancer cells were annotated by a trained pathologist. The detection of epithelial tumor nuclei in both datasets is fairly challenging due to the nature of the malignant epithelial nucleus as describe above.

---

[1] http://mitos-atypia-14.grand-challenge.org/.

Table 2. Detection results. Best results are in bold.

Dataset	Method	P	R	$F1$
MITOS-ATYPIA	Spatially constrained CNN	**0.707**	**0.845**	**0.770**
	Center-of-the-Pixel CNN [8]	0.467	0.594	0.523
Colon	Spatially constrained CNN	**0.731**	**0.778**	**0.754**
	Center-of-the-Pixel CNN [8]	0.366	0.416	0.389

Implementation Details and Experimental Settings. Table 1 shows the detailed architecture of the spatially constrained CNNs used in our experiments. A rectified linear unit (ReLU) activation function was used after each convolution layer and the first fully connected layer. We implemented the proposed CNN using MatConvNet [10].

The input features to the network for each patch are L*a*b* intensities, and Hematoxylin intensity, obtained by a recently proposed color deconvolution method [11]. To alleviate the rotation-variant problem of the input features, we augmented the training data through arbitrary rotation and mirroring. The cutoff values for local maxima are empirically determined on the training set.

Evaluation. Precision (P), Recall (R), and F1-score $(F1)$ were used to quantitatively assess the detection performance. Here, we define the region within the radius of 8 pixels from the annotated center of the nuclei as ground truth. If there are multiple detections within the same ground truth region, only the one closest to the annotated center is considered as true positive.

Results and Discussion. From the visual inspection of the probability maps generated by the proposed method (Fig. 2b), we found that pixels with high probability values are mostly located in the vicinity of the center of nuclei, as imposed by the spatial constraint in (7). Probability maps generated by the center-of-the-pixel CNN [8], on the other hand, exhibit a wider spread of pixels with high probabilities away from the center of nuclei (results are not presented). The compact areas of pixels with high probability values result in a more accurate detection of cancer cells as shown in Table 2. The reported results are from 3-fold cross validation experiments on each of the datasets. Furthermore, on a detailed visual inspection, we found that the proposed method can also detect epithelial tumor nuclei that were missed by the human observer (see cyan rectangle and its close-up on the lower right corner of Fig. 2c, top). It also performs fairly well in cases where nuclei are partly occluded (see cyan rectangle and its close-up on the lower right corner of Fig. 2c, bottom).

A direct comparison of our method with other state-of-the-art algorithms on cell (nucleus) detection would not be appropriate, as these methods assume symmetry of cells (nuclei) [5], or assume that cells (nuclei) appear in the maximally stable extremal region (MSER) [3,12]. However, these assumptions do not hold

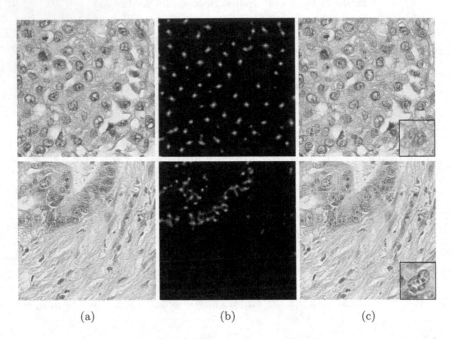

(a)   (b)   (c)

Fig. 2. Example of qualitative results generated by the proposed method on MITOS-ATYPIA (top) and CRC (bottom) datasets: (a) an example image; (b) a corresponding probability map; (c) detection results. In (c), detection results are shown as green dots and the ground truth areas are shown as yellow circles. A cyan rectangle shows a nucleus with weakly stained boundary (top), and overlapping cells (bottom). A close-up of the area inside a cyan rectangle is shown at the lower right corner of the figure (Color figure online).

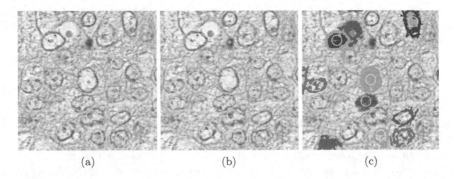

(a)   (b)   (c)

Fig. 3. Detection results generated by (a) spatially constrained CNN, (b) LIPSyM [5], and (c) MSER [12]. In (a)–(b), detection results are shown as green dots and the ground truth areas are shown as yellow circles. In (c), regions detected by MSER are shown in different colors (Color figure online).

true in case of epithelial tumor nucleus detection. This is clearly shown in Fig. 3, where the methods used by [3,5] failed to detect epithelial tumor nuclei.

4   Conclusions

In this work, we proposed a patch-based method for epithelial tumor nucleus detection based on a new design of CNN. Here, we incorporated spatially constrained layers which enforce the known structure of nuclei in the network output. We trained the proposed spatially constrained CNN to regress, for every pixel in a patch, the probability of being the center of a nucleus, where pixels in the vicinity of the center of nuclei must have higher probability values than those further away. Experiments conducted on two fairly challenging datasets of H&E stained histology images have shown quite promising results.

Acknowledgements. This paper was made possible by NPRP grant number NPRP5-1345-1-228 from the Qatar National Research Fund (a member of Qatar Foundation). The statements made herein are solely the responsibility of the authors.

References

1. Yuan, Y., Failmezger, H., Rueda, O.M., Ali, H.R., Gräf, S., Chin, S.F., Schwarz, R.F., Curtis, C., Dunning, M.J., Bardwell, H., et al.: Quantitative image analysis of cellular heterogeneity in breast tumors complements genomic profiling. Sci. Trans. Med. 4(157), 157ra143 (2012)
2. Stewart, B.W., Wild, C.: World cancer report 2014. International Agnecy for Research on Cancer (2014)
3. Arteta, C., Lempitsky, V., Noble, J.A., Zisserman, A.: Learning to detect cells using non-overlapping extremal regions. In: Ayache, N., Delingette, H., Golland, P., Mori, K. (eds.) MICCAI 2012, Part I. LNCS, vol. 7510, pp. 348–356. Springer, Heidelberg (2012)
4. Cosatto, E., Miller, M., Graf, H.P., Meyer, J.S.: Grading nuclear pleomorphism on histological micrographs. In: 19th International Conference on Pattern Recognition, ICPR 2008, pp. 1–4. IEEE (2008)
5. Kuse, M., Wang, Y.F., Kalasannavar, V., Khan, M., Rajpoot, N.: Local isotropic phase symmetry measure for detection of beta cells and lymphocytes. J. Pathol. Inf. 2(2), 2 (2011)
6. Veta, M., van Diest, P.J., Kornegoor, R., Huisman, A., Viergever, M.A., Pluim, J.P.W.: Automatic nuclei segmentation in H&E stained breast cancer histopathology images. PLoS ONE 8(7), e70221 (2013)
7. Ali, S., Madabhushi, A.: An integrated region-, boundary-, shape-based active contour for multiple object overlap resolution in histological imagery. IEEE Trans. Med. Imaging 31(7), 1448–1460 (2012)
8. Cireşan, D.C., Giusti, A., Gambardella, L.M., Schmidhuber, J.: Mitosis detection in breast cancer histology images with deep neural networks. In: Mori, K., Sakuma, I., Sato, Y., Barillot, C., Navab, N. (eds.) MICCAI 2013, Part II. LNCS, vol. 8150, pp. 411–418. Springer, Heidelberg (2013)

9. Krizhevsky, A., Sutskever, I., Hinton, G.E.: Imagenet classification with deep convolutional neural networks. In: Advances in Neural Information Processing Systems, pp. 1097–1105 (2012)
10. Vedaldi, A., Lenc, K.: MatConvNet - convolutional neural networks for MATLAB. abs/1412.4564 (2014)
11. Khan, A.M., Rajpoot, N., Treanor, D., Magee, D.: A nonlinear mapping approach to stain normalization in digital histopathology images using image-specific color deconvolution. IEEE Trans. Biomed. Eng. **61**(6), 1729–1738 (2014)
12. Matas, J., Chum, O., Urban, M., Pajdla, T.: Robust wide-baseline stereo from maximally stable extremal regions. Image Vis. Comput. **22**(10), 761–767 (2004)

3D MRI Denoising Using Rough Set Theory and Kernel Embedding Method

Ashish Phophalia$^{(\boxtimes)}$ and Suman K. Mitra

Dhirubhai Ambani Institute of Information and Communication Technology,
Gandhinagar 382007, Gujarat, India
{ashish_phophalia,suman_mitra}@daiict.ac.in

Abstract. In this paper, we have presented a manifold embedding based method for denoising volumetric MRI data. The proposed method via kernel mapping tries to find linearity among data in the projection/feature space. Prior to kernel mapping, a Rough Set Theory (RST) based clustering technique has been used with extension to volumetric data. RST clustering method groups similar voxels (3D cubes) using class and edge information. The basis vector representation of each cluster is then explored in the Kernel space via Principal Component Analysis (known as KPCA). The work has been compared with state-of-the-art methods under various measures for synthetic and real databases.

Keywords: Image denoising · Magnetic resonance imaging · Rough set theory

1 Introduction

Being a non-invasive technique, Magnetic Resonance Imaging (MRI) is widely used modality (along with X-Ray, CT, etc.) for clinical diagnosis. The acquisition process of medical images is highly sensitive to get accumulated with noise or undesired signals. It has been shown that the noise in Magnetic Resonance (MR) Image is Rician in nature [7]. It has been shown that the intensities of MR images are magnitude of underlying complex data following Rice distribution [6,7]. The real and imaginary parts are modeled as being independently distributed Gaussian with means a_r and a_i respectively, with same variance σ^2. The rician random variable y with PDF can be defined as follows:
$f_Y(y|a,\sigma) = \frac{y}{\sigma^2}e^{\left(-\frac{y^2+a^2}{2\sigma^2}\right)}I_0\left(\frac{ya}{\sigma^2}\right), y > 0$, where $a = \sqrt{a_r^2 + a_i^2}$ is underlying noise free signal amplitude and $I_n(z)$ is n^{th} order modified bessel function of first kind. Let SNR be the signal to noise ratio (here, it is a/σ). When SNR is high, the Rician distribution approaches to Gaussian; when SNR approaches to zero (that is only noise is present, $a \to 0$) the Rician distribution becomes Rayleigh distribution and the PDF becomes $f_Y(y|a \to 0, \sigma) = \frac{y}{\sigma^2}e^{\left(-\frac{y^2}{2\sigma^2}\right)}$.

Many state-of-the-art methods for 3D image denoising are extension of their 2D counterpart version. However, computational complexity becomes a crucial

© Springer International Publishing Switzerland 2015
G. Wu et al. (Eds.): Patch-MI 2015, LNCS 9467, pp. 163–171, 2015.
DOI: 10.1007/978-3-319-28194-0_20

factor during the extension. The 3D MR image denoising was introduced in modern literature in [5] and then followed by [4,8–10,14,16] etc. Instead of playing with patches in 2D images, here a voxel is defined as 3D cube centered at location (i, j, k) in $\mathcal{R}^3$. Hence, a voxel is simply counterpart of a patch with size $w \times w \times w$. Consequently, exploring relationship among intensity values in $\mathcal{R}^3$ is highly sought and thus leads to computational intensive process. There have been many denoising/restoration methods proposed for Medical Images ranging from diffusion filters to dictionary and clustering based filters.

The Non Local Means (NLM) method [1] has been extended to Optimized Blockwise NLM (OBNLM, [5]) for volumetric data. It tweaks the computation of similarity weight between voxels and constrained with predefined criteria for mean and variance of both the voxels. At the same time, it adopted the blockwise strategy to drop restoration of adjacent n voxels which effectively reduce the computation load by n^3 times instead of processing each voxel in the image space. The same has been adopted in [4,8]. In case of ABONLM method [4], denoising is performed under Wavelet framework using adaptive soft wavelet coefficient mixing (ASCM) approach. A non-parametric kernel regression framework has been adopted for 3D MR image denoising in Unbiased Kernel Regression (UKR) method [14]. UKR is rooted on a zeroth order 3D kernel regression and similarity weight between voxels is derived on small sized feature vectors based image intensity and gradient information. The sparseness and self-similarity has been unified in PRI-NLM method [10]. It incorporates rotational invariant NLM and discrete cosine transform hard thresholding for sparsity.

The well-known BM3D method has been extended to 3D MR image denoising as BM4D method [8]. Similar to BM3D, BM4D is also equipped with collaborative filtering notion where similar voxels are arranged in fourth dimension. It is also a two stage method where the output of first stage guides the second stage and uses hard thresholding in first pass and wiener filtering in second pass. Ideally, BM4D is designed for Gaussian noise whereas Variance Stabilization Technique (VST) has been adopted to deal with Rician noise in 3D MRI data. The VST based scheme is also adopted in two phased HOSVD-R method [16]. Recently, another two stage method PRI-NL-PCA [9] was proposed based on sparsity and self-similarity of voxels. It is encompassed with PCA thresholding strategy in first stage where rotational invariant NLM method is deployed in second stage. In this paper, we present manifold embedding based method for MR image denoising. A nonparametric variant of PCA, known as Kernal Principal Component Analysis (KPCA) has been explored for Rician noise removal. The KPCA tries to explore the structure in the data in Feature space instead of data space itself and tries to capture higher-order dependencies in the data.

This paper is organized as follows: Sect. 2 discusses RST based clustering approach followed by overview of Kernel Principal Component Analysis. The proposed method in presented last in Sect. 2. Section 3 presents simulation results of proposed method along with state-of-the-art-method on phantom and real MRI data. The manuscript is concluded in Sect. 4.

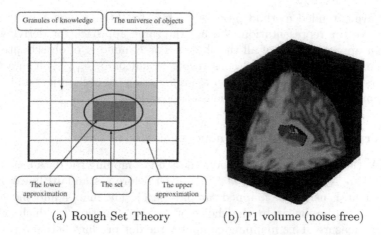

(a) Rough Set Theory   (b) T1 volume (noise free)

Fig. 1. (a) Image granules with upper and lower approximation of an object as conceptualized in Rough Set Theory and (b) Noise free T1 volume data from BrianWeb Database [3].

2   Material and Methods

2.1   Rough Set Based Cluster Formation

Rough Set Theory (RST) can be utilized to explore structural similarity between pixel or set of pixels even in the presence of noise. This classification is defined on predefined attribute(s), Θ, by forming granules within the image space, Ω. This indeed establishes an equivalence classes among the data based on attributes. Rough sets define a class by approximating two sets, namely lower approximation and upper approximation sets of a class with respect to an attribute(s). The lower approximation set of class w.r.t. attribute(s), $\underline{C}_\Theta$, consists of certainly classified granules of Ω whereas the upper approximation set of class with respect to attribute(s), $\overline{C}_\Theta$, constructed by possible granules of that class defined by attribute(s), Θ [12]. The figurative description is given in Fig. 1.

Rough set based derivation of class label (RCL) information and edge details (REM) have been derived in [13]. For given attribute(s), granules can be classified in either lower or upper approximation of an object. The attribute considered is the intensity values at each location in the image space. The objects present in the image are categorized in intensity range by optimizing image histogram. The Rough set based entropy criteria [12] was used in optimizing intensity thresholds. The class label can be assigned by comparing intensity value at each location against the intensity ranges of all the objects. A granule (set of adjacent pixels) is assigned to an object's lower if all the pixels fall in its intensity range. Otherwise it will assign in object's upper approximation only if any pixel in that granule belongs to intensity range. The difference of both the approximations of any objects will generate pixels which are possible edges of the object in the image. Thus, union of all such edges will generate edge map of the image.

We have extended method proposed in [13] to 3D imaging. A voxel is converted to vector representation. We use the same approach for deriving lower and upper approximation of all the objects. For K number of objects present in the image, the number of pool constructed would be $\sum_{i=1}^{K} \binom{K}{i}$. There will be K clusters corresponding to K lower approximations of each object and rest are union approximations of combinations of the objects.

2.2　Kernel Principal Component Analysis

In KPCA, the non-linearity is introduced by first mapping the data into another space F using a nonlinear map $\Phi : R^N \rightarrow F$, before a standard linear PCA is carried out in F using the mapped samples $\phi(x_k)$. The map Φ and the space F are determined implicitly by the choice of a kernel function k, which acts as a similarity measure. This mapping computes the dot product between two input samples x and y mapped into F via

$$k(x; y) = \Phi(x).\Phi(y) \tag{1}$$

One can show that if k is a positive definite kernel, then there exists a map Φ into a dot product space F such that Eq. 1 holds. The space F then has the structure of a Reproducing Kernel Hilbert Space (RKHS) [2]. Equation 1 is important for KPCA since PCA in F can be formulated entirely in terms of inner products of the mapped samples. This has two important consequences: first, inner products in F can be evaluated without computing $\Phi(x)$ explicitly. This allows to work with a very high-dimensional, possibly infinite-dimensional RKHS F. Second, if a positive definite kernel function is specified, we need to know neither Φ nor F explicitly to perform KPCA since only inner products are used in the computations.

In PCA, the covariance matrix is defined as $C = \frac{1}{N-1} X^t X$ where is X is called data matrix containing samples in columns. The covariance matrix in case of KPCA of size $M \times M$, calculated by $C_F = \frac{1}{N} \sum_{i=1}^{N} \phi(\mathbf{x}_i)\phi(\mathbf{x}_i)^T$. Its eigenvalues and eigenvectors are given by $C_F \mathbf{v}_k = \lambda_k \mathbf{v}_k$, where $k = 1, 2, \ldots, M$. Mathematical simplification leads to $\mathbf{v}_k = \sum_{i=1}^{N} a_{ki}\phi(x_i)$ and hence $\mathbf{a}_k$ (N-dimensional column vector of a_{ki}) can be solved by $C_F \mathbf{a}_k = \lambda_k N \mathbf{a}_k$. If projected dataset $\phi(\mathbf{x}_i)$ does not have zero mean, one can use Gram matrix $\tilde{C}_F$ to substitute the kernel matrix C_F which is given by $\tilde{C}_F = C_F - 1_N C_F - C_F 1_N + 1_N C_F 1_N$, where 1_N is the $N \times N$ matrix with all elements equal to $1/N$.

2.3　Proposed Method

MRI data is corrupted with rician noise which is not additive in nature, hence, it is expected in this work that transformation of data into high dimensional space may rise to linearity of data. This work cascades clustering method and manifold embedding method. We derive clusters of similar voxels based on classes present in those. Then KPCA finds the linearity in the higher dimensional space. To denoising voxels, each voxel is projected on the corresponding class basis vectors

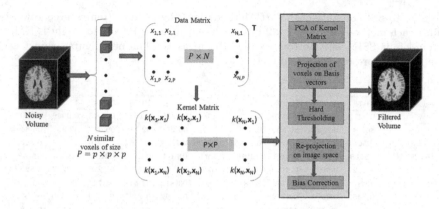

Fig. 2. Flowchart of proposed method

and coefficients below threshold are truncated assumed as noise part in the data. The voxels are reprojected in the image space via invertible basis vectors and bias correction is performed. Figure 2 shows flow of proposed method. The outline of present work can be described as follows:

1. Get the clusters of voxels $(p \times p \times p)$ from the given noisy image using Rough set based method (as described in [13]).
2. For each cluster, get the basis vectors using KPCA method along pixel positions. For cluster matrix of size $p^3 \times N$, kernel matrix would be of size $p^3 \times p^3$, where N is number of voxels in the cluster.
3. Project the noisy image voxels on the obtained basis vectors in the KPCA domain. Apply coefficient shrinkage method on these projected voxels to get the denoised voxels. Transform them back to image space.
4. Remove the bias term from each pixel of the denoised image i.e. $\hat{I}_{unbiased}(i,j,k) = \sqrt{max(\hat{I}(i,j,k)^2 - 2h^2, 0)}$, where h is the standard deviation of noise and $\hat{I}$ is the image obtained by step (4).

3   Experimental Section

This Section encompasses the qualitative and quantitative evaluation of the proposed method along with some of the state-of-the-art methods. The experiments have been carried out on 3D monochrome phantom human brain MRI images obtained from Brain Web Database [3]. The parameters are as follows: Modality = T1, RF = 0, protocol = ICBM, slice thickness = 1 mm, volume size = $181 \times 217 \times 181$ (shown in Fig. 1b). The skull portion have been from the volume and considered four classes: (a) White Matter, (b) Gray matter, (c) Cerebrospinal Fluid and (d) Background. The evaluation measures used are Peak-Signal-to-Noise Ratio (PSNR), Root Mean Square Error (RMSE), Structural

Table 1. Results of state-of-the-art Methods for T1 modality (represented row-wise against each method). In each 2×2 block, top-left figure is PSNR, top-right is RMSE, bottom-left is SSIM and bottom-right is BC measure. The best figure against each noise level is represented in Bold face.

$h \rightarrow$	5		10		15		20		25	
Noise	31.78	06.57	25.76	13.13	22.25	19.69	19.75	26.24	17.82	32.77
	0.3473	0.3497	0.2170	0.2910	0.1583	0.2859	0.1209	0.3033	0.0949	0.3207
UKR	36.04	04.02	30.59	07.53	33.72	05.25	32.11	06.32	32.85	05.81
	0.5084	0.5373	0.3359	0.2760	0.6507	0.7809	0.6364	0.8210	0.7762	0.8902
PRI-NLM	**45.16**	**01.41**	**39.95**	**02.56**	**36.91**	03.64	34.84	04.62	**33.27**	**05.53**
	0.9527	0.9009	0.8769	0.8291	0.8129	0.8173	0.7734	0.8276	0.7297	0.8225
BM4D	43.81	06.57	39.17	02.81	36.50	03.81	34.61	04.74	33.14	05.62
	0.9452	0.9008	0.8729	0.8690	0.8167	0.8597	0.7735	0.8549	0.7390	0.8518
PRI-NL-PCA	40.36	02.45	35.01	04.53	32.0	06.41	29.90	08.16	28.32	09.78
	0.6640	0.4699	0.4918	0.5332	0.4243	0.5705	0.3864	0.5930	0.3662	0.6173
RST-KPCA	44.09	01.59	39.45	02.72	36.83	03.67	32.93	05.76	32.11	06.33
	0.9904	**0.9818**	**0.9770**	**0.9760**	**0.9535**	**0.9641**	**0.9446**	**0.9505**	**0.9391**	**0.9446**

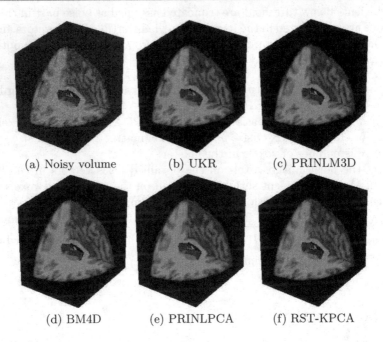

(a) Noisy volume   (b) UKR   (c) PRINLM3D

(d) BM4D   (e) PRINLPCA   (f) RST-KPCA

Fig. 3. Comparison of various methods on T1 from BrainWeb Database

Similarity Index (SSIM) [15] and Bhattacharya Coefficient (BC). The methods used for comparisons are: (a) UKR [14], (b) PRI-NLM [10], (c) BM4D [8], (d) PRI-NL-PCA [9]. In all the experiment, voxels of size $p = 3$ are considered. We have used *simple/linear kernel* only i.e. $k(\mathbf{x}, \mathbf{y}) = \mathbf{x}^T.\mathbf{y}$. Table 1 shows quantitative results over varying level of Rician noise. It can be observed that our methods outperforms state-of-the-art methods in terms of SSIM and BC

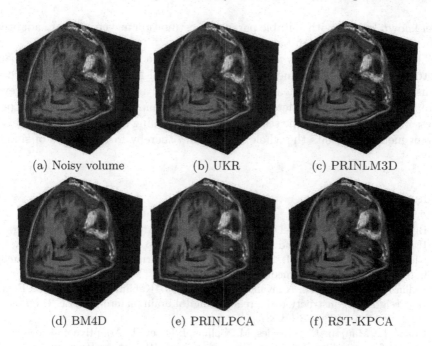

(a) Noisy volume   (b) UKR   (c) PRINLM3D

(d) BM4D   (e) PRINLPCA   (f) RST-KPCA

Fig. 4. Comparison of various methods on subject 018 from OASIS Database

measures. However, our method is behind PRI-NLM method and better than BM4D (at lower noise levels) in terms of PSNR and RMSE measures. Figure 3 shows cross sectional views of denoised volumes from all methods. The proposed method with single threaded MATLAB implementation takes around 45 min on core i7 processor, 2.10 GHz and 8 GB RAM machine. The UKR is observed to have same computational time whereas BM4D with MATLAB/C implementation takes 11 min and others run in less than five minutes.

The subject details from OASIS dataset [11] are as follows: Subject ID: 018, Age: 39 (male) respectively, scan number: mpr-1, type: MPRAGE, voxel resolution: 1.0 mm × 1.0 mm × 1.25 mm, Orientation: Sagittal, TR (ms) = 9.7, TE (ms) = 4.0, TI (ms) = 20.0, Flip angle = 10. The results are shown in Fig. 4 for subject 018 as cross sectional view.

4   Conclusion

Kernel method is explored in this work to deal with Rician noise present in the MRI data. Being signal dependent noise, applicability of linear denoising operation such as PCA is not advisable. It is expected in the present work that kernel method may project the nonlinear data in the linear feature space. We have a extended Rough Set based clustering method to collect similar voxels conditioned on class and edge information. These similar voxels are then used to define kernel matrix via kernel function. However, it can be exercised with other known kernels with suitable parameter estimation method or data adaptive kernel for rician model can be thought of.

The proposed method is non-iterative and single stage method in comparison to some of predecessor methods like BM4D, PRI-NL-PCA etc. In this work, intensity values are used as feature in clustering step and in kernel space however more features can be considered like gradient information as in UKR. The predecessor methods restrict the search space for searching similar voxels. However, current method exploits the whole volume and thereby form clusters of similar voxels.

References

1. Buades, A., Coll, B., Morel, J.M.: A non local algorithm for image denoising. In: IEEE Computer Vision and Pattern Recognition, pp. 60–65 (2005)
2. Charpiat, G., Hofmann, M., Schölkopf, B., et al.: Kernel methods in medical imaging. In: Handbook of Biomedical Imaging (2010)
3. Collins, D.L., Zijdenbos, A., Kollokian, V., Sled, J., Kabani, N., Holmes, C., Evans, A.: Design and construction of a realistic digital brain phantom. IEEE Trans. Med. Imaging **17**(3), 463–468 (1998)
4. Coupé, P., Manjón, J.V., Robles, M., Collins, L.D., et al.: Adaptive multiresolution non-local means filter for 3d mr image denoising. IET Image Process. **6**, 558–568 (2011)
5. Coupe, P., Yger, P., Prima, S., Hellier, P., Kervrann, C., Barillot, C.: An optimized blockwise non local means denoising filter for 3d magnetic resonance images. IEEE Trans. Med. Imaging **27**(4), 425–441 (2008)
6. Foi, A.: Noise estimation, removal in mr imaging: the variance-stabilization approach. In: ISBI, pp. 1809–1814 (2011)
7. Gudbjartsson, H., Patz, S.: The rician distribution of noisy mri data. Magn. Reson. Med. **34**(6), 910–914 (1995)
8. Maggioni, M., Katkovnik, V., Egiazarian, K., Foi, A.: Nonlocal transform domain filter for volumetric data denoising and reconstruction. IEEE Trans. Image Process. **22**(1), 119–133 (2013)
9. Manjón, J.V., Coupé, P., Buades, A.: Mri noise estimation and denoising using non-local pca. Med. Image Anal. **22**(1), 35–47 (2015)
10. Manjón, J.V., Coupé, P., Buades, A., Louis Collins, D., Robles, M.: New methods for mri denoising based on sparseness and self-similarity. Med. Image Anal. **16**(1), 18–27 (2012)
11. Marcus, D.S., Wang, T.H., Parker, J., Csernansky, J.G., Morris, J.C., Buckner, R.L.: Open access series of imaging studies (oasis): cross-sectional mri data in young, middle aged, nondemented, and demented older adults. J. Cogn. Neurosci. **19**(9), 1498–1507 (2007)
12. Pal, S.K., Shankar, B.U., Mitra, P.: Granular computing, rough entropy and object recognition. Pattern Recogn. Lett. **26**, 2509–2517 (2005)
13. Phophalia, A., Rajwade, A., Mitra, S.K.: Rough set based image denoising for brain mr images. Sig. Process. **103**, 24–35 (2014)
14. Rubio, E.L., Nunez, M.N.F.: Kernel regression based feature extraction for 3d mr image denoising. Med. Image Anal. **15**, 498–513 (2011)

15. Wang, Z., Bovik, A.C., Sheikh, H.R., Simoncelli, E.P.: Image quality assessment: From error visibility to structural similarity. IEEE Trans. Image Process. **13**(4), 600–612 (2004)
16. Zhang, X., Xu, Z., Jia, N., Yang, W., Feng, Q., Chen, W., Feng, Y.: Denoising of 3d magnetic resonance images by using higher-order singular value decomposition. Med. Image Anal. **19**(1), 75–86 (2015)

A Novel Cell Orientation Congruence Descriptor for Superpixel Based Epithelium Segmentation in Endometrial Histology Images

Guannan Li[1], Shan E. Ahmed Raza[1], and Nasir Rajpoot[1,2](✉)

[1] Department of Computer Science, University of Warwick, Coventry, UK
Nasir.Rajpoot@ieee.org
[2] Department of Computer Science and Engineering,
Qatar University, Doha, Qatar

Abstract. Recurrent miscarriage can be caused by an abnormally high number of Uterine Natural Killer (UNK) cells in human female uterus lining. Recently a diagnosis protocol has been developed based on the ratio of UNK cells to stromal cells in endometrial biopsy slides immuno-histochemically stained with Haematoxylin for all cells and CD56 as a marker for the UNK cells. The counting of UNK cells and stromal cells is an essential process in the protocol. However, the cell counts must not include epithelial cells from glandular structures and UNK cells from epithelium. In this paper, we propose a novel superpixel based epithelium segmentation algorithm based on the observation that neighbouring epithelial cells packed at the boundary of glandular structures or background tend to have similar local orientations. Our main contribution is a novel cell orientation congruence descriptor in a machine learning framework to differentiate between epithelial and non-epithelial cells.

Keywords: Histology image analysis · Epithelium segmentation · Cell orientation · Superpixels

1 Introduction

Uterine Natural Killer (UNK) cells normally make up no more than 5 % of all cells in the womb lining and it has recently been shown [1] that an over-presence of UNK cells leads to recurrent miscarriage. Thus UNK testing plays a significant role in clinical diagnosis of recurrent miscarriages. The diagnosis protocol devised by Quenby *et al.* in [1] calculates the ratio of UNK cells to stromal cells in histology images of endometrial tissue slides stained with Haematoxylin and CD56, which stains UNK cells brown when used with DAB staining. The task is challenging in that the epithelial cells should not be counted in calculating the ratio, which means that epithelium from glands or luminal epithelium from tissue boundary should be excluded from the counting process. The problems of the detection of UNK and stromal cells, and localisation of luminal epithelium from tissue boundaries were addressed in [2]. However, [2] does not solve the

© Springer International Publishing Switzerland 2015
G. Wu et al. (Eds.): Patch-MI 2015, LNCS 9467, pp. 172–179, 2015.
DOI: 10.1007/978-3-319-28194-0_21

segmentation problem of epithelium from glands. In this paper, we present a method designed for segmenting both glandular epithelium and luminal epithelium (examples are shown in Fig. 1(a)) from tissue boundary.

Existing methods of segmenting glandular structure are mainly based on texture and structure. Farjam et al. [3] proposed a variance filter which produces different texture features on lumen and cell regions and the segmentation is accomplished by clustering the texture features. This method is only capable of segmenting lumen regions in our case, due to epithelium and cell regions having similar texture features. Naik et al. [4] used a Bayesian classifier to detect potential lumens and then initialised level set curve on the boundaries of detected luminal area to finalise the segmentation. The drawback of this method is that level set curve is not capable of approximating epithelium boundaries with complex shape and texture. Nguyen et al. [5] first label nuclei, cytoplasm and lumen by colour space analysis and utilise the constitution of these glandular components to achieve the segmentation. Demir et al. [6] constructed an object graph of a set of circular objects decomposed from the image to identify cell and lumen. Then cell objects are used to form the boundary of glandular structures. Recently, Sirinukunwattana et al. [7] proposed a novel Random Polygons Model (RPM) using epithelial cells as the vertices of a polygon to approximate boundaries of glandular at cost of relatively high computational complexity. A major limitation of such structure-based methods is that they rely on prior knowledge of the glandular structures. In our case, epithelium is characterized by strong inhomogeneity, i.e., discontinuity or multiple layers of epithelial cells.

Epithelium is formed by layers of epithelial cells and identification of these cells is a primary task of the segmentation. Generally, there are not significant distinctive features, in terms of colour and morphology, between epithelial cells and stromal cells. However, we observe that epithelial cells normally surround lumen or are located at the boundary of the background region in a locally and neatly oriented manner. Based on this observation, we propose a novel cell orientation congruence (COC) descriptor using a cell and its neighbours' orientations, which can be used to accurately identify epithelial regions. A major advantage of the proposed algorithm over the above methods is that unlike these methods, our algorithm is not restricted to the detection and segmentation of a closed epithelial structure such as a gland, but it is also capable of segmenting luminal epithelium from the tissue boundary.

2   Materials and Methods

Endometrial biopsies were collected in a clinic at University Hospitals Coventry and Warwickshire NHS Trust from patients suffering from recurrent pregnancy loss or recurrent IVF treatment failure. The biopsy tissue slides are stained with Haematoxylin and CD56 is used as a marker for the UNK cells. More details about the slides preparation can be found in [1]. The image data in our experiment are image regions manually cropped from the high power fields (HPFs) of digitised images of endometrial biopsy slides at 40× resolution.

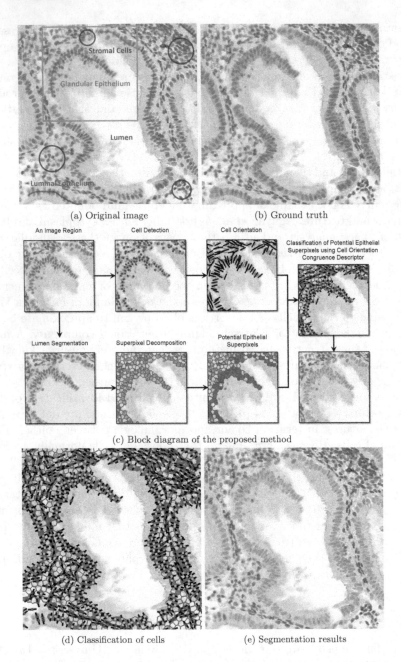

(a) Original image

(b) Ground truth

(c) Block diagram of the proposed method

(d) Classification of cells

(e) Segmentation results

Fig. 1. The cyan window in (a) shows an image region used in (c); ground truth is shown in orange in (b); lumen segmentation is shown in yellow in (c); in (c) and (d), blue dots depict all cells, green dots depict epithelial cells after the classification using the proposed COC descriptor, black bar represents the orientation of a cell, red grids mark superpixels, potential epithelial superpixels are shown in red; and final epithelial segmentation is shown in green in (c) and (e) (Color figure online).

The image regions are saved in the JPEG format with a resolution of $1,700 \times 900$ pixels ($0.25\,\mu m/pixel$).

Figure 1(c) shows a block diagram with the intermediate result of each main step of the proposed method. We first identify lumen and background regions to localise the potential epithelial regions. Second, we detect cells in the potential epithelial regions and compute their cell orientation congruence (COC) descriptors. Third, we perform a two-stage classification process. The first stage is to distinguish epithelial and stomal cells in the potential epithelial regions using their COC descriptors and the second stage is to label true epithelial regions using the epithelial cells. At last, the labelled epithelial regions form the final epithelium segmentation. Experimental results show that the accuracy of the proposed method is competitive compared with 3 state-of-the-art methods.

2.1   Localisation of Potential Epithelial Superpixels

Segmenting epithelial cells is the way of achieving epithelium segmentation. It is difficult to directly segment epithelial cells due to them having very similar stained colour and similar morphological appearances as stromal cells in our case. However, epithelium normally covers the exterior of lumen region or is often located near the non-tissue (background) region. Thus, segmentation of lumen and background regions can be used to locate potential epithelial regions. A sample input image is shown Fig. 1(a).

We first separate the input image into the two underlying stain channels, Haematoxylin and DAB (CD56), using a colour deconvolution method proposed in [8]. The lumen and background regions are segmented on the Haematoxylin channel using a lumen segmentation method proposed in [3], which is based on the observation that lumen and cell regions have distinct local standard deviations. The result of lumen segmentation on an image region from the input image is shown in Fig. 1(c).

Next, we decompose the input image into small image patches, the so-called superpixels using the Simple Linear Iterative Clustering (SLIC) algorithm proposed in [9]. In our cases, the superpixel is a small homogeneous region depicting lumen, background or cell. Superpixels generated on an image region from the input image are shown in Fig. 1(c). We classify superpixels into two types: cell superpixels, which depict either epithelial cell or stromal cell regions, and lumen superpixel, which depict either lumen or background region. We classify a superpixel as lumen superpixel if more than half of its region overlaps with the mask of the lumen mask obtained from the lumen segmentation step, otherwise it is categorised as a cell superpixel. Next, we define that a cell superpixel is a first level potential epithelial superpixel if it immediately connects to lumen superpixels. However, thick epithelium is formed by multiple layers of epithelial cells, a layer of superpixels which immediately connects to lumen superpixels is not enough to represent the epithelium in general. To retrieve as much potential epithelial superpixels as possible, we define that a cell superpixel is a second level potential epithelial superpixel if it immediately connects to the first level epithelial potential superpixels. In addition, we remove a potential epithelial superpixel if more than half of its area is segmented (Otsu thresholding [10]) as non-cell in the Haematoxylin channel, which more likely depicts a background region. The result of potential epithelial superpixel localisation for on an image region from the input image is shown in Fig. 1(c).

2.2   Computation of Cell Orientation Congruency (COC) Descriptor

The Haematoxylin channel of the input image is normalised with zero mean and unit standard deviation in pixel intensities by following the approach introduced in [11]. Let us denote the normalised Haematoxylin channel as $N(i,j)$, where (i,j) denotes pixel coordinates. The directional gradients in x and y directions of $N(i,j)$ are calculated and the local orientation $O(i,j)$ of $N(i,j)$ is estimated as follows,

$$G_{xy}(i,j) = \big((G_x \cdot G_y) \star \Phi\big)(i,j) \tag{1}$$

$$G_{xx}(i,j) = \big(G_x^2 \star \Phi\big)(i,j) \tag{2}$$

$$G_{yy}(i,j) = \big(G_y^2 \star \Phi\big)(i,j) \tag{3}$$

$$O(i,j) = \frac{\pi}{2} + \tan^{-1}\left(\frac{G_{xy}(i,j)}{G_{xx}(i,j) - G_{yy}(i,j)}\right) \tag{4}$$

where $G_x(i,j)$ and $G_y(i,j)$ are gradient images of $N(i,j)$ in x and y direction, respectively, Φ is a 2D Gaussian filter of window size w and standard deviation σ, and $\star$ represents the image convolution operation. $O(i,j)$ is the least squared estimation of the local orientation of $N(i,j)$.

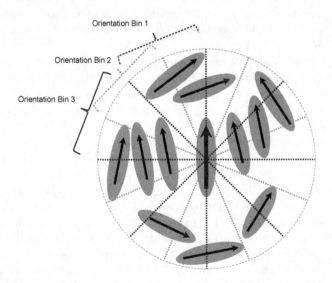

Fig. 2. An illustration of the cell orientation congruence (COC) descriptor. Black arrow represent the orientation vector of a cell.

Li *et al.* in [2] demonstrated that their cell detection method based on phase symmetry attains high accuracy in endometrial histology images. Thus, we employ the detection method in [2] to detect cells in $N(i,j)$. The orientation of a cell with its nucleus centred at the spatial coordinates C is statistically represented by the local orientations using its surrounding pixels as follows:

1. Pixels in a circular neighbourhood with radius α centred at C are sampled, we use $\alpha = 7$ pixels in practice.
2. The local orientation, in radians, of the sampled pixels are rescaled to $[0, \pi]$. To more precisely approximate the cell orientation, we quantise the sampled pixels into seven overlapping orientation bins: $[0, \pi/4]$, $[\pi/8, 3\pi/8]$, $[\pi/4, \pi/2]$, $[3\pi/8, 5\pi/8]$, $[\pi/2, 3\pi/4]$, $[5\pi/8, 7\pi/8]$, $[3\pi/4, \pi]$.
3. The mean of the orientation bin containing the highest number of local orientations is then used to represent the orientation of C, denoted as O_c.

Next, the neighbouring cell detections in a circular neighbourhood with radius λ centred at C are sampled, we use $\lambda = 120$ pixels in practice. The circular neighbourhood is uniformly divided into 16 half overlapping orientation bins of width $\pi/4$. The first bin is from $[O_c, O_c + \pi/4]$, the second bin is $[O_c + \pi/8, O_c + 3\pi/8]$, and so on. An illustration of the overlapping orientation bins is shown in Fig. 2. The cell orientation congruence descriptor of C is then constructed using the orientations of its neighbouring detections as follows,

$$S_d = \sum_{i=1}^{N_d} \Omega_i \cos(\Theta_i) \tag{5}$$

$$\Omega_i = \frac{\omega_i}{\sum_{i=1}^{N_d} \omega_i}, \omega_i = e^{\frac{-D_i^2}{2\sigma^2}} \tag{6}$$

where S_d is the weighted orientation congruence of the d-th orientation bin, N_d is the total number of sampled neighbouring detection in the d-th orientation bin of C, Θ_i is the angle between the orientation vectors of C and the i-th neighbouring detection in the d-th orientation bin, Ω_i is the normalised weight used to indicate the importance of the orientation difference. D_i is the Euclidean distance between C and the i-th neighbouring detection in the d-th orientation bin, and $\sigma = 70$ is used in our case. The cell orientation congruence (COC) descriptor is expressed by a 16 dimensional vector as given below,

$$COC = [S_1, S_2, ..., S_d, ..., S_{16}]^T \tag{7}$$

2.3   Labelling of Epithelial Superpixels

We perform a two-stage classification to distinguish the epithelial and stomal superpixels. First, the cell detections located within potential epithelial superpixels are considered as potential epithelial cell detections. We compute the cell orientation congruence (COC) descriptors of all potential epithelial cells. Then we employ the random forests classifier using the descriptors to classify the potential epithelial cells. These epithelial cells are marked as either false or true. The classification results of epithelial cells are shown in Fig. 1.(d).

Next, a potential epithelial superpixel which contains any false epithelial cell or no cell is initially classified as a non-epithelial superpixel, otherwise it is classified as an epithelial superpixel. A false epithelial superpixel may contain a true epithelial cell, which is also likely to be an epithelial superpixel. A refinement process for the non-epithelial superpixels is performed as follows:

1. Let us denote a non-epithelial superpixel as P, we define that a potential epithelial superpixel which immediately connects to P as level 1 neighbourhood of P, denoted as H_1^i, and a set of level 1 neighbours is denoted as $\{H_1^i\}$;
2. We define that a potential epithelial superpixel which immediately connects to H_1^i and also does not belong to $\{H_1^i\}$ as level 2 neighbourhood of P, denoted as H_2^j, and a set of level 2 neighbours is denoted as $\{H_2^j\}$;
3. We count the number of true epithelial cells and the number of false epithelial cells within P, $\{H_1^i\}$ and $\{H_2^j\}$, denoted as NC_{true} and NC_{false} respectively. Then P is corrected to be an epithelial superpixel if $NC_{true} \geq NC_{false}$, otherwise it remains the same.

The epithelial superpixels after the refinement process are merged to form the final epithelium segmentation. The final segmentation of a sample image in Fig. 1(a) is shown in Fig. 1(e). The ground truth is shown in Fig. 1(b).

3   Results

We calculate the Dice scores of the segmentation results by a gland segmentation accuracy measures introduced in [7] to compare their performance of the proposed method with 3 state-of-the-art methods: [4,5,7]. We trained these methods using 5 sample images and the segmentations using these methods are performed on 30 unseen sample images. Since the algorithms in [4,5,7] are proposed for only segmenting glandular structures, so we remove luminal epithelium (which come from tissue boundaries rather than glands) in the ground truth while calculating the Dice scores. Table 1 shows the segmentation accuracies of the proposed method and the other methods on 30 unseen sample images. The results show that our method offers superior segmentation accuracy compared with [4,5,7].

Table 1. Segmentation accuracies of the proposed method and the other methods on 30 unseen sample images. The Dice scores are reported by the averages ± standard deviations. The best results are in bold.

Methods	Dice	
	Pixel-Level	Object-Level
Naik *et al.* [4]	0.74 ± 0.13	0.73 ± 0.12
Nguyen *et al.* [5]	0.78 ± 0.14	0.76 ± 0.13
Sirinukunwattana *et al.* [7]	0.82 ± 0.08	0.79 ± 0.05
COC (Proposed)	$\mathbf{0.85 \pm 0.07}$	$\mathbf{0.83 \pm 0.06}$

4   Conclusions

In conclusion, we proposed a superpixel based epithelium segmentation method using a novel cell orientation congruence descriptor. The descriptor is used to discriminate between epithelial and stromal cells based on the observation that the epithelial cells in normal endometrium are packed such that their orientation is more or less similar to their neighbouring epithelial cells. The results show that our method attains a good accuracy which is ready to be employed in practice. In future work, we plan to extend the design of the descriptor, e.g., multi-scale nature of the descriptor, and to conduct a large-scale validation of our method.

References

1. Quenby, S., Nik, H., Innes, B., Lash, G., Turner, M., Drury, J., Bulmer, J.: Uterine natural killer cells and angiogenesis in recurrent reproductive failure. Hum. Reprod. **24**(1), 45–54 (2009)
2. Li, G., Sanchez, V., Patel, G., Quenby, S., Rajpoot, N.: Localisation of luminal epithelium edge in digital histopathology images of ihc stained slides of endometrial biopsies. Comput. Med. Imaging Graph. **42**, 56–63 (2014)
3. Farjam, R., Soltanian-Zadeh, H., Jafari-Khouzani, K., Zoroofi, R.A.: An image analysis approach for automatic malignancy determination of prostate pathological images. Cytometry Part B Clin. Cytometry **72**(4), 227–240 (2007)
4. Naik, S., Doyle, S., Agner, S., Madabhushi, A., Feldman, M., Tomaszewski, J.: Automated gland and nuclei segmentation for grading of prostate and breast cancer histopathology. In: 2008 5th IEEE International Symposium on Biomedical Imaging: From Nano to Macro, ISBI 2008, pp. 284–287. IEEE (2008)
5. Nguyen, K., Sarkar, A., Jain, A.K.: Structure and context in prostatic gland segmentation and classification. In: Ayache, N., Delingette, H., Golland, P., Mori, K. (eds.) MICCAI 2012, Part I. LNCS, vol. 7510, pp. 115–123. Springer, Heidelberg (2012)
6. Gunduz-Demir, C., Kandemir, M., Tosun, A.B., Sokmensuer, C.: Automatic segmentation of colon glands using object-graphs. Med. Image Anal. **14**(1), 1–12 (2010)
7. Sirinukunwattana, K., Snead, D., Rajpoot, N.: A stochastic polygons model for glandular structures in colon histology images. IEEE Trans. Med. Imaging (2015)
8. Khan, A.M., Rajpoot, N., Treanor, D., Magee, D.: A non-linear mapping approach to stain normalisation in digital histopathology images using image-specific colour deconvolution. IEEE Trans. Biomed. Eng. **61**, 1729–1738 (2014)
9. Achanta, R., Shaji, A., Smith, K., Lucchi, A., Fua, P., Susstrunk, S.: Slic superpixels compared to state-of-the-art superpixel methods. IEEE Trans. Pattern Anal. Mach. Intell. **34**(11), 2274–2282 (2012)
10. Otsu, N.: A threshold selection method from gray-level histograms. Automatica **11**(285–296), 23–27 (1975)
11. Hong, L., Wan, Y., Jain, A.: Fingerprint image enhancement: algorithm and performance evaluation. IEEE Trans. Pattern Anal. Mach. Intell. **20**(8), 777–789 (1998)

Patch-Based Segmentation from MP2RAGE Images: Comparison to Conventional Techniques

Erhard T. Næss-Schmidt[1,2], Anna Tietze[1,3], Irene K. Mikkelsen[1],
Mikkel Petersen[1], Jakob U. Blicher[1,4], Pierrick Coupé[5],
José V. Manjón[6], and Simon F. Eskildsen[1(✉)]

[1] Center of Functionally Integrative Neuroscience,
Aarhus University, Aarhus, Denmark
seskildsen@cfin.au.dk
[2] Hammel Neurorehabilitation Centre, Aarhus University, Aarhus, Denmark
[3] Department of Neuroradiology, Aarhus University Hospital, Aarhus, Denmark
[4] Department of Neurology, Aarhus University Hospital, Aarhus, Denmark
[5] Laboratoire Bordelais de Recherche en Informatique, PICTURA Research
Group, Unité Mixte de Recherche CNRS (UMR 5800), Talencecedex, France
[6] Instituto de Aplicaciones de las Tecnologías de la Información y de las
ComunicacionesAvanzadas (ITACA), Universitat Politècnica de València,
Valencia, Spain

Abstract. In structural and functional MRI studies there is a need for robust and accurate automatic segmentation of various brain structures. We present a comparison study of three automatic segmentation methods based on the new T1-weighted MR sequence called MP2RAGE, which has superior soft tissue contrast. Automatic segmentations of the thalamus and hippocampus are compared to manual segmentations. In addition, we qualitatively evaluate the segmentations when warped to co-registered maps of the fractional anisotropy (FA) of water diffusion. Compared to manual segmentation, the best results were obtained with a patch-based segmentation method (volBrain) using a library of images from the same scanner (local), followed by volBrain using an external library (external), FSL and Freesurfer. The qualitative evaluation showed that volBrain local and volBrain external produced almost no segmentation errors when overlaid on FA maps, while both FSL and Freesurfer segmentations were found to overlap with white matter tracts. These results underline the importance of applying accurate and robust segmentation methods and demonstrate the superiority of patch-based methods over more conventional methods.

Keywords: Patch-based segmentation · MRI · volBrain · Freesurfer · FSL · MP2RAGE

1 Introduction

The extensive use of imaging techniques to investigate brain diseases and the need to outline specific region of interests (ROIs) for quantitative analysis emphasize the importance of accurate and robust segmentation methods. Accurate tracing of deep

© Springer International Publishing Switzerland 2015
G. Wu et al. (Eds.): Patch-MI 2015, LNCS 9467, pp. 180–187, 2015.
DOI: 10.1007/978-3-319-28194-0_22

brain structures, such as the thalamus and hippocampus, requires a high degree of expertise and preferably standardized outlining protocols. Even though an acceptable intra- and inter-rater reliability can be achieved using standardized protocols [1], manual segmentation is very time consuming. In large datasets, segmentation can become a bottleneck in post-processing and data analysis. Moreover, manual region outlining is prone to inconsistencies. Automatic or semi-automatic segmentation methods have the potential to solve these issues.

Several software solutions for automatic segmentation are publicly available. Functional MRI of the Brain (FMRIB) Software Library (FSL) and Freesurfer are tools frequently used for segmentation and appear to be reasonably reliable [2, 3]. However, there are still a potential to improve the automatic segmentation methods, especially in longitudinal studies [4] and for diseases that cause small structural changes.

Novel segmentation methods utilize redundancy in images to exploit a representative image library with corresponding validated structure labels [5–7]. These methods are called non-local means patch-based segmentation (NLM-PBS), since similar image patches are searched for in a non-local fashion, i.e. spatially located in a neighborhood around the target structure. NLM-PBS has been shown to be superior to conventional atlas-based techniques and even to other library-based methods [5, 6]. State-of-the-art segmentation methods like NLM-PBS have been shown to perform well even in a longitudinal setting [8].

An MRI sequence that has become widely used to obtain T1-weighted (T1w) anatomical images with good grey matter (GM)/white matter (WM) contrast is the magnetization-prepared rapid gradient-echo sequence (MPRAGE). However, at high static field strengths, increasing B1 field inhomogeneity leads to high intensity variations across the image. To mitigate this bias field, an improved MPRAGE sequence was recently proposed. By acquiring two MPRAGE images at different inversion times, this so-called MP2RAGE sequence is less influenced by B1 as well as M0 and T2* [9]. The resulting T1w image contrast is improved, but is also different from conventional MPRAGE images. Thus, current segmentation methods are not performing well on this new sequence [10].

To the best of our knowledge, the accuracy of different automated segmentation methods has not been compared using MP2RAGE images. Furthermore, NLM-PBS has not yet been directly compared to more conventional methods. In this study, we compared the performance of NLM-PBS (with two different libraries) to two widely used methods (Freesurfer and FSL) using manual segmentation as the gold standard. We measured the segmentation accuracy on two deep brain structures, thalamus and hippocampus, imaged with MP2RAGE.

2 Methods

2.1 Participants, MRI Acquisition and Pre-processing

For this study we collected 22 healthy subjects (age range 19–40 years, 12 females) from another internal research project. MP2RAGE images were obtained as part of the study protocol in all subjects, and 10 subjects were additionally examined with diffusion weighted imaging (DWI) as approved by the Regional Ethics Committee.

All subjects were scanned on a Siemens Magnetom Skyra 3T MRI system with a 32 channel head coil. MP2RAGE parameters were TR = 5 s, TI1 = 0.7 s, TI2 = 2.5 s, $\alpha 1 = 4°$, $\alpha 2 = 5°$ reconstructed at isotropic 1 mm^3 resolution (acquisition matrix: 240 × 256, 176 sagittal slices). The final MP2RAGE images were reconstructed by combining the two inversion times as described in [9]. DWI was acquired with 32 directions and 5 B0 maps. Parameters were TR = 10.9 s, TI = 2.1 s, reconstructed at isotropic 2.3 mm^3 resolution (acquisition matrix: 96 × 96, 38 axial slices).

MP2RAGE images have amplified background noise due to the reconstruction process. In our experience, Freesurfer and FSL perform poorly with this artificially amplified background noise, thus we masked out the background noise prior to applying the segmentation methods. Diffusion images were preprocessed using ExploreDTI [11]. We applied eddy current correction, motion correction and distortion correction before calculation of fractional anisotropy (FA) maps and co-registration to the MP2RAGE images. Using the inverse transformation, manual and automatic segmentation masks were then warped to DWI space and overlaid the FA maps.

2.2   Manual Segmentation

The thalamus and hippocampus from the 22 MP2RAGE images were manually segmented by an experienced neuroradiologist (EN) and a trained assistant (TA) using ITK-SNAP (www.itk-snap.org) [12]. First, EN manually traced the thalami in the axial plane using anatomical landmarks. Then, both EN and TA adjusted the thalami in all three principal planes using the protocol outlined by Power et al. [13]. The hippocampi were outlined according to the EADC-ADNI segmentation protocol [1] by TA supervised by EN. All segmentations were performed in MNI space to have similar orientation and make consistent decisions according to the protocols. The final segmentations were transformed back to scanner native space for comparison.

2.3   Automatic Segmentation Methods

We used a publicly available implementation (volBrain) of NLM-PBS [5]. For comparison we selected the publicly available and widely used segmentation tools FSL and Freesurfer. Default settings were used for all pipelines except for the added noise removal as described above. The following provides a brief overview of the three segmentation methods along with the applied settings.

FSL: Images were processed using FMRIB's Integrated Registration & Segmentation Tool (FIRST) from FSL v5.0, a tool to segment subcortical structures [14]. FIRST is a model-based segmentation tool, which uses training data from 317 manually segmented images. The manual labels are parameterized as surface meshes and modelled as a point distribution model. The deformable surfaces are then used to automatically parameterize the volumetric labels in terms of meshes and are constrained to preserve vertex correspondence across the training data. In addition, normalized intensities along the surface normals are sampled and modeled. We omitted the bias field correction step as MP2RAGE images are minimally affected by B1 field inhomogeneity. We used the default settings of FIRST, as they have been empirically optimized and include shape and boundary correction.

Freesurfer: Images were processed with Freesurfer version 5.3 [15]. Briefly, the processing includes removal of non-brain tissue, spatial normalization, segmentation of the subcortical WM and deep GM structures, and intensity normalization. The segmentation maps are created using spatial intensity gradients across tissue classes and are therefore not simply reliant on absolute signal intensity. Therefore, both intensity and continuity information are being carried out in this segmentation method.

volBrain: The volBrain system (http://volbrain.upv.es) is based on an advanced pipeline providing automatic segmentations of several brain structures from T1w MRI. Images are denoised using an adaptive non-local means filter [16], registered to MNI space using ANTS [17], inhomogeneity corrected using SPM8 routines [18], and intensity normalized. Then, thalamus, hippocampus and six other subcortical structures are segmented using and updated version of NLM-PBS [5]. We tested the segmentation method using two different libraries: 1) the default volBrain library (external) of 50 conventional T1w images (MPRAGE and SPGR), and 2) our own manually segmented library of 22 MP2RAGE images in a leave-one-out fashion (local). In both cases, the images were flipped across the mid-sagittal plane to artificially increase the library size as done in related work [6].

For all segmentation methods, error logs were recorded, and quality was visually inspected with ITK-SNAP, overlaying the segmentations onto the T1w image.

2.4   Comparison Metrics

The segmentations obtained from the four automatic methods were compared to the manual segmentations using Dice similarity index (DSI) given by $\frac{2|A \cap B|}{|A| + |B|}$, where A is the set of voxels in the proposed segmentation and B is the set of voxels in the reference (manual) segmentation and $|\cdot|$ is the cardinality. DSI ranges from zero to one where one indicates a perfect match. Furthermore, the false positive and false negative rate (FPR, FNR) of the automatic segmentations were calculated.

3   Results

Figure 1 shows examples of manual segmentations and the corresponding automatic segmentations of the thalamus and hippocampus generated by the four evaluated methods overlaid on the T1w image and the FA map. As the examples illustrate, the thalamus is over-segmented by Freesurfer and to a lesser extent by FSL. As can be seen from the FA map, the internal capsule is partly included in the segmentation. volBrain local does not include any WM tracts, while volBrain external slightly over-segments the thalamus. This observation is reflected in the significantly larger FPRs of FSL and Freesurfer compared to volBrain using both libraries (Fig. 2). The consistent over-segmentation of FSL results in relatively few false negatives, while Freesurfer

Best volBrain local (thalamus DSI=0.929, hippocampus DSI=0.911):

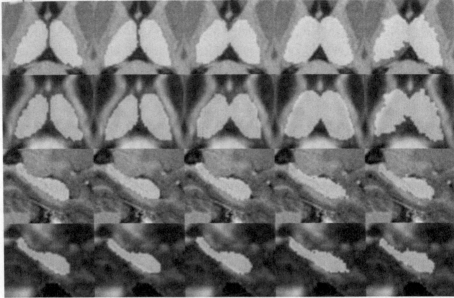

Worst volBrain local (thalamus DSI=0.882, hippocampus DSI=0.885):

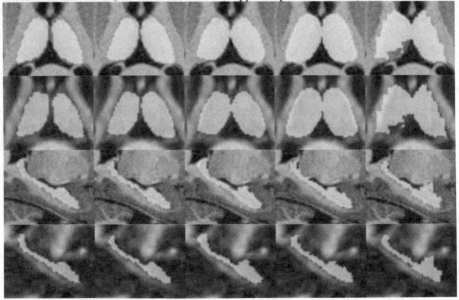

Fig. 1. Examples of manual and automatic segmentations of thalamus and hippocampus overlaid MP2RAGE and FA images. Examples are selected as respectively the best and worst volBrain local cases. From left to right: manual, volBrain local, volBrain external, FSL, Freesurfer.

also suffers from a relatively large FNR. In general, volBrain local performs best on thalamus segmentation with very high DSI (0.913 ± 0.014) followed by volBrain external (0.868 ± 0.024), FSL (0.806 ± 0.034) and Freesurfer (0.798 ± 0.049).

In terms of segmentation accuracy, the hippocampus follows a similar pattern with high DSI for volBrain local (0.892 ± 0.016), followed by volBrain external (0.859 ± 0.014), FSL (0.808 ± 0.017), and Freesurfer (0.771 ± 0.022) (Fig. 2). In terms of FPR and FNR, the pattern for hippocampus is slightly different from that of thalamus. FPR is reflecting the same order as DSI, with volBrain local performing best (8.9 % ± 2.7 %) and Freesurfer performing worst (41.2 % ± 7.2 %). However, in terms of FNR the methods are very similar with a relatively short range (mean FNR: 5.2 %– 12.4 %). The consistent over-segmentation of FSL and Freesurfer naturally leads to relatively low FNRs. volBrain local is the only method with well-balanced FPR and FNR for hippocampus, while volBrain using both libraries demonstrate balanced over- and under-segmentations on thalamus.

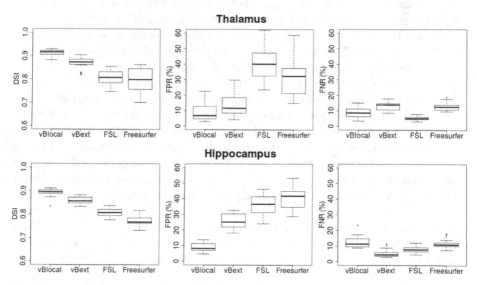

Fig. 2. Dice overlap, false positive rate and false negative rate for segmentations of the thalamus and the hippocampus using the four methods under evaluation. Box lines indicate 1st quartile, median, and 3rd quartile. Whiskers indicate extreme values, which are within the range of two times the length of the box. Dots are values outside this range.

4 Discussion

In this study we evaluated the performance of a recent patch-based segmentation method [5] and compared the results to those of FSL and Freesurfer, two widely applied methods in the neuroimaging community. Using MP2RAGE, a recently proposed T1w MRI sequence with superior soft tissue contrast, we tested the algorithms on two often investigated deep brain structures, the hippocampus and the thalamus.

The results demonstrated that the patch-based method outperforms both Freesurfer and FSL on these structures.

The accuracies we obtained on MP2RAGE images are similar to previously reported accuracies on the hippocampus using conventional MPRAGE [5, 7, 19]. For thalamus, average accuracies are in the same range as hippocampal accuracies for all four methods. However, for FSL and Freesurfer thalamic segmentation accuracies varied more than for hippocampus (Fig. 2). This may be caused by the fuzzy boundary of the thalamus where the image texture is important for making segmentation decisions, not just the image intensity and gradient. Patches can capture texture similarities, and this is perhaps why NLM-PBS attains consistently high accuracy on thalamus.

Using volBrain with a local library provided the best results. In this case the training data was matched perfectly to the test data, while the external library consisted of different imaging sequences from different scanners and manually labeled by different experts. The differences between local and external library reflects the importance of using a coherent labeling protocol and a similar image type within the template library. However, it is worth to note that even with these differences, volBrain external was able to provide good results highlighting the robustness of the method.

FSL and Freesurfer excessively over-segmented the structures with FPRs in the range 15 %–62 %. This resulted in consistent inclusion of WM in the segmentation of the two evaluated GM structures as qualitatively verified using FA maps. This is a major problem for morphometric as well as functional studies, where the over-segmentation leads to increased variance and impaired ability to detect differences and changes. Only volBrain external on hippocampus were found to over-segment. This may be due to differences in how the raters interpret the EADC-ADNI protocol.

The protocols for manual segmentation were based only on T1w images. As can be seen from the overlay on FA maps, it seems that WM voxels are occasionally included in the manual mask. This may be due to difficulty in determining the correct border when using T1w contrast only or simply due to co-registration errors between T1 and DWI. If the former, an improved manual segmentation may be obtained using multi-spectral data combining T1 and FA. Also, the automatic methods will most likely benefit from a multispectral approach. However, for a method to be versatile it is desired to work well on just T1w sequences as acquired in most MRI studies.

References

1. Boccardi, M., et al.: Delphi definition of the EADC-ADNI Harmonized Protocol for hippocampal segmentation on magnetic resonance. Alzheimer's Dement. J. Alzheimer's Assoc. 11(2), 126–138 (2015)
2. Nugent, A.C., et al.: Automated subcortical segmentation using FIRST: test-retest reliability, interscanner reliability, and comparison to manual segmentation. Hum. Brain Mapp. 34(9), 2313–2329 (2013)
3. Han, X., et al.: Reliability of MRI-derived measurements of human cerebral cortical thickness: the effects of field strength, scanner upgrade and manufacturer. NeuroImage 32(1), 180–194 (2006)

4. Mulder, E.R., et al.: Hippocampal volume change measurement: quantitative assessment of the reproducibility of expert manual outlining and the automated methods FreeSurfer and FIRST. NeuroImage **92**, 169–181 (2014)
5. Coupé, P., et al.: Patch-based segmentation using expert priors: application to hippocampus and ventricle segmentation. NeuroImage **54**(2), 940–954 (2011)
6. Eskildsen, S.F., et al.: BEaST: brain extraction based on nonlocal segmentation technique. NeuroImage **59**(3), 2362–2373 (2012)
7. Tong, T., et al.: Segmentation of MR images via discriminative dictionary learning and sparse coding: application to hippocampus labeling. NeuroImage **76**, 11–23 (2013)
8. Coupé, P., et al.: Scoring by nonlocal image patch estimator for early detection of Alzheimer's disease. NeuroImage Clin. **1**(1), 141–152 (2012)
9. Marques, J.P., et al.: MP2RAGE, a self bias-field corrected sequence for improved segmentation and T1-mapping at high field. NeuroImage **49**(2), 1271–1281 (2010)
10. Fujimoto, K., et al.: Quantitative comparison of cortical surface reconstructions from MP2RAGE and multi-echo MPRAGE data at 3 and 7 T. NeuroImage **90**, 60–73 (2014)
11. Leemans, A., et al.: ExploreDTI: a graphical toolbox for processing, analyzing, and visualizing diffusion MR data. In: 17th Annual Meeting of International Society Magnetic Resonance Medicine, Hawaii, USA (2009)
12. Yushkevich, P.A., et al.: User-guided 3D active contour segmentation of anatomical structures: significantly improved efficiency and reliability. NeuroImage **31**(3), 1116–1128 (2006)
13. Power, B.D., et al.: Validation of a protocol for manual segmentation of the thalamus on magnetic resonance imaging scans. Psychiatry Res. **232**(1), 98–105 (2015)
14. Patenaude, B., et al.: A Bayesian model of shape and appearance for subcortical brain segmentation. NeuroImage **56**(3), 907–922 (2011)
15. Dale, A.M., Fischl, B., Sereno, M.I.: Cortical surface-based analysis: I. Segmentation and surface reconstruction. NeuroImage **9**(2), 179–194 (1999)
16. Manjon, J.V., et al.: Adaptive non-local means denoising of MR images with spatially varying noise levels. J. Magn. Reson. Imaging JMRI **31**(1), 192–203 (2010)
17. Avants, B.B., et al.: A reproducible evaluation of ANTs similarity metric performance in brain image registration. NeuroImage **54**(3), 2033–2044 (2011)
18. Weiskopf, N., et al.: Unified segmentation based correction of R1 brain maps for RF transmit field inhomogeneities (UNICORT). NeuroImage **54**(3), 2116–2124 (2011)
19. Morey, R.A., et al.: A comparison of automated segmentation and manual tracing for quantifying hippocampal and amygdala volumes. NeuroImage **45**(3), 855–866 (2009)

Multi-atlas and Multi-modal Hippocampus Segmentation for Infant MR Brain Images by Propagating Anatomical Labels on Hypergraph

Pei Dong, Yanrong Guo, Dinggang Shen, and Guorong Wu[(⊠)]

Department of Radiology and BRIC,
University of North Carolina at Chapel Hill,
Chapel Hill, NC, USA
{pei.dong,yrguo,dgshen,guorong_wu}@med.unc.edu

Abstract. Accurate segmentation of hippocampus from infant magnetic reso-nance (MR) images is very important in the study of early brain development and neurological disorder. Recently, multi-atlas patch-based label fusion methods have shown a great success in segmenting anatomical structures from medical images. However, the dramatic appearance change from birth to 1-year-old and the poor image contrast make the existing label fusion methods less competitive to handle infant brain images. To alleviate these difficulties, we propose a novel multi-atlas and multi-modal label fusion method, which can unanimously label for all voxels by propagating the anatomical labels on a hypergraph. Specifically, we consider not only all voxels within the target image but also voxels across the atlas images as the vertexes in the hypergraph. Each hyperedge encodes a high-order correlation, among a set of vertexes, in different perspectives which incorporate (1) feature affinity within the multi-modal fea-ture space, (2) spatial coherence within target image, and (3) population heuristics from multiple atlases. In addition, our label fusion method further allows those reliable voxels to supervise the label estimation on other difficult-to-label voxels, based on the established hyperedges, until all the target image voxels reach the unanimous labeling result. We evaluate our proposed label fusion method in segmenting hippocampus from T1 and T2 weighted MR images acquired from at 2-week-old, 3-month-old, 6-month-old, 9-month-old, and 12-month-old. Our segmentation results achieves improvement of labeling accuracy over the conventional state-of-the-art label fusion methods, which shows a great potential to facilitate the early infant brain studies.

1 Introduction

The human brain undergoes a rapid physical growth and fast functional development during the first year of life. In order to characterize such dynamic changes *in vivo*, accurate segmentation of anatomical structures from the MR images is very important

---

Dong and Guo-These authors contributed equally to this work.

© Springer International Publishing Switzerland 2015
G. Wu et al. (Eds.): Patch-MI 2015, LNCS 9467, pp. 188–196, 2015.
DOI: 10.1007/978-3-319-28194-0_23

in imaging-based brain development studies. Since hippocampus plays an important role in learning and memory function, many studies aim to find the imaging markers around hippocampus. Unfortunately, the poor image contrast and dramatic appearance change make the segmentation of hippocampus from the infant images in the first year of life very challenging, due to the dynamic white matter myelination progress [1]. Since different modalities convey diverse imaging characteristics at different brain development phases, integration of multi-modal imaging information can significantly improve the segmentation accuracy [2]. However, the modulation of each modality is hard-coded and subjective to the expert's experience.

In medical image analysis area, there has been a recent spike in multi-atlas patch based segmentation methods [3–5], which first register all atlas images to the underlying target image and then propagate the labels from the atlas domain to the target image. The assumption behind is that two voxels should bear the same anatomical label if their local appearances are similar. However, a critical issue in current multi-atlas patch based label fusion methods is that the labels are determined separately at each voxel. As a result, there is no guarantee that labeled anatomical structures are spatially consistent. On the other hand, conventional graph-cut based methods [6] can jointly segment the entire ROI by finding a minimum graph cut. However, only the image information within the target image is utilized during this segmentation.

To combine the power of multi-atlas and graph-based approaches, we propose a novel multi-atlas and multi-modal label fusion method for segmenting the hippocampus from the infant brain images in the first year of life. Hypergraph has shown its superiority in image retrieval [7, 8] and recognition [9]. Our idea is to use hypergraph to leverage (1) the information integration from multiple atlases and multiple imaging modalities, and (2) the label fusion for all target image voxels under consideration.

Specifically, we regard all voxels within the target image and the atlas images as the vertexes in the graph. In hypergraph, we generalize the concept of conventional graph edge (only connects two vertexes at a time) to the hyperedge (groups a set of vertexes simultaneously), in order to reveal the high-order correlations for more than two voxels. In general, our hyperedges in the multi-atlas scenario encode three types of voxels correlations: (1) *feature affinity*: only the vertexes with similar appearance are connected by hyperedge, (2) *spatial coherence*: the vertexes located in a certain neighborhood from target image belong to the same hyperedge, and (3) *atlas correspondence*: each vertex from target image and its corresponding vertexes across all atlas images form the hyperedge. It is worth noting that the hypergraph is very flexible to incorporate the multi-modal information by constructing the above three types of hyperedges w.r.t. different imaging modalities. After constructing the hypergraph, the vertexes from both the atlas image voxels and the target image voxels with high labeling confidence are considered bearing the known labels. Thus, our label fusion method falls into the semi-supervised hypergraph learning framework, i.e., the latent labels on the remaining voxels in the target image are influenced by the connected vertexes with known labels. The principle to propagate the labels is that the vertexes sitting in the same hyperedge should have the same label, with the minimal discrepancy of labels on the vertexes with existing labels before and after label propagation.

Our proposed method has been comprehensively evaluated on segmenting hippocampus from T1 and T2 weighted MR images at 2-week-old, 3-month-old, 6-month-old, 9-month-old and 12-month-old. The segmentation result shows a great improvement compared to the state-of-the-art method [3–5] in terms of labeling accuracy.

2 Method

Given the atlases (including T1, T2 weighted MR images and the ground truth label of hippocampus), the goal is to segment the hippocampus from the unlabeled target image. Since the T1 and T2 weighted images are acquired from the same subject at the same time, it is not difficult to register them to the same space. Due to the dynamic appearance change and poor image resolution, it is challenging to apply deformable image registration for the infant images in the first year of life. Thus, only linear registration is used to map each atlas to the underlying target image domain. After that, our label fusion method consists of two main steps: (1) hypergraph construction (Sect. 2.1) and (2) label propagation (Sect. 2.2), as detailed below.

2.1 Hypergraph Construction

We assume that N atlas images, each with T1 and T2 weighted MR images, are used to label the target image. The hypergraph is constructed to accommodate the complete information from both the multi-atlas and multi-modalities images, where the hypergraph is denoted as $\mathcal{G} = (\mathcal{V}, \mathcal{E}, \mathbf{W})$ with the vertex set $\mathcal{V}$, the hyperedge set $\mathcal{E}$ and its weight $\mathbf{W}$. In order for computation efficiency, only the voxels within a bounding box (shown in the left column of Fig. 1 which covers the hippocampus with enough margin) are used as the vertexes, instead of using the voxels from the entire image.

Hypergraph Initialization: Assume the number of voxels inside the bounding box is q. The hypergraph vertexes are built on every voxel from the bounding boxes of the target image and the atlas images. For each atlas image, we vectorize the voxels in the bounding box into a column vector $\mathcal{V}_s$ with the length of q, where $s = 1, \dots, N$. With the same vectorising order, we can obtain the column vector of graph vertexes from target image, denoted by $\mathcal{U}$. Thus, the vertex set $\mathcal{V}$ is eventually the combination of voxels from the target image and all atlas images, i.e., $\mathcal{V} = \{\mathcal{U}, \mathcal{V}_1, \dots, \mathcal{V}_N\}$ It is worth noting that each element in $\mathcal{V}_s$ bears the known label and the label on each element of $\mathcal{U}$ is currently unknown.

It is clear that the voxels along the interface of multiple structures are more difficult to determine the labels than other points. In light of this, we go one step further to classify the elements in $\mathcal{U}$ into two categories based on their difficulties in labeling. To achieve it, we use an existing label fusion method, such as the majority voting, to predict the label of each element in $\mathcal{U}$ as well as the confidence value in terms of the voting predominance. If the influence for voting one label dominates the other labels, we regard the labeling result on the underlying target image voxel has high confidence to determine its label. Otherwise, we regard the underlying target image voxel needs other heuristics to find its label. Thus, we can divide $\mathcal{U}$ into two parts, $\mathcal{U}^L$ (low confidence) and $\mathcal{U}^H$ (high confidence), where the number of elements in $\mathcal{U}^L$ and $\mathcal{U}^H$ is q^L and q^H ($q = q^L + q^H$), respectively.

The advantage of separate $\mathcal{U}$ to $\mathcal{U}^L$ and $\mathcal{U}^H$ is that it allows the label propagation from not only the atlas images but also the some reliable regions of the target image, which are more specific to label fusion of underlying image. Specifically, for each element in $\mathcal{U}^H$ and $\{\mathcal{V}_s | s = 1, \ldots, N\}$, we assign the label with either 0 (background) or 1 (hippocampus). For each element in $\mathcal{U}^L$, the label value is assigned to 0.5 since the label is uncertain. Following the same order of $\mathcal{V}$, we stack all the label values into a label vector $\mathbf{y}$. As shown in the left bracket in Fig. 1, the first part of $\mathbf{y}$ is the uncertain labels for voxels $\mathcal{U}^L$ (in gray), followed by the known labels from $\mathcal{U}^H$ and $\{\mathcal{V}_s | s = 1, \ldots, N\}$ (hippocampus in white and background in black). Thus, our hypergraph based label fusion turns into a semi-supervised learning scenario, i.e., optimize for a new label vector $\mathbf{f}$ (in the right of Fig. 1) which should be (1) as close to $\mathbf{y}$ as possible and (2) propagate the known labels from $\mathcal{U}^H$ and $\{\mathcal{V}_s | s = 1, \ldots, N\}$ to the difficult-to-label vertexes $\mathcal{U}^L$. The leverage of label propagation is a set of hyperedges, as detailed next.

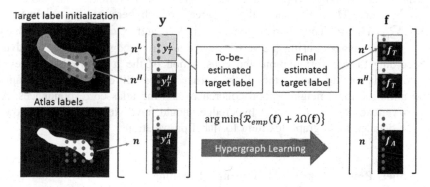

Fig. 1. The framework of hypergraph learning based label propagation.

Hyperedge Construction: Since the goal is to estimate the latent labels for the difficult-to-label voxels in the target image, we only construct hyperedges centered at each vertex $u \in \mathcal{U}^L$ in the low confidence voxel set. In total, we constructed 2×3 types of hyperedges w.r.t. two imaging modalities and three measurements. Specifically, for each modality, we construct the following three hyperedges on each vertex u:

Feature Affinity (FA) hyperedge e^{FA}. It consists of K nearest vertexes ($v \in \mathcal{V}$), where their patchwise similarities w.r.t. the underlying vertex u are the highest K hits in the feature space.

Local Coherence (LC) hyperedge e^{LC}. It consists of all the vertexes $v \in \mathcal{U}$ from the target image and being located within a spatial neighborhood of u.

Atlas Correspondence (AC) hyperedge e^{AC} It consists of all vertexes $v \in \{\mathcal{V}_s | s = 1, \ldots, N\}$ across the atlas images at the corresponding spatial locations w.r.t. u.

Since each of the above hyperedge is centered by u, we call u as the owner of hyperedge e (we omit the superscript of e hereafter).

Incidence Matrix Construction: After the construction of hyperedges for each u, we build a incidence matrix $\mathbf{H}$ with row representing the vertexes and column representing the hyperedges ε, which encode all the information within the hypergraph $\mathcal{G}$. Each entry $\mathbf{H}(v, e)$ in $\mathbf{H}$ measures the affinity between the each vertex v and the owner u of the hyperedge $e \in \mathcal{E}$:

$$\mathbf{H}(v, e) = \begin{cases} exp\left(-\frac{\|\boldsymbol{p}(v) - \boldsymbol{p}(u)\|_2^2}{\sigma^2}\right) & \text{if } v \in e \\ 0 & \text{if } v \notin e \end{cases} \tag{1}$$

where the $\|.\|_2$ is the L_2 norm computed between intensity image patch $\boldsymbol{p}(v)$ and $\boldsymbol{p}(u)$ for vertex v and the hyperedge owner u. σ is the averaged patchwise similarity between u and all vertexes within the hyperedge e. For simplicity, each hyperedge is initialized with an equal weight, $\mathbf{W}(e) = 1$. The degree of a vertex v is defined as $d(v) = \sum_{e \in \varepsilon} \mathbf{w}(e)\mathbf{H}(v, e)$, and the degree of hyperedge is defined as $\delta(e) = \sum_{v \in V} \mathbf{H}(v, e)$. Thus, two diagonal matrices $\mathbf{D}_v$ and $\mathbf{D}_e$ can be formed with each entry along the diagonal using the vertex degree and hyperedge degree, respectively.

According to this formulation, the construction of the hypergraph captures the high-order relationship among the all the vertices across different image modalities, feature affinities, local neighborhood coherences and the atlas correspondences. And any two vertexes within the same hyperedge should have similar labels. Following gives the detailed hypergraph learning for label propagation.

2.2   Labels Propagation via Hypergraph Learning

Given the initialization on the hypergraph, we employed a semi-supervised learning method to perform the label fusion on the constructed hypergraph. The objective function [10] is defined as:

$$\arg\min_{\mathbf{f}}\left\{\mathcal{R}_{emp}(\mathbf{f}) + \lambda\Omega(\mathbf{f})\right\} \tag{2}$$

where $\mathbf{f}$ is the likelihood of hippocampus on each vertex $v \in \mathcal{V}$. The first term $\mathcal{R}_{emp}(\mathbf{f})$ is an empirical loss, which prevent the dramatic change for those the high probability values in $\mathbf{f}$. The second term $\Omega(\mathbf{f})$ is a regularization term on the hypergraph, which restrict the labels at similar range for those vertexes within a same hyperedge. The λ is a positive weighing parameter between the two terms.

The first empirical loss term $\mathcal{R}_{emp}(\mathbf{f})$ is defined by

$$\mathcal{R}_{emp}(\mathbf{f}) = \|\mathbf{f} - \mathbf{y}\|^2 \tag{3}$$

The empirical loss term is designed for the minimization of the differences before and after label fusion.

The second term $\Omega(\mathbf{f})$ is a regularizer on the hypergraph, which defined as follows:

$$\Omega(\mathbf{f}) = \frac{1}{2}\sum_{e \in \varepsilon}\sum_{u,v \in v}\frac{\mathbf{W}(e)\mathbf{H}(u,e)\mathbf{H}(v,e)}{\delta(e)}\left(\frac{\mathbf{f}(u)}{\sqrt{\mathrm{d}(u)}} - \frac{\mathbf{f}(v)}{\sqrt{\mathrm{d}(v)}}\right)^2 = \mathbf{f}^\mathrm{T}(\mathbf{I} - \mathbf{\Theta})\mathbf{f} = \mathbf{f}^\mathrm{T}\Delta\mathbf{f} \tag{4}$$

where $\mathbf{\Theta} = \mathbf{D}_v^{-\frac{1}{2}}\mathbf{HWD}_e^{-1}\mathbf{H}^\mathrm{T}\mathbf{D}_v^{-\frac{1}{2}}$, and Δ can be viewed as normalized hypergraph Laplacian matrix. Here, the regulation term $\Omega(\mathbf{f})$ constrains the labels of vertexes in the same hyperedge should held a similar value during the label propagation. Thus, the objective function, Eq. (2), can be rewritten as:

$$arg\min_{\mathbf{f}}\left\{\|\mathbf{f} - \mathbf{y}\|^2 + \lambda\mathbf{f}^\mathrm{T}\Delta\mathbf{f}\right\} \tag{5}$$

By differentiating the objective function with respect to $\mathbf{f}$, the optimal $\mathbf{f}$ can be computed iteratively as below:

$$\mathbf{f} = (\mathbf{I} + \frac{1}{\lambda}(\mathbf{I} - \mathbf{\Theta}))^{-1}\mathbf{y} \tag{6}$$

Given the estimated $\mathbf{f}$, the anatomical label on each difficult-to-label target voxel $u \in \mathcal{U}^L$ can be determined by

$$\begin{cases} Hippocampus & f(u) > 0.5 \\ Background & otherwise \end{cases} \tag{7}$$

It should be noted that using the semi-supervised learning to perform the binary classification on the hypergraph allows prediction of the entire target image voxels simultaneously, while combining several correlations across all the voxels between the target image and atlas images.

3 Experiments

3.1 Date Acquisition and Preprocessing

In the experiments, MR images of 10 healthy infant subjects are acquired from a Siemens head-only 3T scanner. For each subject, both T1- and T2-weighted MR images were acquired in five data sets at 2 weeks, 3 months, 6 months, 9 months and 12 months of age. T1-weighted MR images were acquired with 144 sagittal slices at a resolution of $1 \times 1 \times 1\,\mathrm{mm}^3$, while T2-weighted MR images were acquired with 64 axis slices at resolution of $1.25 \times 1.25 \times 1.95\,\mathrm{mm}^3$. For each subject, the T2-weighted MR image is linearly aligned to the T1-weighted MR image at the same age and then further resampled to $1 \times 1 \times 1\,\mathrm{mm}^3$. Standard preprocessing was performed including skull stripping [11], intensity inhomogeneity correction [12]. The manual segmentations of the hippocampal regions for all 10 subjects are available and used as ground-truth for evaluation.

3.2   Evaluation of the Proposed Method

For all the experiments, the patch size is set as $5 \times 5 \times 5$ voxels. The number of nearest neighborhood vertexes K is 10 in constructing e^{FA}. The spatial neighborhood in constructing e^{LC} and e^{AC} is set to $3 \times 3 \times 3$ voxel. Parameter λ in Eq. (2) is 10.

To evaluate the performance of the proposed method, we adopted the leave-one-out cross-validation. In each cross-validation step, one subject is used as target images and the remaining 9 subjects were used as the atlas images. Our proposed hypergraph patch labeling (HPL) method is compared with three state-of-the-art multi-atlas patch-labeling methods: local-weighted majority voting (LMV) [3], non-local mean (NLM) [4] and sparse patch labeling (SPL) [5].

Table 1 gives the average dice ratio of four comparison methods for 2-week, 3-month, 6-month, 9-month and 12-month data respectively. It can be seen that our method can achieve better segmentation accuracy than all other three counterpart methods. Figure 2 further shows the impact of using our proposed method for segmenting the infant hippocampus compared with other different labeling methods under different modalities.

Finally, Fig. 3 shows the final segmentation results by the four methods and their corresponding manually segmentations for one typical subject at 2-week-old. Through visual inspection, our estimated labeling results (bottom line) are closer to the ground truth (yellow contours).

Table 1. The average dice ratio and standard deviation of four comparison methods: local-weighted majority voting, non-local mean, sparse patch labeling and hypergraph patch labeling for 2 week, 3 month, 6 month, 9 month and 12 month data. (* indicates the significant improvement of HPL over other compared methods ($p < 0.05$), T1 + T2).

	LMV	NLM	SPL	HPL
2 week	0.45 ± 0.12*	0.51 ± 0.12	0.57 ± 0.10	0.60 ± 0.11
3 month	0.49 ± 0.09*	0.54 ± 0.10*	0.61 ± 0.04	0.64 ± 0.04
6 month	0.48 ± 0.09*	0.58 ± 0.11	0.65 ± 0.06	0.67 ± 0.07
9 month	0.46 ± 0.07*	0.59 ± 0.08*	0.66 ± 0.04	0.67 ± 0.04
12 month	0.48 ± 0.10*	0.61 ± 0.05*	0.70 ± 0.04	0.71 ± 0.04

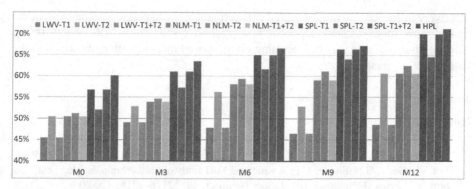

Fig. 2. Comparison of the average dice ratio of the ten infant subjects between different labeling methods across five time points: 2-week (M0), 3-month (M3), 6-month (M6), 9-month (M9) and 12-month (M12)

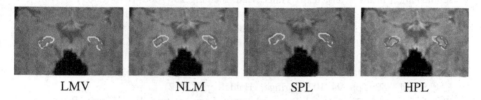

Fig. 3. Infant hippocampus segmentation comparison between the automatic segmentation using the four methods (red circles) and the ground truth (yellow circles) (Color figure online)

4 Discussion and Conclusion

With our proposed method, we achieved a better segmentation result with fewer atlases compared with the state-of-the-art patch-based method. The reasons are due to the followings: (1) the label propagation based on the hypergraph can adaptively combine the complementary information both from T1- and T2- weighed images; (2) for each image modality, three types of voxels correlations are considered, i.e. feature affinity, local spatial neighborhood and atlas corresponding spatial regions, which extensively exploits the high order correlations among a group of voxels; (3) Instead of labeling each voxel independently as in the existing methods, our semi-supervised hypergraph learning method performs a global optimization to predict the anatomical labels for all the voxels in the target image simultaneously. (4) Through the label propagation process, we allow the high confidence voxels to guide the nearby low confidence voxels, which provides valuable heuristics to overcome the uncertainty in label fusion.

In this paper, we propose a multi-atlas and multi-modal label fusion method for the segmentation of the hippocampus from infant MR images. We combine the advantages of conventional multi-atlas and graph-based approaches by encoding the feature affinity within the multi-modal feature space, spatial coherence, and the atlas information via hypergraph. Then, the whole label fusion procedure falls into the semi-supervised hypergraph learning framework, where the estimation of the latent anatomical labels is adaptively influenced by the connected counterparts in the hypergraph. The experiment results show more accurate hippocampus labeling results from MR images in the different phases of first year of life, using our proposed method with comparison to the state-of-the-art methods.

References

1. Knickmeyer, R.C., Gouttard, S., Kang, C., Evans, D., Wilber, K., Smith, J.K., Hamer, R.M., Lin, W., Gerig, G., Gilmore, J.H.: A structural MRI study of human brain development from birth to 2 years. J. Neurosci. Off. J. Soc. Neurosci. **28**, 12176–12182 (2008)
2. Wang, L., Shi, F., Yap, P.-T., Gilmore, J.H., Lin, W., Shen, D.: 4D multi-modality tissue segmentation of serial infant images. PLoS ONE **7**, e44596 (2012)
3. Isgum, I., Staring, M., Rutten, A., Prokop, M., Viergever, M.A., van Ginneken, B.: Multi-atlas-based segmentation with local decision fusion–application to cardiac and aortic segmentation in CT scans. IEEE Trans. Med. Imaging **28**, 1000–1010 (2009)
4. Coupé, P., Manjón, J.V., Fonov, V., Pruessner, J., Robles, M., Collins, D.L.: Patch-based segmentation using expert priors: application to hippocampus and ventricle segmentation. NeuroImage **54**, 940–954 (2011)
5. Zhang, D., Guo, Q., Wu, G., Shen, D.: Sparse patch-based label fusion for multi-atlas segmentation. In: Yap, P.-T., Liu, T., Shen, D., Westin, C.-F., Shen, L. (eds.) MBIA 2012. LNCS, vol. 7509, pp. 94–102. Springer, Heidelberg (2012)
6. Shi, J., Malik, J.: Normalized Cuts and Image Segmentation. IEEE Trans. Pattern Anal. Mach. Intell. **22**, 888–905 (2000)
7. Gao, Y., Ji, R., Cui, P., Dai, Q., Hua, G.: Hyperspectral image classification through bilayer graph-based learning. IEEE Trans. Image Process. **23**(7), 2769–2778 (2014)
8. Gao, Y., Wang, M., Zha, Z.-J., Shen, J., Li, X., Wu, X.: Visual-textual joint relevance learning for tag-based social image search. IEEE Trans. Image Process. **22**(1), 363–376 (2013)
9. Gao, Y., Wang, M., Tao, D., Ji, R., Dai, Q.: 3-D object retrieval and recognition with hypergraph analysis. IEEE Trans. Image Process. **21**(9), 4290–4303 (2012)
10. Zhou, D., Huang, J., Schölkopf, B.: Learning with hypergraphs: clustering, classification, and embedding. In: Proceedings of NIPS, vol. 19, pp. 1601–1608 (2006)
11. Shi, F., Wang, L., Dai, Y., Gilmore, J.H., Lin, W., Shen, D.: LABEL: pediatric brain extraction using learning-based meta-algorithm. NeuroImage **62**, 1975–1986 (2012)
12. Sled, J.G., Zijdenbos, A.P., Evans, A.C.: A nonparametric method for automatic correction of intensity nonuniformity in MRI data. IEEE Trans. Med. Imaging **17**, 87–97 (1998)

Prediction of Infant MRI Appearance and Anatomical Structure Evolution Using Sparse Patch-Based Metamorphosis Learning Framework

Islem Rekik, Gang Li, Guorong Wu, Weili Lin, and Dinggang Shen[✉]

Department of Radiology and BRIC, University of North Carolina
at Chapel Hill, Chapel Hill, NC, USA
dgshen@med.unc.edu

Abstract. Magnetic resonance imaging (MRI) of pediatric brain provides invaluable information for early normal and abnormal brain development. Longitudinal neuroimaging has spanned various research works on examining infant brain development patterns. However, studies on predicting postnatal brain image evolution remain scarce, which is very challenging due to the dynamic tissue contrast change and even inversion in postnatal brains. In this paper, we unprecedentedly propose a dual image intensity and anatomical structure (label) prediction framework that nicely links the geodesic image metamorphosis model with sparse patch-based image representation, thereby defining spatiotemporal metamorphic patches encoding both image photometric and geometric deformation. In the training stage, we learn the 4D metamorphosis trajectories for each training subject. In the prediction stage, we define various strategies to sparsely represent each patch in the testing image using the training metamorphosis patches; while progressively incrementing the richness of the patch (from appearance-based to multimodal kinetic patches). We used the proposed framework to predict 6, 9 and 12-month brain MR image intensity and structure (white and gray matter maps) from 3 months in 10 infants. The proposed framework showed promising preliminary prediction results for the spatiotemporally complex, drastically changing brain images.

1 Introduction

Studying early brain development and neurodevelopmental disorders has been at the heart of various recent neuroimaging studies that aim to improve our limited understanding of early brain workings as well as the dynamics of brain abnormalities [1]. Part of the ongoing research in this exploding field aims to not only understand how infant brains grow, but also to learn how to predict their evolution in space and time. In other words, given a single MR image acquired at a specific timepoint, can we build a learning framework that can robustly output how the brain looks like at late timepoints (in both image appearance and

G. Wu et al. (Eds.): Patch-MI 2015, LNCS 9467, pp. 197–204, 2015.
DOI: 10.1007/978-3-319-28194-0_24

anatomical structure)? This will greatly help understand the dynamic, nonlinear early brain development and provide fundamental insights into neurodevelomental disorders.

To the best of our knowledge, the problem of jointly predicting both image appearance (intensity) and structure (e.g., brain tissue labels: white and gray matters) during the first postnatal year from a single acquired image has not been explored yet. In the sate-of-the art, a few methods [2,3] have dealt with extrapolating image appearance at earlier or late timepoints (backward or forward prediction) using geodesic shape regression models to estimate diffeomeorphic (i.e. smooth and invertible) deformation trajectories; however, they required at least two images for prediction or extrapolation. This confined scope of publications for predicting postnatal early brain development can be partly explained by the drastic change of tissue contrast and anatomical structures in developing brains, which renders prediction more challenging (Fig. 1).

In this paper, we propose the first **dual image and label prediction framework** that nicely links the geodesic image metamorphosis model [4] (training stage) with sparse patch-based image representation (prediction stage). The image-to-image metamorphosis model elegantly solves the problem of contrast change between different MR brain images (see 3-month vs. 6-month T1-w images in Fig. 1) as it morphs a baseline image I_0 into a target image I_T by jointly estimating optimal spatiotemporal velocity deformation vector field v_t (i.e. dynamic kinetic path) and intensity scalar field I_t (dynamic photometric path), with $t \in [0, T]$. In the learning stage, we first propose an extension of the image-to-image metamorphosis into a spatiotemporal metamorphosis that exactly fits the baseline image to subsequent observations in an ordered set $\Im = \{I_0, I_1, \ldots, I_N\}$ of images.

The training stage comprises the estimation of a spatiotemporal metamorphosis for each training subject using a patch-based image encoding. A wide spectrum of patch-based methods has been for infant images labeling and registration [5,6]. The richness and locality of a patch made it a good candidate for examining individual and population-based image variation. Besides, the in-vogue sparse patch-based image representation methods take into account the neighborhood of corresponding patches and simultaneously select the best candidate patches for representation, unlike patch-based non-local mean or majority voting methods. *In the prediction stage*, for each voxel x in the testing baseline image I_0, we sparsely encode each patch $p(x)$ centered at x using a dynamic dictionary composed of patches from the training subjects. For prediction, the sparse representation will be propagated to late timepoints as each patch is *dynamic* and has a metamorphosis path $p(x, t)$ estimated during the training stage. The propagation is applied to both dynamic label map dictionaries and intensity dictionaries; thereby allowing a simultaneous image and label prediction. We test the proposed framework through progressively upgrading the richness of the dynamic patch from an *appearance-based patch* to an *appearance-and-structure-based patch* up to a *multimodal kinetic patch*. Finally, we predict for each of these baseline patches their intensity and structure evolution paths up to the last timepoint in the training dataset.

2 Spatiotemporal Image Metamorphosis Framework (Training Stage)

As introduced by [4], the metamorphosis image theory presents a solid mathematical ground for tracking both local intensity and shape changes in images; which is fundamental to learning early brain dynamic growth. The idea of metamorphosis stems from integrating the infinitesimal variation of the image appearance (i.e. residual) with the *diffeormophic metric* used to estimate image deformation trajectories; therefore accounting for intensity change and producing the *metamorphic metric*. Basically, a baseline image I_0 morphs under the action of a velocity vector field v_t that advects the scalar intensity I_t (i.e. time-evolving image intensity) [4]. Solving the advection equation with a residual allows to estimate both image intensity evolution and the velocity at which it evolves (Fig. 1). In other words, this model registers one source image I_0 to a target image I_T while estimating two optimal evolution paths linking these images: (1) a geometric path $\{v_t\}_{[0,T]}$ encoding the smooth velocity deforming one image into another, and (2) a photometric path $\{I_t\}_{[0,T]}$ representing the change in image intensity.

The definition of the metamorphic metric requires the use of appropriate spaces to which the images, the force acting on the images, and the velocity driving the evolution of the baseline image towards the target image belong. **An image I** is an element of the square integrable set of functions L^2 considered as a Riemannian manifold denoted M (the object space). A curve $(t \mapsto I_t, t \in [0,T])$ on M is the path of evolution of a baseline image I_0 (Fig. 1). M is equipped with the usual metric on L^2. We denote by Ω the space where an image I is defined. **The action (force) ϕ** is a diffeomorphic transformation (a mapping) that belongs to a Lie group G endowed with a Lie algebra $\mathcal{G}$. In classical diffeomorphic deformation theory, we associate to the action ϕ a velocity v that satisfies the flow equation:

$$\begin{cases} \frac{d\phi_t}{dt} = v(\phi_t(x)), \ t \in [0;T] \\ \phi_0(x) = x, \ x \in \Omega \end{cases}$$

A curve $(t \mapsto \phi_t, \ t \in [0,T])$ on G acting on an image $I \in M$ describes a deformation path morphing I over the time interval $[0,T]$. **The velocity field** v_t, for all $t \in [0,T]$, belongs to the vector space V, which is the tangent space to the action group G. We adopt similar construction as in [7] for V with an inner product $< .,. >_V$ defined through a differential Cauchy-Navier type operator L (with adjoint $L^\dagger$) given by: $< f,g >_V = < Lf, Lg >_{L^2} = < L^\dagger Lf, g >_{L^2})$ where $< .,. >_{L^2}$ is the standard L^2 inner-product for square integrable vector fields on M and $L = (-\alpha\nabla^2 + \gamma)I_d$ (I_d is the identity matrix and α and γ two deformation parameters).

We estimate the optimal metamorphosis path (I_t, v_t) from I_0 to I_T by minimizing the following cost functional U using a standard alternating steepest gradient descent algorithm [8]:

$$U(I,v) = \int_0^T |v_t|_V^2 dt + \frac{1}{\sigma^2} \int_0^T \left| \frac{dI(t)}{dt} + \nabla I_t.v_t \right|_{L^2}^2 dt$$

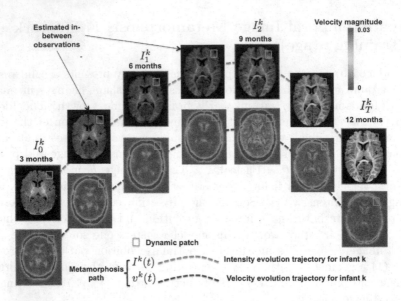

Fig. 1. *Spatiotemporal image metamorphosis.* For each infant k in the training dataset, we estimate a dynamic photometric I_t^k and kinetic v_t^k paths (vector field is displayed); which can be more locally traced within a dynamic patch (Color figure online).

σ weighs the trade-off between the deformation smoothness (first term) and fidelity-to-data (second term). The term $\nabla I_t.v_t$ represents the spatial variation of the moving image I_t in the direction v_t. Furthermore, the moving intensity scalar field I_t is defined under the action of the diffeomorphism ϕ_t on a baseline image I_0 : $I_t = \phi_t.I_0$.

We extend the image-to-image metamorphosis to a spatiotemporal metamorphosis passing through the images $\Im = \{I_0, I_1, \ldots, I_N\}$ by adding to the boundary conditions for the intensity path I_t beginning at $I(t = 0) = I_0$ and reaching $I(t = T) = I_N$ the intermediate conditions, where we force the evolving metamorphic path I_t to successively fit a set of observations $\{I_1, \ldots, I_{T-1}\}$.

3   Sparse Patch-Based Image Intensity and Label Prediction from Baseline (Testing Stage)

Weighted sparse representation of a new image using estimated metamorphosis path. The idea that similar brain images in appearance and structure will deform in a similar way was recently used for image registration prediction in [9]. In the context of prediction from a single image, we also adopt the same idea within a patch-based image representation framework. Indeed, the local anatomical structure can be better captured within the richness of local patches. Besides, the patch size can explore different scales of the image and can be easily adjusted to upgrade the method performance. For a new testing image, we first sample cubic overlapping patches at each voxel $x \in \Omega$. Then we trace forth the photometric evolution path for each patch in every training subject k (Fig. 1-gray curve), thereby defining a set of dynamic patches centered at x: $p^k(x,t)_{[0,T],s=1...S}$, where S denotes the number of the training subjects. We use these training patches in a column-wise manner to define a dynamic dictionary at each voxel x: $D(x,t)_{[0,T]}$. To overcome the possible registration error, we expand $D(x,t)$ by adding all patches centered at y, s.t. $y \in W_x$, where W_x is a search window centered at x. Next, for a new testing baseline *appearance* patch $p(x,0)$, we select the most similar patches in $D(x,0)$ using the squared absolute difference as a metric, thus generating a 'filtered' dictionary $D_{select}(x,0)$. Last, we sparsely represent $p(x,0)$ by the coefficient vector α and $D_{select}(x,0)$ through minimizing the following functional:

$$\min_{\alpha \geq 0}||p(x,0) - D_{select}(x,0)\alpha||_2^2 + \eta||\alpha||_1$$

where $D_{select} \in \mathbf{R}^{d \times S_W}$, $p(x,0) \in \mathbf{R}^d$, $\alpha \in \mathbf{R}^{S_W}$ and $\eta > 0$. d is the patch dimension and S_W is the total number of patches in the dictionary, which depends on both the number of training subjects S and the number of patches inside the window W. The first term measures the discrepancy between the baseline patch $p(x,0)$ and the reconstructed baseline patch $D_{select}(x,0)\alpha$, and the second term is L_1 LASSO regularization on the coefficient vector α.

Patch-wise prediction of both photometric and label evolution paths for a testing subject. To predict the image intensity $\hat{I}(x,t)$ located at x, at a specific timepoint t, we use the sparse coefficient vector α to select and weigh patches from the built dictionary at t as follows: $\hat{p}(x,t) = D_{select}(x,t)\alpha$; where for $t > 0$ $D_{select}(.,t)$ contains only appearance patches. Then we take the center value of the appearance patch as a predicted value $\hat{I}(x,t)$.

Assuming that we have Y possible labels $\{l_1, \ldots, l_Y\}$ in the training images, we predict the label $\hat{L}(x,t)$ associated with $\hat{I}(x,t)$ by weighted majority voting as follows:

$$\hat{L}(x,t) = arg\max_{m=1,\ldots,m_Y} \sum_{p=1}^{S_W} \alpha \cdot \delta(l_p, l_m)$$

where l_p denotes the label of the patch p center in $D_{select}(x,t)$ and the Dirac function $\delta(l_p, l_m) = 1$ when $l_p = l_m$ and 0 otherwise.

Multiple strategies for baseline dictionary construction. To investigate the role of the baseline dictionary $D(.,0)$ building and its richness in sparse prediction performance, we define three methods to build $D_{select}(x,t)$ for $t \in [0,T]$ in addition to the *default method M0* which only considers appearance (intensity) patches (Fig. 3):

⋆ *Appearance-and-deformation-based dictionary (Method1 or M1).* To incorporate the kinetic information provided by the metamorphosis model, which may be of value, we estimated the total deformation map, integrated over the dynamic kinetic path (red curve in Fig. 1) of a testing image when morphed into the estimated 4D photometric atlas (Fig. 3). This provides a *mean photometric evolution* of a baseline testing image –that may help guide the prediction

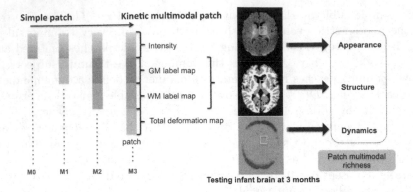

Fig. 2. Multiple strategies for baseline dictionary construction (Color figure online).

of its local changes. Thus, we stack up the total deformation patch behind the appearance patch (Fig. 2–M1).

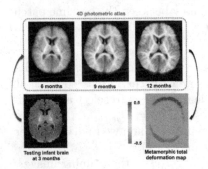

Fig. 3. Spatiotemporal testing image metamorphosis into a 4D photometric atlas to generate total deformation map.

⋆ *Appearance-and-structure-based dictionary (Method2 or M2).* We build the dictionary using column patches, each composed of three sub-patches: the top patch encodes the image appearance, the middle patch represents the GM (gray matter) label map and the bottom patch represents the WM (white matter) label map (Fig. 2–M2). This enables to upgrade the richness of the column patch by incorporating guiding structural information.

⋆ *Multimodal kinetic dictionary (Method3 or M3).* We build multimodal patches including appearance, structure, and kinetic local information to construct the baseline dictionary (Fig. 2–M3).

4   Results and Discussion

Data and parameters setting. We evaluated the proposed framework on T1-w images in 10 infants, each with MRI scans acquired at 3, 6, 9 and 12 months of age. We fixed the metamorphosis parameters at the same values for all infants: $\alpha = 0.01$, $\sigma = 4$ and $\gamma = 0.05$. For patch-based representation, the window size W is of the patch size; $\eta = 0.01$. Patch-size was set to $3 \times 3 \times 3$, and $5 \times 5 \times 5$ for comparison.

Leave-one-out cross validation and evaluation metrics. We use Dice index $D(A, B) = \frac{2|A \cap B|}{|A \cup B|}$ to evaluate label prediction accuracy (Table 1) and

Table 1. Mean Dice index across 10 infants (patch size $3 \times 3 \times 3$)

Method		Method1	Method2	Method3
6 months	GM	0.7530 ± 0.0636	0.7660 ± 0.0564	**0.7690 ± 0.0572**
	WM	0.6320 ± 0.0636	**0.7080 ± 0.0432**	0.6970 ± 0.0481
9 months	GM	0.7640 ± 0.0519	0.7510 ± 0.0428	**0.7740 ± 0.0504**
	WM	0.6340 ± 0.0640	**0.7080 ± 0.0329**	0.6740 ± 0.0430
12 months	GM	0.7500 ± 0.0503	0.7210 ± 0.0423	**0.7600 ± 0.0523**
	WM	0.6590 ± 0.0647	**0.7350 ± 0.0334**	0.6890 ± 0.0482

normalized sum of squared differences (NSSD) and peak signal-to-noise ratio (PSNR) to evaluate intensity prediction accuracy (Table 2). Interestingly, the multimodal kinetic patch (Method 3) showed the best performance in GM prediction accuracy, while the appearance-and-label based patch (Method 2) led to a better prediction for WM. The former results can be explained by the high dynamics of the GM well captured in the total deformation map (i.e. cortical growth) (Fig. 2), unlike the WM deformation map which is less dynamic and lacks details, eventually due to the fuzziness of the 4D photometric atlas. One could further improve WM prediction results when using the multimodal kinetic patch through estimating a sharper 4D atlas that preserves the anatomical details. For the intensity prediction, method 1 displays the best performance (appearance-and-deformation patch). As the image domain differs from the label domain, one could easily expect different performances. One way to solve this inconsistency in performance in both domains is to bridge the gap between both domains through the estimation of a mapping that separately evolves the appearance dictionary towards the structure or deformation dictionaries.

Besides, when we used a larger patch ($5 \times 5 \times 5$), we noticed that the prediction accuracy for Method 3 (appearance-and-label patch) remarkably increased up to (GM $= 0.84 \pm 0.043$, WM $= 0.71 \pm 0.063$) at 6 months, (GM $= 0.811 \pm 0.038$, WM $= 0.676 \pm 0.042$) at 9 months and (GM $= 0.778 \pm 0.039$, WM $= 0.70 \pm 0.043$) at 12 months; however, the intensity prediction became more blurry. Our prediction results shown in (Fig. 4) are promising with regard to the dynamics and complexity of brain development and the contrast drastic shifts (Fig. 1 3 months vs. 12 months).

Table 2. Average intensity prediction error across 10 infants (patch size $3 \times 3 \times 3$).

Month	Method1		Method2		Method3	
	PSNR	NSSD	PSNR	NSSD	PSNR	NSSD
6 months	**31.23**	**0.0239**	30.39	0.0282	30.15	0.0306
9 months	**28.28**	**0.0438**	28.12	0.0455	27.59	0.0508
12 months	**28.57**	**0.0389**	28.61	0.0413	28.2	0.0419

5   Conclusion

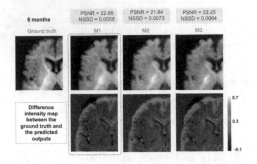

Fig. 4. Prediction results in a representative infant at 6 months for the 3 tested methods: M1 (appearance-and-deformation), M2 (appearance-and-labels), and M3 (appearance-labels-and-deformation).

We proposed the first sparse meta-morphosis patch-based prediction model for dual image intensity and structure evolution during early brain development. The results are quite promising and can be further improved through including more shape information as well as sharpening the 4D photometric atlas. Furthermore, in our future work, the selection of the best patches from the dynamic baseline dictionary can be further refined by including multimodal features (e.g., shape or anatomical structure) –instead of only relying on the 3 month image intensity; and these multimodal features can in turn be appropriately selected.

References

1. Knickmeyer, R., Gouttard, S., Kang, C., Evans, D., Wilber, K., Smith, J., Hamer, R., Lin, W., Gerig, G., Gilmore, J.: A structural mri study of human brain development from birth to 2 years. J. Neurosci. **28**, 12176–12182 (2008)
2. Fletcher, P.: Geodesic regression and the theory of least squares on riemannian manifolds. Int. J. Comput. Vis. **105**, 171–185 (2013)
3. Niethammer, M., Huang, Y., Vialard, F.-X.: Geodesic regression for image time-series. In: Fichtinger, G., Martel, A., Peters, T. (eds.) MICCAI 2011, Part II. LNCS, vol. 6892, pp. 655–662. Springer, Heidelberg (2011)
4. Trouvé, A., Younes, L.: Metamorphoses through lie group action. Found. Comput. Math. **5**, 173–198 (2005)
5. Wu, G., Kim, M., Sanroma, G., Wang, Q., Munsell, B., Shen, D.: Hierarchical multi-atlas label fusion with multi-scale feature representation and label-specific patch partition. Neuroimage **106**, 34–46 (2015)
6. Shi, F., Wang, L., Wu, G., Li, G., Gilmore, J., Lin, W., Shen, D.: Neonatal atlas construction using sparse representation. Hum. Brain Mapp. **35**, 4663–4677 (2014)
7. Beg, M., Miller, M., Trouvé, A., Younes, L.: Computing large deformation metric mappings via geodesic flows of diffeomorphisms. Int. J. Comput. Vis. **61**, 139–157 (2005)
8. Garcin, L., Younes, L.: Geodesic image matching: a wavelet based energy minimization scheme. In: Rangarajan, A., Vemuri, B.C., Yuille, A.L. (eds.) EMMCVPR 2005. LNCS, vol. 3757, pp. 349–364. Springer, Heidelberg (2005)
9. Wang, Q., Kim, M., Shi, Y., Wu, G., Shen, D.: Predict brain MR image registration via sparse learning of appearance and transformation. Med. Image Anal. **20**, 61–75 (2015)

Efficient Multi-scale Patch-Based Segmentation

Abinash Pant[1,2(✉)], David Rivest-Hénault[1], and Pierrick Bourgeat[1]

[1] CSIRO Digital Productivity Flagship, The Australian e-Health Research Centre,
Herston, QLD, Australia
{David.Rivest-Henault,Pierrick.Bourgeat}@csiro.au
[2] University of Burgundy, Le Creusot, France
Abinash_Pant@etu.u-bourgogne.fr

Abstract. The objective of this paper is to devise an efficient and accurate patch-based method for image segmentation. The method presented in this paper builds on the work of Wu et al. [14] with the introduction of a compact multi-scale feature representation and heuristics to speed up the process. A smaller patch representation along with hierarchical pruning allowed the inclusion of more prior knowledge, resulting in a more accurate segmentation. We also propose an intuitive way of optimizing the search strategy to find similar voxel, making the method computationally efficient. An additional approach at improving the speed was explored with the integration of our method with Optimised PatchMatch [11]. The proposed method was validated using the 100 hippocampus images with ground truth segmentation from ADNI-1 (mean DSC = 0.892) and the MICCAI SATA segmentation challenge dataset (mean DSC = 0.8587).

1   Introduction

Proliferation of atlas images along with the growing availability of computational resources has made multi-atlas based segmentation techniques popular. These techniques primarily revolve around using multiple atlas images to introduce expert knowledge into the segmentation process. These atlases are registered to the target images space and the information is propagated to determine the label of the target image. Heckemann et al. [1] pioneered such techniques using 30 normal brain MR images providing accurate segmentation. Aljabar et al. [2] proposed improvements by selecting only a subset of the complete atlas set that are more anatomically similar to the target image. In contrast to global selection of atlases, various patch-based techniques [6,7] that look at patch wise similarity have gained popularity. A local weight is computed for each of the local patch extracted from the atlas. These computed weights are based on intensity similarity with the target patch and are then used in the label fusion process to produce the final segmentation. Sparse representation, with its success in face recognition [4], have been extensively used [8,9,14] to estimate these weights.

However, calculating these weights can be very costly especially when larger 3D patches are required to capture the appropriate level of information. Pre-selections strategies for discarding atlases or patches [5,6] have been employed

© Springer International Publishing Switzerland 2015
G. Wu et al. (Eds.): Patch-MI 2015, LNCS 9467, pp. 205–213, 2015.
DOI: 10.1007/978-3-319-28194-0_25

to alleviate this problem. Even though these strategies ease the process of calculating weights, they discard information, which could lead to sub-optimal results [11]. The use of large patches introduces another problem in segmenting small structures, as pointed out by [14]. Patch similarity of large anatomical structures could misguide the labeling of small structures around it.

Another common technique used in patch-based methods is to define a search window, around the target voxel, where similar patches are searched. They are used to increase the accuracy of the method as similar patches would lie in the vicinity of the target voxel in a well registered atlas. This also provides a computational boost as the search is limited to a small window rather than the whole image. However, these windows are constant and do not evolve depending on the knowledge provided by the atlases or the anatomy of the structure under consideration. This results in identical effort being exerted in calculating weights for each patch. But in reality the effort required is not uniform and can be approximated using prior information available. For example effort required to label a patch near the centre of a solid sphere should be much less, as a majority of atlas labels would belong to sphere class, than a patch which is closer to its surface. Similarly a large search window might adversely affect the segmentation result of a small well registered structure, by bringing in more outliers.

In this paper, we use a compact multi-scale feature to avoid the use of pre-selection strategies while still being discriminative. We also propose a search criterion that evolves according to the confidence level of a region provided by the atlas, to lower the execution time. We have also integrated our method with Optimised PatchMatch as an additional approach to make our method computationally efficient. Our method is validated against the ADNI and MICCAI SATA data set. A comprehensive validation is performed to show the efficacy of the proposed enhancements.

2   Method

The main objective of any multi-atlas segmentation approach is to estimate a label map L_t for a given target image I_t. This is achieved by using a set of N atlas of images $I = \{I_s | s = 1, 2 \cdots I_N\}$ and their corresponding label map $L = \{L_s | s = 1, 2 \cdots N\}$ which is registered to the target image. For each voxel x ($x \in I_t$) a set of Q voxels are selected from the atlas around a search neighbourhood $n(x)$. A feature vector v_b ($b = 1, 2 \cdots Q$) is created for each of these voxels and assembled column wise into a matrix V. A set of weights w_b is estimated to reconstruct the target voxel's feature vector A using V. The label for the target voxel $L_t(x)$, out of M possible labels, can be calculated by $\arg\max_{m=1 \cdots M} \sum_{b=1}^{Q} (w_b . \delta(l_b, L_m))$ where l_b is the label corresponding to each feature vector v_b. This gives a general overview of the method used for segmentation. Details of each component after the registration step has been explained below.

2.1   Multi-scale Feature

Patch-based techniques traditionally use only a single scale patch, which puts a hard limit on the available information. These methods [6,7,9] generally use a larger patch to compensate for the lack of high level information which leads to an increase in computation time. Multi-scale approaches have been proposed [14] to increase the prior information, but, somewhat surprisingly, they dedicate a majority of the voxels to represent the coarser scale making them bulky. We argue that there is no compelling benefit in assigning a large number of voxels to represent these coarser scale. It is especially true when these scale are not crucial in determining the final label of the target voxel and a downsampled version could prove to be equally effective. To overcome this problem we use a simple multi-scale patch consisting of δ patches (one per scale) of size $\epsilon \times \epsilon \times \epsilon$ at different scales. It can also be naturally extended to include variable patch size for each scale. For a typical feature vector ($\delta = \epsilon = 3$) the size of the vector would be 81, which is an order of magnitude smaller than the vectors used in related work [14].

The effectiveness of the proposed feature vector is illustrated by a simple example shown in Fig. 1, which shows the response of different feature vectors of the emphasized voxel over the whole image. We can observe that multi-scale patch response (c) and (d) is more precise and localised than that of single scale patch response (a) and (b). It is also evident that the response of our patch (d) is much more targeted than that of (c). This may be attributed to the fact that the patch used in (c) uses a Gaussian filter at the original scale without sub-sampling thus would require a much larger patch to encode the same level of information as compared to ours (d).

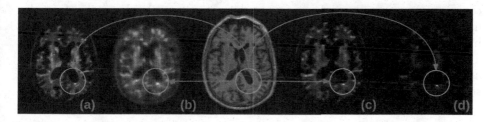

Fig. 1. Response of the feature using sum of squared differences. (a) Small scale patch (b) Large scale patch (c) Multi-scale patch of Wu et al. [14] (d) Our multi-scale patch

Patch-based techniques by design are computationally very expensive therefore most of the proposed methods use pre-selection techniques to limit the atlas/patches to make it computationally efficient. As pointed out by [11], this reduces the problem scope, which might lead to less desirable results. The size of the feature vector also contributes to the computational burden, thus using a light weight feature vector allows to include rich information while staying computationally efficient.

2.2   Sparse Label Fusion

Sparse representation is the method of representing an input data using a linear combination of a small part of an over-complete dictionary leading to a compact representation. Such representation has been proven very successful in classification applications such as face recognition [4]. The use of these techniques, for multi-atlas segmentation, was first proposed by [8,9]. Here the target feature vector v_t can be represented as a combination of the selected vectors v_b weighted by factor w_b such that $v_t = \sum_{b=1}^{Q}(w_b.v_b)$. The whole system can be represented as $A = V \times W$ where W is the matrix formed by concatenating the weights. This being an under-determined system does not have a unique solution. Therefore, a sparse constrain $min\|W\|_1$ is added, which converts the problem into a ℓ_1 minimization problem where a majority of the weights w_b are zero. The weights can be obtained using Eq. 1. The weights obtained are used to estimate the target label from atlas labels providing the final segmentation. This optimization problem has been solved using the SLEP package [3].

$$\hat{W} = \arg\min\frac{1}{2}\|A - V \times W\|_2 + \lambda\|W\|_1. \tag{1}$$

2.3   Hierarchical Pruning

During the process of finding the sparse coefficients to determine the label of the target, a hierarchical pruning step proposed by Wu et al. [14] has been used. This process has been found to improve accuracy and reduce computational burden. The basic idea of hierarchical pruning is to break the complex task of obtaining the sparse coefficients into several stages. Initially, information from all the scales is used to determine a set of candidate patches. Information from coarser scale and weak patches is removed iteratively until only patches from the finest scale remains. This ensures that final set of patches are similar to target patch at all scales and that no scale, particularly the coarse ones, dominates. This technique, with reduced iterations at earlier stage, can also act as a holistic and robust pre-selection criteria which is in tune with the overall optimization strategy.

3   Speed Improvements

In addition to computing the labels of each voxel in parallel and caching the computed feature vector v we will discuss two strategies used to increase the speed of the overall process.

3.1   Search Optimization

Patch-based methods determine the label for a particular voxel by a weighted voting scheme where each selected voxel casts a vote depending on its label. The task becomes relatively easy when most of the voxels belong to the same class and have the same label. In this scenario there is no need to find the exact voting power or weight of every voxel as the label of the target would be determined by the majority, regardless of the weights. Conversely the process becomes quite challenging when there is roughly an equal distribution of voxels from different classes making the weight calculation step crucial.

This information has been utilized to adaptively change the behaviour of the algorithm so that most of the computational time is spent in regions of high uncertainty. The throttling of speed is obtained by defining a search window for each level θ ($\theta \in \{0, 1, 2 \ldots\}$). The search window at each level is set to $\omega \times \omega \times \omega$ where $\omega = 2.\theta + 1$. A threshold g_θ is defined for every level θ such that each level would only handle regions which satisfies this condition $g_\theta \geq \beta > g_{\theta-1}$ where β is the percentage of majority voxels with the same label. β is calculated dynamically for each voxel, in a computationally inexpensive step, by looking at the all the atlas labels corresponding to each voxel's location. The complete search strategy is defined as $\{g_0, g_1, \ldots\}$ such that level 0 would handle regions where at-least $g_0\%$ of voxels have the same label. The remaining region would be handled by level 1 and so on. For example a search strategy of $\{100\}$ would process all patches that have the same label at level 0 and the rest of the patches are handled by level 1; this corresponds to using a window of $3 \times 3 \times 3$ in traditional approaches. The number of iterations at each of the θ levels is also set to compensate for the change in the total amount of patches being selected while increasing or decreasing the window size.

In Fig. 2(a), (b) and (c) a search optimization strategy has been created using the atlas labels. Figure 2(d), (e) and (f) show their corresponding manual delineation. The dark gray region, which denotes an easy region, would require a small search window with fewer number of iterations as the majority of voxels belong to the object. The opposite is the case for the white region, where there is an equal distribution of classes. A larger patch with a greater number of iteration is required. This strategy works very well providing faster execution time without any significant decrease in accuracy. This method is generic and can be used with any patch-based method. It can also be extended to include the anatomical information linked with the label to create a strategy tuned for a particular anatomy.

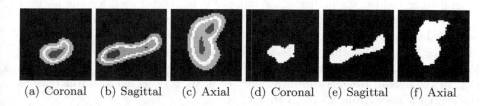

(a) Coronal   (b) Sagittal   (c) Axial   (d) Coronal   (e) Sagittal   (f) Axial

Fig. 2. Search optimization strategy ($\{95,65\}$) obtained from the atlas images (see text above). (a)–(c) shows the strategy and (d)–(f) their corresponding manual delineation

3.2   Integration with Optimised PatchMatch

Ta et al. [11] proposed Optimised PatchMatch (OPAL) that provides very accurate segmentation of MR images in a comparatively short time. The algorithm works by first generating k-Approximate Nearest Neighbour (ANN) from a given atlas and then uses a label fusion technique to obtain the desired segmentation. The algorithm runs with a constant complexity and doesn't discard any *a priori* information, the details of this algorithm have been omitted for brevity. The integration with OPAL was done primarily as an experiment to reduce the overall computational complexity by introducing a pre-selection stage in our pipeline.

To integrate OPAL within our proposed pipeline, the number k was increased while reducing the number of iteration in order to obtain a wide variety of patches which could later be fed to our method. This was done in order to reduce the probability of the same voxel being selected multiple times while still having a large collection of relevant voxels to choose from for our segmentation pipeline. This resulted in drastic reduction in overall time with comparable accuracy.

4   Results

4.1   Hippocampus Segmentation

The imaging data used for this experiment used the Harmonized Protocol[1] for Hippocampal volumetry. We used 100 T1-weighted MR images acquired following the ADNI-1 imaging protocol of 37 AD, 34 MCI and 29 Normal subjects along with their manual delineation.

For all the experiments, the atlases have been affinely registered using the robust block matching approach MIRORR [15]. To provide a fair comparison, all the other factors have been kept constant. The value for λ, used for label fusion, has been set to 0.2 for all the experiments. The values of δ and ϵ has been set to 3 giving us a feature vector that consists of $3 \times 3 \times 3$ patches at 3 different scales (1, 1/2 and 1/4 of the original image size). A 12 core Intel Xeon(R) system clocked at 3.20 GHz with 16 GB RAM was used for all the experiments.

A leave-one-out cross validation has been used to validate the proposed method. The proposed method with $5 \times 5 \times 5$ window using pruning and multi-scale feature yielded the highest Dice score of 0.892 and is used for comparison with other methods. To show the effectiveness of the proposed improvements, degraded versions of our method has been compared with this variant as shown in Table 1. We can see that multi-scale feature increased the accuracy by 0.022. Pruning provided an improvement of 0.006 in the Dice score with a slight reduction in the overall time. An improvement of 0.007 is observed when increasing the search window from $3 \times 3 \times 3$ to $5 \times 5 \times 5$.

The proposed search optimization strategy, with a configuration of {95,65}, gave a comparable result with the best variant leading to an approximate 60 % reduction in the overall time. The integration with Optimised PatchMatch, with

---

[1] http://www.hippocampal-protocol.net.

Table 1. Dice ratios and time taken for 6 variations of our method

Method	Time (s)	DSC
5 × 5 × 5 window with pruning and multi scale	**428**	**0.892**
No multi-scale	167	0.870
No pruning	689	0.887
3 × 3 × 3 window	91	0.885
Optimised search {95,65}	182	0.890
Proposed + Optimised PatchMatch ($k = 200$)	51	0.885

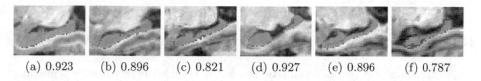

(a) 0.923   (b) 0.896   (c) 0.821   (d) 0.927   (e) 0.896   (f) 0.787

Fig. 3. Segmentation of left(a–c) and right(d–f) hippocampus of subjects with best, median and worst Dice scores (red and blue denote over and under segmentation) (Color figure online).

$k = 200$, provided a drastic reduction in overall time with just a slight reduction in the Dice score. A visual summary of the segmentation result provided by our method is shown in Fig. 3.

We compared our mean dice coefficients with other published results on ADNI-1 dataset. Roche et al. (BMAS) [12] and Gray et al. (LEAP) [13] reported an average dice score of 86.6 ± 1.70 and 87.6 ± 2.07 respectively on the ADNI-1 dataset. Our method yielded an average dice score of 89.2 ± 2.22 on the same dataset. It can be seen that the accuracy of our proposed method is comparable to the accuracy reported by the above mentioned methods.

4.2 MICCAI SATA Challenge

Our algorithm was validated using MICCAI SATA challenge [10]. The standardized registered diencephalon dataset containing 35 training samples and 12 testing samples were used for the validation. The images were acquired using MPRAGE (Magnetization Prepared Rapid Acquisition Gradient Echo) having a resolution of $1 \times 1 \times 1\,mm^3$. All the images were already registered to remove any variability introduced due to the registration algorithm.

An automated system for submission provided by the challenge organisers was used to validate the result. Our method, "*HALF_R_1_4*", gave an average(median) Dice score of 0.8587(0.8696), which is just 0.0084 lower than the current leading method "*UNC MCseq*". It should be noted that this challenge does not take into account the computational complexity to evaluate the results.

5 Conclusion

The use of a smaller patch representation made it possible to include more prior knowledge which improved the overall accuracy of the method. This was validated by comparing it with a degraded version version of our method. The proposed dynamic search optimization technique was used while searching for similar patches. This approach proved to be computationally efficient and also provided comparable accuracy. A further decrease in the overall computational time was achieved by integrating our method with OPAL. Encouraging results has been obtained on the ADNI and MICCAI SATA datasets when compared with the state of the art.

References

1. Heckemann, R.A., et al.: Automatic anatomical brain MRI segmentation combining label propagation and decision fusion. NeuroImage **33**(1), 115–126 (2006)
2. Aljabar, P., et al.: Multi-atlas based segmentation of brain images: atlas selection and its effect on accuracy. Neuroimage **46**(3), 726–738 (2009)
3. Liu, J., Ji, S., Ye, J.: SLEP: sparse learning with efficient projections. Ariz. State Univ. **6**, 491 (2009)
4. Wright, J., et al.: Robust face recognition via sparse representation. IEEE Trans. Pattern Anal. Mach. Intell. **31**(2), 210–227 (2009)
5. Coupé, P., Manjón, J.V., Fonov, V., Pruessner, J., Robles, M., Collins, D.L.: Non-local patch-based label fusion for hippocampus segmentation. In: Jiang, T., Navab, N., Pluim, J.P.W., Viergever, M.A. (eds.) MICCAI 2010, Part III. LNCS, vol. 6363, pp. 129–136. Springer, Heidelberg (2010)
6. Rousseau, F., Habas, P.A., Studholme, C.: A supervised patch-based approach for human brain labeling. IEEE Trans. Med. Imaging **30**(10), 1852–1862 (2011)
7. Coupé, P., et al.: Patch-based segmentation using expert priors: application to hippocampus and ventricle segmentation. NeuroImage **54**(2), 940–954 (2011)
8. Zhang, D., Guo, Q., Wu, G., Shen, D.: Sparse patch-based label fusion for multi-atlas segmentation. In: Yap, P.-T., Liu, T., Shen, D., Westin, C.-F., Shen, L. (eds.) MBIA 2012. LNCS, vol. 7509, pp. 94–102. Springer, Heidelberg (2012)
9. Tong, T., et al.: Segmentation of brain MR images via sparse patch representation. In: MICCAI Workshop on Sparsity Techniques in Medical Imaging (STMI) (2012)
10. Asman, A., et al.: Miccai 2013 segmentation algorithms, theory and applications (SATA) challenge results summary. In: MICCAI Challenge Workshop on Segmentation: Algorithms, Theory and Applications (SATA) (2013)
11. Ta, V.-T., Giraud, R., Collins, D.L., Coupé, P.: Optimized PatchMatch for near real time and accurate label fusion. In: Golland, P., Hata, N., Barillot, C., Hornegger, J., Howe, R. (eds.) MICCAI 2014, Part III. LNCS, vol. 8675, pp. 105–112. Springer, Heidelberg (2014)
12. Roche, F., et al.: Accuracy of BMAS hippocampus segmentation using the harmonized hippocampal protocol. Alzheimer's Dementia J. Alzheimer's Assoc. **10**(4), P705–P706 (2014)
13. Gray, K.R., et al.: Integration of EADC-ADNI harmonised hippocampus labels into the LEAP automated segmentation technique. Alzheimer's Dementia J. Alzheimer's Assoc. **10**(4), P119–P120 (2014)

14. Wu, G., et al.: Hierarchical multi-atlas label fusion with multi-scale feature representation and label-specific patch partition. NeuroImage **106**, 34–46 (2015)
15. Rivest-Hénault, D., et al.: Robust inverse-consistent affine CT-MR registration in MRI-assisted and MRI-alone prostate radiation therapy. Med. Image Anal. **23**(1), 56–69 (2015)

Author Index

Printed in the United States
By Bookmasters